Demand and Supply of Skills in Ghana

A WORLD BANK STUDY

Demand and Supply of Skills in Ghana

How Can Training Programs Improve Employment and Productivity?

Peter Darvas and Robert Palmer

THE WORLD BANK
Washington, D.C.

© 2014 International Bank for Reconstruction and Development / The World Bank
1818 H Street NW, Washington, DC 20433
Telephone: 202-473-1000; Internet: www.worldbank.org

Some rights reserved

1 2 3 4   17 16 15 14

World Bank Studies are published to communicate the results of the Bank's work to the development community with the least possible delay. The manuscript of this paper therefore has not been prepared in accordance with the procedures appropriate to formally edited texts.

This work is a product of the staff of The World Bank with external contributions. The findings, interpretations, and conclusions expressed in this work do not necessarily reflect the views of The World Bank, its Board of Executive Directors, or the governments they represent. The World Bank does not guarantee the accuracy of the data included in this work. The boundaries, colors, denominations, and other information shown on any map in this work do not imply any judgment on the part of The World Bank concerning the legal status of any territory or the endorsement or acceptance of such boundaries.

Nothing herein shall constitute or be considered to be a limitation upon or waiver of the privileges and immunities of The World Bank, all of which are specifically reserved.

Rights and Permissions

This work is available under the Creative Commons Attribution 3.0 IGO license (CC BY 3.0 IGO) http://creativecommons.org/licenses/by/3.0/igo. Under the Creative Commons Attribution license, you are free to copy, distribute, transmit, and adapt this work, including for commercial purposes, under the following conditions:

Attribution—Please cite the work as follows: Darvas, Peter, and Robert Palmer. *Demand and Supply of Skills in Ghana: How Can Training Programs Improve Employment and Productivity?* World Bank Studies. Washington, DC: World Bank. doi:10.1596/978-1-4648-0280-5. License: Creative Commons Attribution CC BY 3.0 IGO

Translations—If you create a translation of this work, please add the following disclaimer along with the attribution: *This translation was not created by The World Bank and should not be considered an official World Bank translation. The World Bank shall not be liable for any content or error in this translation.*

Adaptations—If you create an adaptation of this work, please add the following disclaimer along with the attribution: *This is an adaptation of an original work by The World Bank. Responsibility for the views and opinions expressed in the adaptation rests solely with the author or authors of the adaptation and are not endorsed by The World Bank.*

Third-party content—The World Bank does not necessarily own each component of the content contained within the work. The World Bank therefore does not warrant that the use of any third-party-owned individual component or part contained in the work will not infringe on the rights of those third parties. The risk of claims resulting from such infringement rests solely with you. If you wish to reuse a component of the work, it is your responsibility to determine whether permission is needed for that re-use and to obtain permission from the copyright owner. Examples of components can include, but are not limited to, tables, figures, or images.

All queries on rights and licenses should be addressed to the Publishing and Knowledge Division, The World Bank, 1818 H Street NW, Washington, DC 20433, USA; fax: 202-522-2625; e-mail: pubrights@worldbank.org.

ISBN (paper): 978-1-4648-0280-5
ISBN (electronic): 978-1-4648-0281-2
DOI: 10.1596/978-1-4648-0280-5

Cover photo: © Robert Palmer. Used with permission. Further permission required for reuse.
Cover design: Debra Naylor, Naylor Design, Inc.

Library of Congress Cataloging-in-Publication Data has been requested

Contents

Foreword	*xi*
Acknowledgments	*xiii*
About the Authors	*xv*
Abbreviations	*xvii*

Executive Summary		**1**
	Country and Sector Context	1
	Social and Economic Demand for Technical and Vocational Skills in Ghana	2
	TVET Supply, Coordination, and Financing	4
	Policy Recommendations	7
	Notes	10
Chapter 1	**Context, Drivers, and Challenges of Technical and Vocational Skills Development Reform**	**11**
	Introduction	11
	The Global Rise in Importance of Technical and Vocational Skills Development	14
	Technical and Vocational Skills Development Drivers in Ghana	15
	TVET Policy, 2002–13	17
	A Framework for Assessing Market and Nonmarket Imperfections Related to TVET in Sub-Saharan Africa	19
	Concluding Comments	26
	Notes	26
Chapter 2	**Demand for TVET**	**29**
	Introduction	29
	Social Demand for TVET	30
	Economic Demand for TVET	34
	Skill Demand and Supply in Selected Sectors	40
	Concluding Comments	44
	Notes	45

Chapter 3	**TVET Supply, Performance, and Assessment**	47
	The Suppliers of Technical and Vocational Education and Training in Ghana	47
	Formal Public TVET Providers	48
	Private Institution TVET Providers	57
	Enterprise-Based TVET Providers	58
	Concluding Comments	61
	Notes	61
Chapter 4	**TVET Coordination**	63
	Introduction	63
	The Coordination of TVET Supply and Demand	65
	Coordination of Government Strategies, Plans, and Development Partner Support	66
	TVET Quality Assurance and Qualifications	68
	Concluding Comments	70
	Notes	70
Chapter 5	**TVET Financing**	73
	Systemic TVET Financing	73
	TVET Financing Modalities	79
	Outcomes and Issues	83
	Concluding Comments	86
	Notes	87
Chapter 6	**Policy Recommendations**	89
	TVET Policy Development and Governance	89
	A Demand-Driven, Responsive TVET System	90
	Equity Considerations	92
	TVET Financing	92
	Data, Monitoring and Evaluation, and Information Systems	94
	Notes	95
Appendix A	**Demand for Skills in Selected Economic Sectors**	97
	Information and Communication Technologies Sector	97
	Construction Sector	100
	Oil and Gas Sector	102
	Livestock Sector	104
	Tourism and Hospitality Sector	106
	Notes	108
Appendix B	**TVET Provision in Ghana**	109
	The Technical Training Institutes	109
	National Vocational Training Institute	118
	Social Welfare Centers, Department of Social Welfare	124

Contents

	The Integrated Community Centers for Employable Skills	126
	Opportunities Industrialization Center—Ghana	132
	The Youth Leadership and Skills Training Institutes of the National Youth Authority	136
	Community Development Vocational/Technical Institutes	140
	Ghana Regional Appropriate Technology Industrial Service	144
	National Apprenticeship Program	148
	Local Enterprise and Skills Development Program	151
	The Skills Training and Entrepreneurship Program	152
	The Rural Enterprise Project (IFAD, 1995 and Ongoing)	154
	Private Vocational Training Institutes	156
	Informal Apprenticeship Training	162
	Private Formal Enterprise-Based Training	167
	The Ghana Industrial Skills Development Center	169
	Notes	171

References   177

Boxes

B.1	Two-Week Courses for Industry at the Accra Technical Training Centre	115
B.2	ATTC Income, Approximate Breakdown	116
B.3	Training Services Offered by GRATIS	144
B.4	Training Output and Other Services Offered by GRATIS since Its Establishment (to 2006)	146
B.5	Don Bosco Technical Institute, Ashaiman (Tema)	157

Figures

1.1	Framework for Skills Assessment	20
2.1	Firms Identifying Labor Skill Levels as a Major Constraint, by Size: Ghana, 2007, and Sub-Saharan Africa and World, 2006 or Most Recent Year	36
2.2	Portion of Firms Identifying Labor Skill Levels as a Major Constraint: Ghana, 2007, Compared with Other Sub-Saharan Africa Countries, 2006 or Most Recent Year	37
2.3	Skills Lacking in Existing Employees	40
3.1	Firms Offering Formal Training, by Size, Ghana, 2007, and Sub-Saharan Africa and World, 2006 or Most Recent Year	60

A.1	Mapping the ICT Sector	98
A.2	Supply of Skilled Labor in the Ghana Construction Industry, 2000–10	101
A.3	Typical Petroleum/O&G Value Chain	103
A.4	COTVET Survey Conducted among Students from Two Polytechnics (Accra and Cape Coast) to Assess Students' Opinions on Their Study Program	107
B.1	Key Actions to Address Hard-to-Fill Vacancies	168

Tables

1.1	Total Enrollment in Primary and Lower Secondary Schools in Ghana	16
1.2	Global Competitive Ranking Index of 144 Countries, Selected Sub-Saharan African Countries, 2012/13	17
2.1	AGI Business Barometer, Top Challenges, by Enterprise Size	37
3.1	Main Public and Private TVET Providers, by Backer, 2012/13	48
3.2	Coverage and Location of Public TVET Institutes, by Type, 2012	49
3.3	TVET Enrollment of Full-Time Students, by Type of Institute and Gender, Latest Year	50
3.4	TVET Staff and In-Service Training, by Type of Institute and Gender, Most Recent Year	53
3.5	Public TVET Training Environment, by Type of Institute, 2012	54
3.6	Private TVET Institutes Covered by EMIS Sample, 2006/07 to 2010/11	57
4.1	National TVET Qualifications Framework	69
5.1	TVET Funding Recommendations, 2002–08	74
5.2	Skills Development Fund Applications and Approvals	78
5.3	Technical Training Institutes' Actual Unit Costs, 2006–09	80
5.4	ICCES Financing Modalities and Implications	81
A.1	Demand-Supply Gap for ICT Skills in Ghana's Labor Market	98
A.2	Firm Cost for Training ICT Personnel in Ghana	99
A.3	Domestic Meat Production, 2004–08	105
B.1	Enrollment Data for TVET Institutions under the Ministry of Education, 2001/02 to 2011/12	111
B.2	Teaching and Nonteaching Staff, 2007/08 and 2011/12	111
B.3	Unit Costs for Technical Training Institutes Compared with Junior High School and Senior High School, 2006–10	117
B.4	Trainee Enrollment, 2005–07	119
B.5	Number of Trade and Proficiency Tests Taken, 2006 and 2007	123
B.6	Enrollment in ICCES Ashanti, 2001–12	128
B.7	Enrollment and Dropout Figures, 2001–12	133

B.8	Enrollment Figures, 2001/02 to 2011/12	136
B.9	Number of Teaching and Nonteaching Staff, Various Years	137
B.10	Enrollment, 2001/02 to 2011/12	141
B.11	Total Number of Teaching and Nonteaching Staff, 2008 and 2012	141
B.12	Enrollment in the Three-Year Technical Apprentice Training Program, 2001/02 to 2007/08	145
B.13	Craft Certificates Examination Results, May/June 2007	147
B.14	Number of Instructors in TVET Providers	160
B.15	Apprentices in Ghana with Less Than a Complete Basic Education	164

Foreword

Over the past 15 years, Ghana has experienced an unprecedented period of steady economic growth, declining poverty, increasing prosperity, and peace and democracy. As a lower middle income country, Ghana is now better positioned to leverage its competitiveness and to attract foreign investment. Developing skills for continued competitiveness, growth, and prosperity is one of the country's important new frontiers. The right skills matter at many levels: equipping young Ghanaians to find or create well-paying jobs, helping the private sector to become more productive and, ultimately, ensuring that the economy diversifies and that productive jobs are created in labor-intensive sectors. Ghana's economic growth is linked with mining and commodities, which account for a relatively low share of employment. Labor-intensive sectors (such as construction, hospitality, and agriculture) suffer from persistently low productivity and are not competitive in global export markets. In addressing these bottlenecks, more attention is needed to the quality of basic and secondary education, as well as access to higher level knowledge, both of which have developed unevenly.

Ghana's technical and vocational education and training (TVET) sector is in many ways at the intersection of these opportunities and challenges. The TVET sector is tasked with building human capital, helping youth find jobs, and raising labor productivity—but it is often unable to live up to these expectations. The quality and relevance of vocational training are considered low, training is often expensive and inefficient, and investments into the sector are not sustainable. The government has been trying to reform and expand the TVET sector for more than a decade. Recently, these efforts have gained further urgency due to the country's deepening youth employment challenge.

This report assesses the economic and social demand for vocational skills and the scope and scale of supply; and looks at various institutions, policies, and financing mechanisms. The report also pays special attention to vocational training for those working in the informal economy, and nonformal (private) training providers and analyzes new initiatives and policies. It demonstrates that demand for vocational skills by employers is constrained by various market failures and addressing these requires policies that effectively stimulate increasing demand for skills in the private sector. On the supply side, the report demonstrates considerable diversity of training providers ranging from public, school-based programs toward higher technical skills to private and also informal training activities that improve job-specific skills. Training services also show large variations in terms of quality, effectiveness, and efficiency. The report calls for government policies that help address some of these challenges without inhibiting the diversity of training providers. The report is based on background studies completed by Ghanaian, international, and World Bank experts; it was completed in conjunction with the World Bank–supported Ghana Skills and Technology Development Project.

It is hoped that the report will serve well Ghanaian policy makers, stakeholders in vocational training, and the public by advising on a better balance between demand and supply and clearly demonstrating how effective policies and financing, and engagement of the private sector, can help achieve the country's strategic goals as it gears up to meet the youth employment challenge.

Peter N. Materu
Sector Manager
Education, Central and West Africa
Africa Region
The World Bank

Acknowledgments

This report was authored by Peter Darvas and Robert Palmer. The report findings reflect a close partnership between the government of Ghana, the World Bank, various development agencies supporting skills development in Ghana, and Ghanaian and international experts. As a background to the report, assessments of key economic sectors were completed by Petra Righetti and Anubha Verma (information and communication technology), Gerald Kojo Ahorbo and Øystein Førsvoll (oil and gas industry), Divine K. Ahadzie (construction industry), and Victor Antwi (livestock sector). The Council for Technical and Vocational Education and Training (COTVET) provided a sector report on demand for TVET in the hospitality and tourism sectors. Priyam Saraf provided an analysis of demand for skills in the cocoa industry, and she also ably summarized all the analyses of demand for the selected economic sectors analyzed in the main section and presented in the appendix of the book. In the World Bank, Eunice Ackwerh, Peter N. Materu, and Deborah Mikesell provided continuous support to the analysis and the preparation of the book. From the government side, Dan Baffour Awuah, Executive Director (2008–12); Sampson Damptey, Acting Executive Director (2012–13); and other COTVET staff provided generous feedback and guidance. Official peer reviewers were Amit Dar, Allan Moody, Venkatesh Sundararaman, Alexandria Valerio, and Andrea Vermehren from the World Bank; George Afeti from the Ghana National Inspectorate Board; Jeanette Burmester from Gesellschaft für Internationale Zusammenarbeit; Jorgen Billetoft from the Danish International Development Agency; and Kenneth King from the University of Edinburgh and from Network for International Policies and Cooperation in Education and Training (NORRAG). The authors appreciate the editorial support by David Anderson, Burton Bollag, Rumit Pancholi, Chandrani Ray, and Kavita P. Watsa.

About the Authors

Peter Darvas has worked on basic, secondary, and higher education and training in Ghana since 2005. He also lived in Ghana between 2006 and 2009 where, as the education sector coordinator for the World Bank and as the sector leader for the development partners, he provided strategic support to the government of Ghana in its effort to develop the Education Strategic Plan (2010–2020) and lead partnership in the annual sector performance reviews and in other multidonor partnerships. For the World Bank, Peter led various investment projects including the Education Sector Project, the Education for All Fast Track Initiative, and the Ghana Skills and Technology Development Project. He also led a number of World Bank–sponsored sector analyses including Education in Ghana; Improving Equity, Efficiency, and Accountability of Education Service Delivery; Basic Education beyond the Millennium Development Goals in Ghana; and also the sector analyses focusing on skills and technology development, which also led to the completion of this book. Peter works with the World Bank Senior Education Economist at the Human Development Department of the Africa Region and is based in Washington, DC.

Robert Palmer has worked on technical and vocational education and training issues in Ghana since 2001, and at various levels: in a rural vocational school for a year, as an academic researcher, and as a policy and program advisor. His PhD, from the University of Edinburgh, was on skills development in the informal economy in Ghana. He has worked on several large education research projects in the country including on the Department for International Development–funded projects: Post-Basic Education and Poverty Reduction in Sub-Saharan Africa and South Asia (2004–2006); and the Research Consortium on Educational Outcomes and Poverty (2005–2009). He has been a consultant for the World Bank in Ghana on numerous occasions since 2008. Robert currently works between the United Kingdom and Jordan as an independent international education and skills development consultant.

Abbreviations

AGI	Association of Ghana Industries
ATTC	Accra Technical Training Center
CBT	competency-based training
COTVET	Council for Technical and Vocational Education and Training
CSSPS	Computerized School Selection and Placement System
DFID	Department for International Development (United Kingdom)
EMIS	Education Management Information System
ESP	Education Strategic Plan
GDP	gross domestic product
GEA	Ghana Employers Association
GES	Ghana Education Service
GET Fund	Ghana Education Trust Fund
GISDC	Ghana Industrial Skills Development Center
GIZ	Gesellschaft für Internationale Zusammenarbeit (German Society for International Cooperation)
GLSS	Ghana Living Standard Survey
GNI	gross national income
GoG	Government of Ghana
GPE	Global Partnership for Education
GRATIS	Ghana Regional Appropriate Technology Industrial Service
GRSCDP	Gender Responsive Skills and Community Development Project
GSDI	Ghana Skills Development Initiative
GSS	Ghana Statistical Service
GYEEDA	Ghana Youth Employment and Entrepreneurial Agency
ICCES	Integrated Community Center for Employable Skills
ICT	information and communication technology
IT	information technology
ITAC	Industrial and Training Advisory Committee of COTVET
JHS	junior high school
JSS	junior secondary school

LESDEP	Local Enterprise and Skills Development Program
LI	Legislative Instrument
MC	master craftspeople
MoELR	Ministry of Employment and Labor Relations
MoESW	Ministry of Employment and Social Welfare
MoFA	Ministry of Food and Agriculture
MoLGRD	Ministry of Local Government and Rural Development
MoTI	Ministry of Trade and Industry
MoYS	Ministry of Youth and Sports
MSE	micro and small enterprise
NAC	National Apprenticeship Committee of COTVET
NACVET	National Coordinating Committee for Technical and Vocational Education and Training
NAP	National Apprenticeship Program
NDPC	National Development Planning Commission
NER	New Education Reform
NERIC	National Education Reform Implementation Committee
NGO	nongovernmental organization
NTVETQC	National TVET Qualifications Committee of COTVET
NTVETQF	National TVET Qualifications Framework
NVTI	National Vocational Training Institute
NYA	National Youth Authority
NYEP	National Youth Employment Program
OICG	Opportunities Industrialization Center—Ghana
OJT	on-the-job training
PPP	public-private partnership
REP	rural enterprise project
SDF	Skills Development Fund
SHS	senior high school
STEP	Skills Training and Entrepreneurship Program
TPSAT	Technology Promotion and Support to Apprentices Training
TQAC	Training Quality Assurance Committee of COTVET
TTI	Technical Training Institute
TVE	technical and vocational education
TVED	Technical and Vocational Education Division of GES
TVET	technical and vocational education and training
UNICEF	United Nations Children's Fund
VSP	Vocational Skills and Informal Sector Support Project
VTI	Vocational Training Institute

Currency Equivalents

As of January 2014
$1 = Gh₵ 2.3525

As of mid-2011
$1 = Gh₵1.50

As of mid-2008
$1 = Gh₵1

All dollar amounts are U.S. dollars unless otherwise indicated

Executive Summary

Country and Sector Context

Ghana has a youthful population of 24 million and has shown impressive gains in economic growth and in poverty reduction over the last two decades. The discovery of oil promises to increase government revenues by about $1 billion per year in the coming years. However, as with most African countries, the foundations on which both growth and poverty reduction are being built need strengthening. Ghana will require several more decades of sustained efforts and solid growth for most of its citizens to sustainably break out of poverty. (Despite reductions in poverty nationwide, about 30 percent of the population still live below the poverty line.)

The necessary sustained growth requires three critical steps: (1) increase productivity in the strategic economic sectors, (2) diversify the economy, and (3) expand employment. Raising the level and range of skills in the country provides a key contribution to these core drivers of sustained growth.

Skills development in Ghana encompasses foundational skills (literacy, numeracy), transferable and soft skills, and technical and vocational skills. These skills are acquired throughout life through formal education, training, and higher education; on the job through work experience and professional training; through family and community; and via the media.

This report focuses on one segment of Ghana's skills development system: formal and informal technical and vocational education and training (TVET) at the pretertiary level. TVET in Ghana is often associated with the outcomes of formal public TVET, despite the fact that the sector is responsible for less than 10 percent of the technical and vocational skills acquired. Some of Ghana's public TVET system is part of the educational system; some of it is not but is formalized through laws and regulations and overseen by government agencies other than by the Ministry of Education; some is privately provided. The majority of young Ghanaians acquire technical and vocational skills on the job through informal apprenticeships. Although the scale and scope of Ghana's TVET system are difficult to pin down, they clearly represent a major intersection between education, youth, and the labor market.

Ghana's technical and vocational skills development system experiences an adverse cycle of high costs, inadequate quality of supply, and low demand, leading to further declines in financing, supply, and demand. The government has long promised the population that increasing technical and vocational skills training opportunities will help solve youth unemployment. But this adverse cycle means that the promise of skills development is at risk of remaining unfulfilled.

Social and Economic Demand for Technical and Vocational Skills in Ghana

Over the last decade or more, Ghana has seen rapid increases in educational enrolment; nonetheless, the overall skill level of Ghana's labor force remains relatively low. Of the total employed population, 62 percent either dropped out of primary or lower secondary school or have no formal schooling, and only 9 percent has completed education at the senior secondary level or higher. In the last decade, Ghana's Free, Compulsory and Universal Basic Education program, along with subsequent long-term education strategic plans, has led to some of the largest cohorts of students leaving primary school ever witnessed. Total enrollment in primary and junior high school (JHS) increased by more than 50 percent between 2001/02 and 2010/11. This has increased demand for post–basic education and training opportunities. Of those who complete the three years of JHS, half (more than 200,000 students) do not make it to further formal education or training. About 8 out of every 10 youth 15–17 years of age are not enrolled in a senior high school, and only 5–7 percent of JHS graduates can expect to find a place in either public or private TVET institutes.

Although education attainment has significantly increased in terms of access to and completion of basic education (though Ghana still has about a million 6–16-year-old children out of school), the quality of learning has not followed suit. In fact, nearly three-fourths of the students leave basic education without proficient level of literacy and numerical skills. Learning assessments and the basic education completion exam show significant disparities in the distribution of those academic skills. Those coming from poorer families, rural areas, or deprived districts also have lower learning results, providing them with insufficient skills to progress academically. Very few of these youth have opportunities to improve their weak basic skills through second chance programs because they are generally obliged to engage in unskilled, often unpaid household jobs, in agriculture, or in street peddling. Some of these youth get into informal apprenticeships. However, informal apprenticeships, as the report shows, do not provide some basic literacy or numeracy skills. Consequently, although basic education has significantly expanded over the last decade, it has created a wedge between those who are stuck in unskilled jobs and those who have some level of success transitioning from school to work. Social cohesion and competitiveness in Ghana is weakened by the fact that the majority of youth have such low basic skills and are thus stuck in jobs with low productivity and limited upward mobility.

TVET remains less popular than general education, which is regarded by many as better preparation for the available formal employment opportunities. Choosing technical or vocational training upon completion of basic education is the result mostly of mediocre academic performance rather than being attracted to a vocation. Social demand for TVET is undoubtedly influenced by its relatively low prestige, which, in turn, is related to economic issues: its perceived and actual relevance to the labor market, the low graduate pay, lack of jobs in the formal economy, and limited growth potential in the informal micro- and small-enterprise (MSE) sector. Between 2002/03 and 2009/10 enrollment in senior secondary schools increased from 301,120 to 537,332 students, clearly underlining the social demand for general education. In the meantime, enrollment in virtually all public TVET institutes has been either static or in decline over the last few years.

Despite more than 20 years of robust economic growth, little change has taken place in the structure of Ghana's labor market; an insufficient number of formal job opportunities remain, and the bulk of all employment opportunities continue to be in the large informal economy. The structure of the economy continues to be dominated by micro and small enterprises, which typically have low productivity. In fact, this structure has worsened over the last decade as few of the micro and small enterprises managed to grow in size and the larger ones appear to be able to substitute investment in labor with investment in capital. Among the sectors, agriculture remains dominant, while the role of services continues to grow, but both have low productivity. The sectors producing the bulk of the revenues for the country are mining, natural resources, and other commodities, whereas manufacturing, the sector that tends to require labor at higher skill levels, continues to lag behind.

Sustained and shared growth in Ghana requires diversification and improvements in productivity. The present economic and labor market structure sustains long-term risks for the country. Overreliance on resources such as oil and gas can lead to further pressures on manufacturing and other tradable sectors as well as pressures on long-term sustained growth. Growth in Ghana is boosted by favorable trends in global commodity prices, but no guarantees are at hand that these trends will continue or remain stable. These sectors are also typically not labor intensive, and skilled labor can often be substituted with investment in capital and technology. Youth unemployment and underemployment remain key social and political challenges. However, the assumption by politicians and policy makers that the provision of skills to youth will ease unemployment and underemployment for those newly leaving school remains an unfulfilled promise.

The government is pursuing the strategic development of its economy through diversification and private sector growth. These efforts could be made more effective by better taking into account the dominance of microenterprises and the persistence of their low productivity and high rate of market failure. Assessments of the competitiveness of the economy demonstrate that improvements are needed in the regulatory framework and infrastructure, as well as access to credit, land, and technology. To effectively address these challenges, priority sectors need to be identified and targeted.

Perhaps surprisingly, the overwhelming majority of Ghanaian firms, regardless of their size, surveyed as part of the 2007 World Bank Enterprise Survey did not perceive the skill level of the workforce as a major constraint. Furthermore, according to the Association of Ghana Industries Business Barometer, none of the top 10 challenges cited by Ghanaian businesses include mention of education or skill constraints. This is likely a result of the low-skills equilibrium that the economy and its private sector—from micro and small enterprises to larger companies—finds itself in. Ghanaian enterprises appear to have adapted to the low skills level in the country by adopting low-level technologies, which in turn means that there are relatively few high-skill job opportunities. Poaching externalities mean that the country sees a lack of incentive for enterprises to invest in training for their employees when they fear that these employees might be lured away by another firm. This helps keep skill levels low.

However, other studies show opposite results. Furthermore, in the light of the known inadequacy of the supply of skills in terms of relevance and quality, it is clear that a more careful interpretation of these studies is required to understand the apparent inadequate economic demand for skills.

Assessments completed in 2010 suggest that the priority economic sectors cannot grow to full potential without expansion of the skills pool. As part of this report, the demand and supply of skills was analyzed in some selected priority sectors. Among the findings was that earnings and livelihoods in various agricultural sectors can be significantly improved through value chain approaches that require improved skills and technology introduction. Sectors amenable to such improvements range from farming and animal husbandry to postharvest activities including conservation, packaging, marketing, and transportation. The expected expansion of the residential real estate market in Ghana could potentially employ more than one million additional (semi-)skilled workers in construction-related jobs. The quality of services in hospitality and tourism has been persistently low because of the low skills of the sector's employees. In the oil and gas sector, Ghana is primarily operating in the upstream part of the industry value chain (exploration, drilling, production). Many of the jobs created here require specialized skills that Ghana cannot provide. Direct job creation in this sector is limited; Ghana is looking at creating only 10,000 oil- and gas-related jobs in the next five years.

TVET Supply, Coordination, and Financing

The last decade in Ghana has seen a significant amount of national policy debate around TVET reform, and this has resulted in a series of policy documents over the 2002–13 period related in whole or in part to TVET. Ghana's TVET coordinating body, the Council for TVET (COTVET),[1] now plans to develop a single, overall, national TVET strategy.

The Ghanaian government acts as a large provider of skills development in the country. There are more than 200 public TVET institutes, including 45 technical training institutes (TTIs) under the Ministry of Education (MoE), 116 vocational institutes under the Ministry of Employment and Labor Relations (MoELR) (National Vocational Training Institutes [NVTIs], Integrated Community Centers for Employable Skills [ICCESs], Social Welfare Centers, and Opportunities Industrialization Centers), and the remainder under different ministries. Public institutional TVET providers can be found in all 10 regions of the country. Most tend to be located in urban areas, with the exception of the publicly funded Integrated Community Centers for Employable Skills and the Youth Leadership and Skills Training Centers, which are predominantly rural.

TVET in Ghana is delivered by a large number of entities, including eight ministries, private for-profit and nonprofit institutes, and nongovernmental organizations (NGOs), and through informal apprenticeships. (Up to twice as many students are enrolled in private institutes as in public ones; 10 times as many students are in informal apprenticeships as in public institutes.) Earlier governments have attempted—and ultimately failed—to coordinate Ghana's TVET sector: first, through the establishment of the NVTI in the 1970s, initially mandated to coordinate all aspects of vocational training nationwide, and then, following the NVTI's failure, through the National Coordinating Committee for Technical and Vocational Education and Training (NACVET) in the 1990s. NACVET ultimately failed to impose order on the unwieldy system as well.

In 2006, the new TVET coordination body, COTVET was established, and it has already made progress toward better coordination of the supply side of TVET. On the demand side, it will be important to better engage with the private sector and to collect more demand-side data, including at both the national and institutional levels. Furthermore, insufficient coordination with government plans has led to the development of parallel agendas, plans, programs, and committees. A recent example is the Local Enterprise and Skills Development Program, which has been granted a budget of Gh¢96 million for 2011/12 (about $50 million); this is more than the entire (recently established) Skills Development Fund[2] budget ($45 million).

Total public enrolment is about 47,000 students, with the MoE's technical training institutes accounting for a large proportion of this total. All the data from the public TVET providers themselves clearly show that enrollment levels over the last several years are either stagnant or in slight decline. For example, over the period 2001/02 to 2009/10, TTI enrollment remained largely stagnant at around 20,000 students; NVTI enrollment dropped by close to 10 percent over two years between 2005 and 2007, from 7,297 to 6,710; ICCES enrolment dropped by almost 40 percent (2008–11); and, over 2001/02 to 2011/12, enrollment in the Community Development Vocational/Technical Institutes was more or less stagnant, with a slight decline in the most recent year.

The largest provider of skills training remains the informal apprenticeship system, which trains in excess of 440,000 youth at any one time; there are about four informal apprentices for every trainee in formal public and private training centers combined. The fact that so many young people are being trained at no cost to the state is surely a major achievement. Several attempts have been made to support informal apprenticeship training in Ghana, but no intervention has yet had any systemic and sustainable impact. The latest government attempt to improve informal apprenticeship is via the National Apprenticeship Program, which is a relatively small-scale program providing additional classes and services to about 1 percent of the 440,000 youth in informal apprenticeship.

The labor market relevance of formal institution- and school-based TVET has been generally poor. Curricula tend to be excessively theoretical; instructors with marketable and up-to-date skills are difficult to attract and retain, and teachers are not encouraged to acquire the required practical experience through industrial attachments. Courses are typically three years in duration, and certification does not rely on competency-based assessment. Other market links such as industry liaison officers, training for the informal sector, short courses, and posttraining support are almost absent. Institutes lack the autonomy needed to respond to market changes.

Ghana's formal TVET system tends to exclude the poorest segment of the society. The share of individuals having followed a TVET course rises with families' level of wealth. Opportunity costs and direct costs of training, combined with lack of (merit-based) scholarships and untargeted public spending on TVET that is captured by those who are less in need, widen inequalities. As a result, the share of individuals from the highest-income quintile having technical or vocational training is seven times that of those from the poorest quintile. Educational entry requirements set by most formal TVET providers, public and private, are often not met by poorer pupils. The majority of those entering *informal* apprenticeships are also JHS dropouts—but those with lower aggregate grades or from poorer backgrounds.

A diverse array of financing modalities disconnected from one another and demonstrating a variety of incentives or lack thereof can be found. On top of the hierarchy of vocational training at the secondary level are the technical training institutes,[3] which are basically financed based on inputs not unlike general secondary schools. Allocations are largely based on historical allocations and student enrollments. Unit costs are routinely calculated by the MoE, but these are of limited use because they do not take internally generated funds into account (for example, training fees, parent-teacher association fees, or the proceeds of other income-generating activities) or recurrent costs associated with the depreciation of equipment. This results in salaries and teaching hours outweighing materials and equipment costs. The financing of other public Vocational Training Institutes (VTIs) represents a mixture: salaries, administration, and services are subsidized by the government, and other costs are covered by fees. For private VTIs, the main source of income is the school fees collected from students. At the opposite end of the scale is apprenticeship, the financing of which is unregulated. Its costs are borne by apprentices and their families with no input from the government or communities. In between are various types of formal and informal training programs financed through externally initiated, often temporary, programs and projects or internally based on user fees and other revenues.

Consequently, TVET financing represents at the same time inefficiencies, high unit costs and underfinancing especially in terms of quality inputs. As a result, a wide range of perceptions is present about the costs of training, with providers, especially public providers, believing that TVET is acutely underfinanced by employers (especially micro and small enterprises), for whom the true cost of training would often be prohibitively high and bears the risk of poaching externalities. In between are students and employees who either feel excluded from publicly subsidized formal training or may be reluctant to invest in their own training, especially in view of the opportunity costs.

The public financing approach and general lack of incentives to improve TVET in Ghana help to perpetuate a supply-driven, low-quality skills system that responds very poorly to the needs of the economy and especially its growth sectors. Public financing incentives are lacking for training providers to deliver better services, for employees to improve their skills and employability, and for employers to provide more training. Where public funding has been used to support private informal apprenticeships, it often does so in a way that risks displacing private financing, and where it has been used to support short duration skills training, it has often done so in an inefficient way.

Policy Recommendations

A national skills development strategy is in preparation under the auspices of COTVET. It will be useful if this strategy is

- responsive to the challenges stemming from social demand (employment, equity)
- relevant to the private sector and labor market demand
- informed by market and nonmarket failures
- harmonized with the national economic development priorities (diversification, shared sustainable growth)
- effective in terms of incentivizing the training providers to align with these expectations

The national skills strategy should aim to complement, and be complemented by, reforms that are underway in related sectors (for example, private sector development and employment, the informal economy, information and communication technologies, and agriculture).

Parallel with the strategic agenda, capacity-building efforts in COTVET and other TVET stakeholders will better enable coordination, implementation and monitoring, and the development of policies to stimulate both demand and supply. A key capacity will be COTVET's ability to coordinate across sectors, government agencies, and various types of providers, including by ensuring (1) standards for training services and a qualification framework, (2) monitoring and use of information systems, and (3) development partner and NGO support.

Under COTVET's guidance, training providers may want to go through a needs-assessment and rationalization process; they would then need to be provided with adequate support and incentives to be able to make the change to a demand-driven approach. Such a rationalization process would likely result in the institutions being more specialized in fewer trade areas, rather than offering a wide range of courses that may or may not be in demand. TVET institutes require sufficient autonomy and incentives to (re)connect with industry requirements. Decentralization can play a key role in bringing training supply closer to market needs.

The government and COTVET would do well to revisit the design of the very well-intentioned National Apprenticeship Program—although it appears to have been built more on good intentions and less on evidence-based experience of past programs. It contains several elements (for example, the one-year duration, the government's taking over fee payment, and the offering of stipends to apprentices) that have either not worked in the past, have been shown to reduce the quality of "graduates," or have proven to be unsustainable. Efforts would be well directed toward providing literacy and second-chance education opportunities to masters and apprentices, offering technical and pedagogical training and improved access to technology for masters, and improving quality through certification and workplace monitoring.

A more rigorous social profiling of the country's youth is required to enable the development and delivery of different types of training (and complementary) interventions. Better targeting is required. A well-targeted and well-designed program can really contribute a public good. A targeted scholarship scheme could promote access to TVET, especially for the poor, and for women, who could be enabled to enter trades that traditionally do not employ females. Improving access to and completion of a quality JHS education will help to make access to post-JHS TVET programs more equitable. Policies and initiatives related to reducing direct and opportunity costs of training will also help.

The government can best help the TVET system by being less directly involved in training provision and more involved in coordination, as well as providing incentives, standards, accreditation, quality assurance, and information. Any government intervention would be more effective if cognizant of current market offerings and the risks of creating undesirable market distortions. Moreover, if the government promotes the creation of an effective qualification system as the cornerstone of quality assurance, such a quality assurance system should be independent of government control, since the government cannot be expected to provide objective judgment over a service (public TVET) that it provides.

The national qualification system will be more effective if focused on training and skills that are more closely linked to improving the chances of youth to find employment and improve individual earnings, enterprise growth, and productivity. Furthermore, the qualification framework would need to be developed in sync with the competency-based training system that is being gradually introduced in Ghana. This system focuses less on the inputs, courses completed, and years spent in training, and more on the skills and competencies acquired. Also, a key cornerstone of the national qualifications framework is the recognition of prior learning, which effectively integrates apprenticeship and other informal and nonformal types of training into one qualification framework.

TVET financing will be more effective if it is based on a funding formula focused on results and performance. Planners should be cognizant of the risk that public funding could distort the training market or lead to market failures by artificially bolstering certain segments of the TVET provider network. Financing and incentive systems can be used to promote demand-driven training, to reward quality and productivity, and to promote equality and breaking out of a low-skills equilibrium. Incentives could help to improve the performance of trainee and instructor industry attachments and to encourage industry associations to provide employment.

One of the more innovative elements of the ongoing reform has been the establishment of sustainable financing for the Skills Development Fund (SDF). Channeling the majority of TVET resources through a SDF would make it easier for funds to be allocated in line with general national socioeconomic priorities and specific priorities identified by COTVET. At the same time, the allocation mechanism could encourage a demand-driven approach, linked to effective training delivery focusing on market skills requirements. In the meantime, making it mandatory for employers to contribute could put a excessive burden especially on the MSEs and could contribute to these MSEs' remaining small and informal.

TVET information systems, providing for the monitoring and evaluation of TVET supply, demand, and financing, require significant improvements. For example, such information systems will be effective if they capture not only the various types of formal provision and informal apprenticeships noted in this report, but also other forms of informal skill acquisition and learning that are taking place in the informal economy in Ghana. On the demand side, for example, more (disaggregated) wage data need to be collected via regular labor force surveys; this would reveal what the market is demanding in terms of skills. Effective data collection instruments that capture more information than just inputs (such as the number of students) would be useful; they could be extended to collect data on outputs (such as the number that graduate) and outcomes (such as the proportion of graduates that find work). Key stakeholders' capacities require strengthening, including at the institutional and district levels and within informal trade associations. The MoELR, which delivers most public non-MoE training, requires capacity-building efforts to strengthen its ability to formulate TVET policy and deliver services.

In parallel to the development of information systems, technical capacity to collect and analyze data needs to be improved. Furthermore, the capacity of Ghanaian institutions, governmental and nongovernmental, to conduct TVET research needs to be strengthened.

The political economy of the TVET reform process is a critical factor, but not well understood. We note on several occasions in this report the strong influence of politics on TVET policy making and how politicians are sometimes quick to jump on TVET as a solution to youth unemployment. However, a better understanding of the political economy of the reform process is required, including a clearer analysis of TVET's impact on reducing unemployment, and ways to strengthen that role. Further research in this area would be useful.

Notes

1. COTVET: www.cotvet.org.
2. Skills Development Fund: www.sdfghana.org.
3. The report does not cover polytechnics, which are tertiary-level training institutions.

CHAPTER 1

Context, Drivers, and Challenges of Technical and Vocational Skills Development Reform

Introduction

Ghana's Socioeconomic and Labor Market Context

Ghana has a youthful population of about 24 million (2010) (GSS 2010) and has shown impressive gains in economic growth and poverty reduction over the last two decades. The country has experienced about two decades of sustained economic growth (in the range of 4–5 percent)[1] and in 2011 was one of only seven countries in the world, and the only country in Sub-Saharan Africa, to have double-digit growth (14.4 percent) (IMF 2012a, 2012b), with the recent discovery of oil accounting for about half of the 2011 growth. In 2011, Ghana was reclassified as a (lower-) middle-income country with a gross national income (GNI) per capita (Atlas method) of $1,230 in 2010.[2] Economic growth is expected to be 8.2 percent in 2012, quite above the projected average for Sub-Saharan Africa (5 percent) (IMF 2012b). Poverty rates have dropped significantly since the early 1990s;[3] absolute poverty was reduced from its 1990 level by more than 43 percent by 2005/06 (GSS 2005/06). Nonetheless, about 30 percent of the population (more than 7 million people) still live in poverty (below $1.25 purchasing power parity) (UNDP 2011).

As with most African countries, both growth and poverty reduction are building on weak foundations. Ghana will require several more decades of sustained efforts and solid growth for most of its citizens to sustainably break out of poverty.

Economic growth has been mostly based on high revenues from the extractive and agricultural sectors due to sound macroeconomic policies and favorable global commodity prices. If managed well, recently found oil and gas reserves will constitute another source of significant growth and revenue. Ghana has also been using its resources well, investing in human capital through education, health, and infrastructure, stimulating the expansion of domestic markets and consumption. However, the sustained growth needed to reach long-term development now requires three critical steps: (1) increase productivity in the strategic economic sectors, to make sure that future growth in these sectors is sustained and that the country can build solidly on its comparative advantages, (2) diversify the Ghanaian economy and protect it from future price fluctuations in key revenue sectors, and (3) expand employment so that growth is truly and sustainably shared among all citizens.

The key strategic documents promoting economic growth and social development (GoG 2003a, 2005; NDPC 2008, 2010a, 2010b) uniformly identify human capital development as a cornerstone of the country's development. Within the general objective of human capital development, education has played a key role almost since independence. Although there have been variations in education policy directions and financing, the sustained commitment to the sector has brought about impressive results and contributed strongly to growth and poverty reduction.

At the end of the last decade, a new social consensus emerged in Ghana proposing that long-term national strategic needs go beyond educational attainment and focus increasingly on other aspects of human capital development including skills, the creation and adaptation of technologies, and what are increasingly known as "innovation systems."[4]

Adequate levels and ranges of skills contribute to three core drivers of sustained growth: productivity, diversification, and employment. Skills also have a cumulative impact on other productivity factors, including land, capital, labor, and technology. In regions where natural resources are scarce, or even where such resources are abundant but there is a risk of "Dutch disease,"[5] skills can be among the most critical success factors in diversifying the economy and boosting domestic markets. With other factors held constant, employment is unambiguously linked to job seekers' skills.

What Skills Are Necessary to Improve Productivity, Employment, and Economic Diversification?

The scale and scope of skills required by local or national economies are difficult to estimate in detail. Of course, the necessary skills include general cognitive skills such as literacy, numeracy, and scientific literacy; noncognitive skills such as creativity, persistence, reliability, and communication; and more specific, technological, vocational, and professional skills. These skills are developed at home, at school, or in the workplace, and only a minority of them are certified or even certifiable.

Often, skills are associated with the outcomes of formal public technical and vocational education and training (TVET),[6] despite the fact that the sector accounts for less than 10 percent of the technical and vocational skills acquired (roughly one and a half times as many trainees attend private TVET institutes than public ones, and 10 times more are in informal apprenticeships; see chapter 3). However, all types of TVET need to be taken into account (including school- and nonschool-based, formal and informal, public and private, initial and continuous types) when considering the impact of the TVET sector on the country's economic performance, and when proposing policies aimed at improving productivity, economic diversification, and employment.

The momentum in growth and poverty reduction efforts in Ghana requires that the focus be placed on the skills of youth, for one good reason: the median age of Ghana's population is about 20 years old (UNDP 2011). Although this new generation of future employees has the highest schooling attainment, it is also the most dependent on salaried employment: many Ghanaian youth have moved to urban areas and can no longer rely on agriculture to sustain themselves and their families.

Although TVET alone does not guarantee productivity gains or job creation, it is generally agreed that a blend of cognitive, noncognitive, intermediate, and higher technical skills is crucial to enhance the country's competitiveness and contribute to social inclusion, acceptable employment, and the alleviation of poverty.

A large number of young Ghanaians have few or no employable skills. Those who do, predominantly acquire them through informal apprenticeships, with few advantages and significant constraints. The main advantages of the informal apprenticeship system are that it is private, sensitive (if not responsive) to changes in demand, and capable of generating private resources. The disadvantages include the lack of clear and reliable standards, the absence of quality assurance, the generally low quality of training, inefficient operation, and significant equity problems. These will each be analyzed later in the report.

The key problems with formal TVET programs are their being of small scale, providing training to only a minority of youth, their fragmented programs, and the quality of the service offered. Although little is known about the outcomes, little evidence shows that they are better than for informal apprenticeships. Furthermore, the position of formal TVET programs within the education system is unclear at best. Indeed, the absence of academic prestige and limited training opportunities within students' school careers result in weak performance, poor learning results, and difficult school-to-work transitions.

There is also an adverse cycle involving high costs, inadequate quality of supply, and low demand, leading to further declines in financing, supply, and demand. This adverse cycle means that the technical and vocational skills development promise is at risk of remaining unfulfilled. That promise, long proffered to the population by government and politicians, is that increasing skills training opportunities will help solve youth unemployment. This adverse cycle effectively generates lost opportunities: As long as the quality of skills is low and the cost of training is high, key economic sectors will invest in other production factors to substitute for skills. Indeed, profitable production in key Ghanaian industries does not currently rely on improved labor productivity (see chapter 2).

Productivity, diversification, and employment fail to improve as a result. Economic diversification is slow at best, and so are changes in the structure of the labor market. Consequently, TVET sector reforms and policies tend to focus on the promise instead of the results. These reforms and policies focus to a large extent on the investment implications of the need to expand TVET, rather than on the high recurrent costs and lackluster present performance.

The first part of this chapter outlines the global drivers of technical and vocational skills development and the factors contributing to the increased global interest in TVET. Second, it summarizes the Ghanaian national context and country specific drivers of TVET. Third, it highlights the key challenges for Ghana's TVET system as reflected by recent key policy documents: the Education Strategic Plan (GoG 2003c) and its revision (GoG 2009b) and the New Education Reform (NER) (GoG 2004a). Last, it outlines a conceptual framework that can be used to assess the various kinds of market and nonmarket imperfections related to TVET in Ghana.

The Global Rise in Importance of Technical and Vocational Skills Development

Skills development is a broad concept of a new development agenda that encompasses basic academic skills learned mostly in schools; life skills learned through socialization in schools, family, community, and workplace; and technical and vocational skills learned in schools, training institutes, and on the job. Added to this, for a portion of the workforce, are professional skills acquired at higher-level educational institutions and in various training programs on the job. Within this context, TVET's role is to provide improved mobility, employability, higher earnings to wage earners, and improved productivity and competitiveness to the economy as a whole. The critical challenge for policy makers is to integrate TVET services into the broader skills agenda.

The first decade of the twenty-first century saw TVET gradually move up the agenda of donor agencies and governments in Sub-Saharan Africa (King, McGrath, and Rose 2007; King and Palmer 2007, 2010; Wegner and Komenan 2008). This renewed interest in skills is being driven by a number of different factors (King and Palmer 2010), including the following:

- *The success of universal primary education and the challenge of postprimary provision.* Agencies such as United Nations Educational, Scientific, and Cultural Organization (UNESCO), the United Kingdom's Department for International Development, and others report rising pressure for both TVET and secondary school expansion.
- *The notion of skills for competitiveness, enterprise productivity, individual prosperity, and poverty reduction.* Countries increasingly perceive the availability of skills as a crucial factor.
- *The sectorwide agenda.* There is a growing emphasis on holistic, sectorwide approaches to education and training, including a diverse post–basic education system with public and private providers and public and private financing, rather than simply prioritizing universal basic education. Also, it is believed that countries and the international development community need to go beyond Education for All (EFA), in part to achieve it (Palmer et al. 2007).
- *The political agenda.* In many developing countries, a strong political assumption is made that the development of skills can help tackle unemployment.

- *The security agenda.* In relation to the poverty reduction agenda, it is believed that the provision of skills to disenfranchised youth in fragile states, or fragile regions within states, can contribute to improving countries' security situations.

In Sub-Saharan Africa, a major force behind this renewed interest in TVET, and linking all the above drivers, is the fact that Africa's youth unemployment problem has not been resolved. Indeed, the situation has not improved even in the countries with solid growth rates over longer periods (five to seven years).

Since the start of the twenty-first century's second decade, TVET has been receiving even more attention and has shifted from being seen as a subsector area of interest only to specialists, to a cross-cutting issue of wide concern.

Against the backdrop of the global financial and economic crisis since 2008, international organizations have reaffirmed the importance of workforce skills and TVET as a key factor in future growth and productivity (ILO 2009, 2010, 2012; UNESCO 2011). In 2012–13, the World Congress on TVET in Shanghai (UNESCO 2012a, 2012b), the OECD *Skills Strategy* report (OECD 2012), the World TVET Report (UNESCO 2013), and the Education for All Global Monitoring Report 2012 (UNESCO 2012c) all bring increased focus on TVET and skills development more broadly. The financial and economic crisis has led to a (formal) jobs crisis in many countries, leaving more and more people to seek work in the informal economy.

Technical and Vocational Skills Development Drivers in Ghana

In the 1990s, in response to the World Declaration on Education for All,[7] the government launched a program focusing primarily on access: the Free, Compulsory, and Universal Basic Education program. Over the 15-year period from 1987 to 2002, the World Bank and other donors provided close to $600 million in soft loans and grants to support a series of education reform programs.

The other development of particular relevance to Ghana's education sector has been the grant approved by the Fund of the Global Partnership for Education (GPE).[8] To qualify for GPE funds, a country has to prepare a credible strategy for achieving Education for All goals by 2015 and demonstrate the existence of a funding gap. Ghana prepared its Education Strategic Plan (ESP) in 2003.

In the last decade, the Free, Compulsory, and Universal Basic Education program has produced some of the largest cohorts of students completing primary school ever witnessed; total enrollment in primary and junior high school (JHS) has increased by more than 50 percent: total primary enrollment from 2,586,434 in 2001/02 (GoG 2003b) to 3,962,779 in 2010/11 (GoG 2011a), and total JHS enrollment from 865,636 to 1,335,400 (GoG 2003b, 2011a). This has occurred at a time when Ghana's formal sector has been unable to generate sufficient employment and income opportunities, despite more than 20 years of sustained economic growth. The great majority of all those leaving school are therefore obliged to enter the informal, microenterprise economy, urban and rural, and receive informal training through apprenticeships or other types of on-the-job learning.

Table 1.1 Total Enrollment in Primary and Lower Secondary Schools in Ghana

	2001/02	2010/11
Primary school	2,723,300	3,962,779
Junior high school/junior secondary school	895,928	1,335,400

Sources: 2001/02 data from GoG 2004d; 2010/11 data from GoG 2011a.

The rapid expansion of primary and lower secondary enrollment as part of the Education for All process (table 1.1) has increased demand for post–basic education and training opportunities.[9] This has led to concerns about youth lacking the opportunity to continue their education beyond JHS.[10] In response, policy makers and politicians have proposed to dramatically increase support to post–basic levels, including TVET.

The major drivers for the government's interest in the development of technical and vocational skills are divided between social and economic considerations:

1. *Social concerns* include the increased demand for post–basic education and training opportunities by individual students and their families, and concerns about youth unemployment (World Bank 2008a, 2008b). The issue of unemployed JHS graduates who are unable to pursue their education and training (because of the scarcity of positions, lack of information, or weak performance) is a serious concern to the government at the highest level, as is the fact that the majority of JHS graduates find employment only in low-productivity informal jobs
2. *Economic concerns* include the predominance of the informal economy, the low productivity of most industries, and the limited sustainability of economic growth, given, among others, the vulnerability of leading industries to fluctuations in commodity prices.

The New Education Reform program is based on a 2004 White Paper (GoG 2004a) and was introduced in 2007. It aimed to correct some of the inefficiencies and inadequacies of the formal education system. TVET features prominently in these NER reforms because the sector is perceived as an alternative to general secondary education, on the assumption that it can help link the provision of skills with both employment and poverty reduction. The assumption that the provision of skills to youth (through schools or special vocational institutes) will ease unemployment among those who complete school has been longstanding (see Palmer 2007a), and so are the concerns over the ability of the education and training system to supply the skills demanded by a diversified and competitive economy (World Bank 2008a).

The 2004 "Draft TVET Policy Framework for Ghana" also specifically mentions concerns about both poverty reduction and economic competitiveness as being key drivers of TVET reform in Ghana (GoG 2004b).

Ghana is considered a factor-driven economy (World Economic Forum 2011, 2012) and competes based on its factor endowments—primarily unskilled labor and natural resources. To become more competitive, for example, through

Table 1.2 Global Competitive Ranking Index of 144 Countries, Selected Sub-Saharan African Countries, 2012/13

	Overall Index	4th Pillar: Health and Primary Education	5th Pillar: Higher Education and Training	7th Pillar: Labor Market Efficiency	9th Pillar: Technological Readiness	11th Pillar: Business Sophistication	12th Pillar: Innovation
South Africa	52	132	84	113	62	38	42
Rwanda	63	100	117	11	113	70	51
Botswana	79	114	95	60	106	95	73
Namibia	92	120	119	74	104	102	101
Ghana (2011/12)[a]	114	124	109	79	113	99	98
Ghana (2012/13)	103	112	107	97	108	101	95
Kenya	106	115	100	39	101	67	50
Nigeria	115	142	113	55	112	66	78
Tanzania	120	113	132	47	122	106	75
Chad	139	144	140	95	143	138	113

Sources: World Economic Forum 2011, 2012.
Note: The index denotes ranking; the lower the index, the more competitive the countries are.
a. Out of 142 countries.

increasing efficiency and quality without increasing item costs, higher education and training have an important role to play (ibid.).

According to the Global Competitive Index ranking of 144 countries, Ghana ranks poorly in terms of education and training when compared with the rest of the world (see table 1.2). However, Ghana's overall ranking has shown improvement between 2011/12 and 2012/13. When compared with the 30 Sub-Saharan Africa countries included in the index, Ghana ranked eighth in 2012/13 and 11th in 2011/12. Furthermore, in 2012/13, Ghana overtook Kenya—often regarded as a good comparator country to Ghana—in overall ranking compared to 2011/12.

TVET Policy, 2002–13

In the last decade, a significant amount of national policy debate has been focused around TVET reform, and this has resulted in a series of policy documents related in whole or in part to TVET over the 2002–13 period. However, there is no single, overall, national skills or TVET strategy that contains clear strategic reform objectives, targets to be achieved, benchmarks, indicators, and timelines.[11]

Between 2002 and 2008 the government simultaneously elaborated and followed two separate policy documents—an approach that one major bilateral agency in Ghana described as a dual-track education policy-making process (Palmer 2005).

The Education Strategic Plan

Up until its revision in 2009 (see below), the main education policy framework was the 2003–15 Education Strategic Plan (ESP) (GoG 2003b, 2003c), which we shall refer to as ESP I. ESP I was arguably a donor-driven document that was developed with support from various donor agencies with an interest in basic education.

It was an education strategy linked to constitutional requirements to provide free compulsory universal basic education, in line with the targets set out in the Ghana Poverty Reduction Strategy, Education for All—one of the Millennium Development Goals, defining targets through 2015. With regard to TVET, the ESP I—being a Ministry of Education (MoE) strategic document—focused entirely on school-based technical and vocational education (TVE) and set targets for 2015 related to enrollments, percentage of enrolled females, and extent of industrial attachments.

The New Education Reform

In parallel to ESP I, the government pursued its New Education Reform program. A key objective of NER was to shift the policy focus to post–basic education, based on the assumption that Ghana was on track to achieve full access to basic education in a time frame shorter than expected.

The NER originated from a panel of academics and other education specialists commissioned by the then president to examine the education system in Ghana. In October 2002, this panel, led by Professor Anamuah-Mensah, published its report, "Meeting the Challenges of Education in the Twenty First Century" (GoG 2002).[12]

In 2004, the "White Paper on the Report of the Education Reform Review Committee" (GoG 2004a) presented ministers' agreed position on the recommendations made in the Anamuah-Mensah Report. The White Paper, among other things, proposed to expand post–basic education and training as well as the vocational track at the upper secondary level. This led to the establishment of the National Education Reform Implementation Committee (NERIC) in early 2007 and to the launch of NER later in 2007.

Comparison of ESP I and NER

Whereas the TVET components of ESP I track of the policy-making process were contained in the one main ESP I reference document, the TVET components of the NER track were contained in various policy documents that were never really synthesized, including (1) the 2002 Anamuah-Mensah Report and the 2004 White Paper (GoG 2002, 2004a), (2) the 2007 report of the TVET subcommittee of NERIC (GoG 2007d), (3) the latest draft of the TVET policy framework, from August 2004 (GoG 2004b), (4) the 2006 Council for TVET (COTVET) Act (GoG 2006e), (5) the 2007 "Operationalizing COTVET Act" report (CPTC 2006), and (6) the Singapore Action Plan.[13]

A key issue is that although ESP essentially refers to TVET falling under the aegis of the MoE, the remit of NER was much wider. Its key documents covered TVET across multiple ministries as well as nongovernmental TVET, including informal apprenticeships.

There is one more component to the policy discussion. In late 2008, the National Development Planning Commission (NDPC) produced a medium- to long-term development plan for the 2008–15 period (NDPC 2008), which contains a discussion of skill development. This was later updated by the NDPC in its "Medium-Term National Development Policy Framework" (NDPC 2010a).

The Revised Education Strategic Plan and the Status of Overall TVET Policy

In 2009, a revised ESP (2010–20) (hereafter ESP II) was drawn up (GoG 2009b) with the aim of harmonizing the TVET and skills development components of ESP I with the TVET components of NER. The ESP II Strategies and Work Program document (GoG 2009c) does a reasonable job of trying to draw in several of the various TVET domains in Ghana, including the MoE secondary technical schools, the MoE technical vocational institutes, the MoE polytechnics, and—on a superficial level—apprenticeship, agricultural education, and nonformal training. For each of these areas, ESP II outlines objectives, indicative targets, and activities. However, this revised ESP fails to cover all providers of TVET; the focus was again mostly on MoE TVET provision and the activities of COTVET itself (because COTVET was placed under the MoE).

It should be recalled that at the second cycle level, NER specified that there should be four streams: academic, technical, (formal) apprenticeship, and agricultural. As a result, ESP II, which is an MoE-produced strategy, of course, was obliged to attempt to cover these non-MoE areas, in addition to nonformal education, which also falls under the MoE (but has traditionally been associated in Ghana with adult literacy programs and not nonformal technical skills training). However, it is clear that the strategies related to apprenticeship, for example, are weak; the main provision related to this simply states: "Where appropriate, institutionalize formal and informal apprenticeship programs with local master-craftspersons" (GoG 2009c: objective SC11). This, of course, refers to apprenticeships under the National Apprenticeship Program (see appendix B).

What Ghana continues to need is an overarching TVET strategy document, a national skills strategy that harmonizes all the policy positions related to TVET and defines objectives, targets, indicators, and timelines for *all* domains of TVET. As of June 2013, this had not been elaborated, and the TVET policy framework of August 2004 (GoG 2004b), although it technically never went beyond a draft stage, remains the only real framework for TVET to date. In late 2011, COTVET commissioned a consultant to review the 2004 policy framework, with the aim of informing the development of a national skills strategy. Indeed, it is encouraging that the 2012–16 COTVET strategic plan includes the preparation of a 10-year national strategic plan for technical and vocational skills development (even if it is not expected to be completed until 2016) (COTVET 2012b). Discussions between NDPC and COTVET are ongoing on the development of such a strategy. NDPC is leading the process, and COTVET is providing needed data and other input.

A Framework for Assessing Market and Nonmarket Imperfections Related to TVET in Sub-Saharan Africa

The purpose of this section is to outline a specific framework that can help to assess the various kinds of market and nonmarket imperfections related to TVET in Sub-Saharan Africa.[14] This framework is drawn upon in the later sections of this report.

Several frameworks are being developed and adopted to examine the wider skills universe: for example, all levels of education and training from early

Figure 1.1 Framework for Skills Assessment

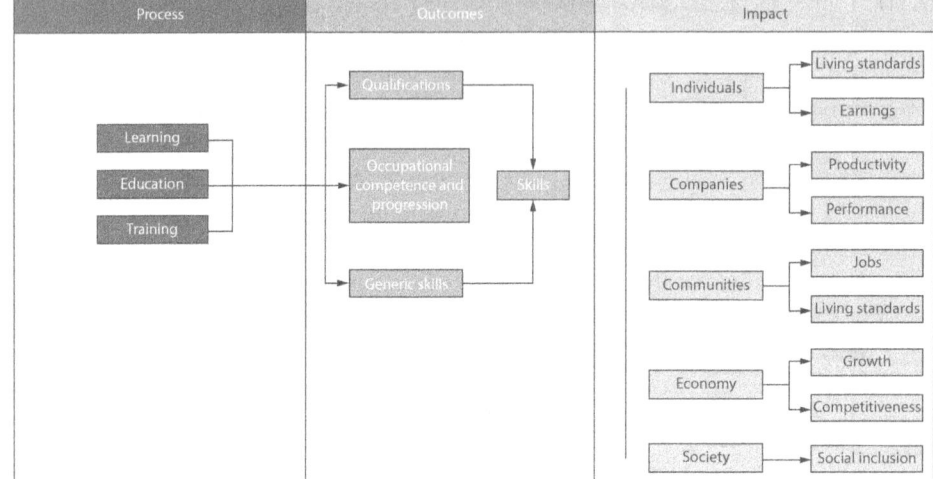

Source: Campbell 2002.

childhood to tertiary, and all types of cognitive, technical, and noncognitive skills. The framework shown in figure 1.1, which is illustrated by the case of Ghana in this report, complements existing frameworks, some of which are noted here:

- The World Bank, *Skills toward Employment and Productivity* (World Bank 2010c). This report goes into more detail on one part of the program framework, Skills toward Employment and Productivity 3: building job relevant skills, by focusing on the TVET aspect of "job relevant skills."
- The World Bank, *System Assessment and Benchmarking for Education Results* (Tan, McGough, and Valerio 2010). This report adds value to this framework by specifically examining TVET from the perspective of market and nonmarket imperfections.
- The Inter-Agency Working Group on TVET Indicators. *Proposed Indicators for Assessing Technical and Vocational Education and Training* (IAWG on TVET Indicators 2012).
- The G20 Development Working Group Working Draft, *Developing Indicators of Skills for Employment and Productivity* (G20DWG 2011).

Market Imperfections

Noncompetitive Markets

Low-Skills Equilibrium in a Large Part of the Private Sector. Countries with low-skill levels can get stuck in a low-skills equilibrium, where the whole economy—or parts or sectors of it—becomes adjusted to a low-skill level (Lall 2000, 22). Many factors are associated with a low-skill equilibrium that are often both causes of and symptomatic of the phenomenon. In low-skill environments, enterprises adapt to the low-skills level in a country by adopting simple, low-level technologies (Lall 2000), therefore resulting in relatively few high-skill job opportunities. In turn, the lack of high-skill job opportunities means that individuals have less incentive to invest in higher skills. Another cause (and symptom) of a low-skills equilibrium is the imperfect competition for skills (poaching externalities) that exists in many countries; there is a lack of incentive for enterprises to invest in training for their employees when they fear that these employees might be poached by another firm. This helps keep skill levels low. Many Sub-Saharan Africa countries have (very) large informal economies, which results in additional contributing factors to the perpetuation of a low-skills equilibrium. For example, among informal micro and small enterprises (MSEs), training is not seen as a priority or major constraint, and hence there is a low demand for upgrading skills from these groups. Furthermore, informal MSEs often operate in low-income domestic markets where purchasing power is low; as a result, predominant demand is for low-cost items that, in many cases, also tend to be low-quality items. The inability of many customers to buy higher-quality items suppresses demand among enterprises to up-skill to meet such a need. Moreover, those individuals who are learning on the job (for example, through informal apprenticeships or via casual labor) usually acquire only skills to produce cheap, low-quality items (on an intermittent basis) and find themselves trapped in a low-skills, low-productivity vicious cycle.[15]

Where there is a lack of competition between training providers (see below), the quality of training often gets suppressed, and the competencies that individuals can acquire are often reduced, again contributing to a low-skills equilibrium.

Where there is a perceived or actual lack of formal employment opportunities—which are seen as providing higher income than informal work, but which invariably require higher levels of skill attainment—or where there is a perceived or actual difficulty in accessing further education and training, not only can social demand for higher-skill levels to be suppressed, but completion rates of lower-skill levels (for example, lower secondary level) can actually be reduced; this all helps to perpetuate a supply of individuals with lower-skill levels.

In many countries in Sub-Saharan Africa, access to credit, technology, land, and regulatory frameworks is low; the demand for skills is constrained by these issues. For example, enterprises have an incentive to borrow to finance training as long as the increase in labor productivity and earnings (and hence the internal rate of return) is higher than the interest rate charged. However, financial institutions usually have little information on the benefits of training to individual productivity, as well as little information on the employer or individual—and so may not lend.

Thus, individuals, employers, and enterprises can become stuck in a low-skills equilibrium in which the potential to up-skill is there, but there is no incentive to raise skill levels. "Countries with the lowest skill levels—and so the greatest skill needs—face the greatest difficulty in providing new skills" (Lall 2000: 23–24).

Labor Markets. In Sub-Saharan Africa, many labor markets are segmented; formal labor markets are typically small and uncompetitive, whereas informal labor markets are normally large but unproductive. Moreover, such segmented labor markets typically do not enable those in low-skill, low-wage employment to move to high-skill, high-wage employment; in other words, mobility from informal to formal labor markets is difficult. In such contexts, enterprises' and individuals' relationship with TVET changes. For example, enterprises may not regard low-skill levels, or training to raise them, as a priority concern (see above), while individuals may see little benefit in seeking to attain higher-skill levels since their mobility up the jobs ladder, where they might put such skills to use, is constrained.

Providers. The public sector training market in many developing countries remains highly uncompetitive due to many factors (see, for example, Johanson and Adams 2004). Government policies in many developing countries have, over the years, helped to create and maintain supply-driven training systems, within which uncompetitive providers operate and, crucially, are not incentivized to behave any other way. Financing of public TVET providers remains largely focused on inputs (numbers of students, staff, buildings, and so on) rather than outcomes; this input focus typically does nothing to promote quality, competition, and improvements in outcomes (for example, higher percentage of students graduating with a certain competency level, or percentage of TVET leavers who are working in their trade area 12 months after graduating). Public financing mechanisms also tend to create and perpetuate long chains of accountability between the provider (the school or training institute) and the client (youth and their parents). Salaries of teachers and instructors in public providers are paid by the government, not directly by parents, and they know that they will get paid regardless of how many students pass their exams or gain adequate practical competencies. And they are not easily fired for underperforming, coming to class late, or not coming at all for extended periods.[16] Staffing regulations remain delinked from incentives that would drive improvements in industry-related skills (for example, linking participation in industrial attachments to career progression and salary increase); rather, they tend to be focused more on encouraging TVET teachers to get higher and higher academic-related qualifications. Public TVET providers typically have relatively limited levels of autonomy to hire and fire staff, introduce new short courses, generate, retain, and allocate revenue beyond school fee collection, procure equipment, and so on.

In some contexts, public training providers are so geographically dispersed that there is simply no competition among providers.

In many developing countries, the largest training offering is from the large informal apprenticeship system—not from formal TVET provision. Here, too, the training market remains uncompetitive, largely because of the uncompetitive nature of the informal enterprises within which the training takes place.

Inequalities
The segmented labor markets of many countries in Sub-Saharan Africa coincide with inequalities that are geographical, social, educational, and economic.

One type of inequality breeds another. For example, educational inequalities at the basic education level, or geographical inequalities in access to formal (and informal) TVET, lead to inequalities of access to, and mobility within, the labor market. Inequalities are themselves exacerbated by the presence of segmented labor markets, inequalities of access to and/or quality of public services, and, further, weak private sector development with low productivity.

Although one can identify various reinforcing cycles of inequality, as noted above, the existence of such cycles suggests that virtuous cycles of equality could also be created; for example, improving equality of access to quality basic education should help to improve equality of access to TVET, the externalities of which should help to address key forms of youth exclusion.

Information Asymmetries and Inadequacies

Information Asymmetries. There is often an information imbalance about the benefits of and returns to learning, which can result in underinvestment in skills, especially by employers.

Inadequate Information. Individuals often have limited information about the quality of training providers; as a result, they have difficulty in identifying which provider to choose and may end up with low-quality training. Information is often lacking on what skills are demanded by the labor market (as well as what skills are likely to be in demand in several years). Individuals, therefore, are usually not able to select training courses or specializations based on current or projected need; instead, they revert to dominant perceptions regarding "valuable" trade areas, rely on family and social connections to suggest areas, or—for women—simply end up going into trade areas that are deemed suitable for their gender.

Nonmarket Imperfections

Developing country governments often don't respond to market imperfections, respond in ineffective ways, or respond in ways that actually make things worse. Key problems with the approach to TVET taken by governments of many developing countries are related to imperfections in institutions and policies.

Institutions
At the level of the institution, the most obvious (but least evidence-based) nonmarket imperfection is the fact that many trainees complete their training with inadequate or irrelevant skill sets. In many developing countries, large numbers of young people are undertaking public institution–based TVET programs, usually from one to three years, but are graduating with skill competency levels that are below market needs or with skills that are no longer demanded in the market. This imperfection at the level of the public training institute stems from systemic policy imperfections (see below).

Most governments still act as a large provider of skills without creating incentive systems to encourage equity, quality, and competition. At the same time rigid public sector regulations and policies don't provide the flexibility needed by providers to quickly react to changes in market demand; examples of such rigidities include centralized decision making and lack of autonomy at the institutional/school level, as well as civil service regulations for recruiting, moving, and firing staff.

Policies

Financing Policies. Typically the TVET financing and incentive approaches used in developing countries help to perpetuate a supply-driven, low-quality skills provision.

Public financing incentives are lacking for training providers to deliver better services, for employees to improve their skills and employability, and for employers to provide more training. In many cases, government financing approaches end up distorting markets.

As noted earlier, at the level of the public provider, funding for public TVET institutes and salaries for their instructors are not linked to performance or to any minimum level of quality. Rather, budgets are usually linked to historic allocations, number of students, and the like. Salary and promotion systems for TVET teachers and instructors are often similar to those for their counterparts in general education schools; they are based on years of experience and further academic degrees obtained. But incentivizing TVET teachers to pursue higher academic study may not be in the best interest of the young people they are training. Technical education in higher education institutions (universities, colleges, polytechnics) is often very theoretically focused and detached from industry, so that after completing the program the TVET instructor may be no better off when it comes to delivering industry-relevant practical competencies. There are usually no policies that link TVET teacher salaries (or incentives) to industrial connections to improve their understanding of, and competency in, industry-demanded practical skills.

Public subsidies for TVET are often used inefficiently. For example, where subsidized (or free at point of use, or including free or subsidized equipment use), short-term training programs can result in trainees dropping out of longer-term training that they are paying for. In another case, when TVET institutes or other training providers receive direct government subsidies, competition is reduced and individuals tend to migrate to subsidized programs. In many cases, the government does not base its choice of training provider or modality on evidence of demand or expected return, but on populist and political decisions, as well as on assumptions about the relationship between skills provision and reduction in unemployment.

Public financing can easily substitute for private financing. Governments can end up paying for something that the private sector would have paid for anyway.

Coordination Policies. One of the most serious nonmarket imperfections regarding TVET is coordination of providers, qualifications, strategies, polices, information, legislation, and development partner support. When set up, TVET coordinating councils are often not given sufficient power, resources, and autonomy from any one ministry. Nonmarket imperfections in coordination and in collecting (and disseminating) the needed supply and demand information can result in supply-demand mismatches, which lead to skills shortages, gaps, and surpluses.

Targeting Policies. Governments may fail to react to market inequalities that inhibit the access of marginalized groups to TVET.

Typically public TVET programs are not good at targeting and don't cater well to specific needs (of different categories of people). As a result, public funding can be captured by those who are less in need, thus widening inequalities.

An additional consequence of inadequate coordination (above) is that policy makers can receive an incomplete picture of the entire public TVET domain and, although some public providers (especially MoE TVET) are well known and have policy champions to capture support, many others remain neglected, misunderstood, and very underfunded.

Enabling Environment Policies. Developing country governments typically fail to do enough to promote skill utilization (and demand) through designing and implementing policies to promote an enabling environment for the use of skills. There is usually much more government focus on getting young people into, and out of, TVET programs than there is on putting in place policies, mechanisms, and incentives to promote a better utilization of these acquired skills. Part of this is also due to an inadequate policy coordination to coordinate policies across sectors to promote better skill utilization overall.

Comments on the Policy-Making Process

In many cases, TVET policies are the result of policy borrowing; popular assumptions about TVET-development linkages or short-term outlooks linked to political campaigns.

Policy borrowing, rather than policy learning: Countries sometimes borrow (or are "sold") approaches that work in other countries, without taking into account their own specific local context. Examples include the widespread take-up of national qualification frameworks by many developing countries, even when there are growing concerns about their applicability (Young 2005).

Popular assumptions about TVET-development linkages, rather than evidence-based approaches: In many developing countries, policy makers hold a rather linear view of the links between TVET and youth unemployment, poverty reduction, or growth. Expanding TVET provision is very frequently seen as a solution to the challenge of large numbers of unemployed youth; in many cases, however, far too much is expected of what TVET alone can do.

Unsustainable, campaign-related TVET approaches, rather than strategic evidence-based thinking: Since TVET is so closely linked to dealing with youth employment issues, in too many cases TVET programs and policies spring up that promise to deliver quick fixes or quick political gains. Such approaches are typically unsustainable.

Where approaches are based on deeply ingrained assumptions about what TVET can do, and/or on short-term attempts to get quick wins, public expenditure is typically not being allocated efficiently and may even be functioning in ways to crowd out private financing.

Concluding Comments

Having explored some of the contextual issues related to TVET reform in Ghana, as well as outlining a conceptual framework that we shall refer back to at the end of each subsequent chapter, this report proceeds as follows. Chapter 2 explores issues of TVET demand, looking at both social and economic demand issues. Chapter 3 looks at TVET supply, performance, and assessment and provides an analysis of the landscape of TVET providers, formal and informal, public and private. Chapter 4 looks at the critical issue of TVET coordination and describes the current efforts to improve this via COTVET. Chapter 5 explores TVET financing, public and private, from the institutional and enterprise levels, to macrofinancing policies and new financing developments. Chapter 6 concludes with policy recommendations.

Notes

1. Real GDP growth: 8 percent (2010), 4 percent (2009), 8.4 percent (2008), 6.5 percent (2007), 6.1 percent (2006), 6 percent (2005), 5.3 percent (2004), 5.1 percent (2003), 4.5 percent (1993–2002) (2011, 185; IMF 2012b, 196).
2. See http://data.worldbank.org/country/ghana. In 2010, Ghana's GDP was rebased, and the new national account estimates showed that Ghana was a little wealthier than previously estimated.
3. Ibid.
4. While this report will focus on skills development, the World Bank has also taken an active part in the dialogue on Science, Technology, and Innovation.
5. The Dutch disease is an economic concept that explains the apparent relationship between the increase in the exploitation of natural resources and a decline in the manufacturing sector, related to the revaluation of the exchange rate.
6. This report uses the terms "Technical and Vocational Education and Training" (TVET) and "Technical and Vocational Skills Development" interchangeably.
7. World Declaration on Education for All and Framework for Action to Meet Basic Learning Needs, adopted by the World Conference on Education for All—Meeting Basic Learning Needs, held in Jomtien, Thailand, March 5–9, 1990.
8. Previously known as the Fast-Track Initiative.

9. This expansion has, of course, also resulted in the dilution of the quality of primary and lower secondary schooling.
10. Under the new education reforms introduced in September 2007, basic education in Ghana consists of two years of preprimary, six years of primary, and three years of JHS.
11. The closest that the government has come to this is the 2007 TVET subcommittee of the National Education Reforms Implementation Committee, although this is in need of revision.
12. This report is hereafter referred to as the "Anamuah-Mensah Report."
13. In January/February 2008 the World Bank organized a "Leaders in Education and Training for Sustained Growth in Africa (LETSGA) Workshop" in Singapore. At this workshop, Ghanaian participants developed a TVET Action Plan, which came to be known in Ghana TVET circles as the Singapore Action Plan.
14. This framework was developed by the authors, drawing on Campbell (2002) and World Bank (2010a, 2011a). See also Almeida, Behrman, and Robalino (2012).
15. The skills acquired by on-the-job learners, such as informal apprentices or casual laborers, largely depend on what is produced, which in turn is driven by market demand.
16. In contrast, private training providers tend to have relatively shorter chains of accountability; parents pay school fees to the school, and teachers and principals aim to deliver good service and be seen to deliver good outcomes (high proportions of students getting high marks, or going on to higher education and training). If they don't, parents are quite free to take their money (and child) to another private school.

CHAPTER 2

Demand for TVET

Introduction

For technical and vocational education and training (TVET) to promote economic growth and poverty reduction, policy should consider both the supply of and the demand for skills.[1] This chapter reviews the main demand-side issues concerning technical and vocational skills in Ghana.

A World Bank report, "Ghana Job Creation and Skills Development" (World Bank 2008a), examined the economic demand-side issues noted above but did not fully address the social demand-side issues.[2] This chapter aims to complement that report, first, examining the social demand for TVET and, second, providing further discussion of some aspects of an economic demand-side analysis related to the skill needs of formal industry and informal micro and small enterprises (MSEs) and to the returns on informal apprenticeships.

The demand-side analysis should consider both social and economic demand issues:

1. *Social demand issues* to be addressed include (i) the level (past, current, and projected) of social demand for TVET on behalf of those who complete basic education and their parents, (ii) enrollment in different types of TVET programs and how this reflects social demand, and (iii) the strength of social demand for Ghana's large private training system (including informal apprenticeships and private vocational institutes).
2. *Economic demand issues* to be addressed include (i) recent economic trends and economic growth prospects that may signal a future demand for skills, (ii) the structure of the market demand for skills and the driving economic forces, (iii) labor market policies, (iv) nonlabor policies that affect the labor market (such as foreign direct investment and technological development), (vi) employment and earnings trends and what they tell us about the demand for skills, and (vii) the skill needs of formal industry and informal MSEs.

Social Demand for TVET

As noted earlier, politicians and policy makers in Ghana increasingly perceive TVET as an effective policy option to deal with the large numbers of those who complete school and concerns over youth unemployment. *However, is this demand from policy and political communities matched by a demand from parents and youth?*

Social Demand from Youth Who Complete and Those Who Do Not Complete JHS

Ghana's progress toward Education for All has resulted in some of the largest cohorts of youth completing lower secondary school ever witnessed. Between academic years 2001/02 and 2011/12, enrollment in junior high school (JHS) (public and private combined) increased by almost 50 percent, from 895,928 to 1,434,211 pupils (GoG 2004d, 2012a). Despite this overall increase, still only two-thirds of students who start JHS complete it (GoG 2012a), leaving many locked out of further formal education and training options.

As the number of those who complete JHS increases, it is inevitable that the social demand for post–basic education and training will increase.[3] The pressure for expansion is backed by the analysis of household data, offering evidence of positive economic returns to post–basic education, which provides access to better paying jobs and higher earnings. TVET is also assumed to play an important role in promoting access to both wage- and self-employment (World Bank 2008a, 78).

However, opportunities for post-JHS education and training remain limited; of those who complete the three years of JHS, half do not make it to further formal education and training. The 2011 Basic Education Certificate Examination (BECE) was taken by a total of 372,799 pupils in 2011, of whom 46 percent were placed in second cycle formal education (GoG 2012a). More than 200,000 young people completing JHS, therefore, were unable to pursue formal post–basic education or training.

Net enrollment in senior high school (SHS) is 24 percent (2011/12; GoG 2012a). This means that about 8 out of every 10 youth 15–17 years of age are not enrolled in SHS (although some of these youth may still be enrolled in lower levels of education if they have been repeating one or more grades). Only 5–7 percent of JHS graduates can except to find a place in either public or private TVET institutes (World Bank 2008a, 60–61). The bulk of all post–basic education and training opportunities, therefore, will continue to be provided by informal apprenticeships or on-the-job learning (World Bank 2008a, 60–61, 78).

TVET Enrollment Trends

What do recent trends in TVET enrollment tell us about the social demand for different types of TVET?

Enrollment in virtually all public TVET institutes has been either static or in decline over the last few years[4] (see chapter 3):

- Over the period 2001/02 to 2009/10, enrollment in MoE technical training institutes (TTIs) has remained largely stagnant at around 20,000 students (see appendix section "The Technical Training Institutes"). A senior MoE civil servant commented that it will be difficult to increase enrollment in TTIs because "people don't want it [Technical and Vocational Education]."[5] In other words, TVET is not in demand.
- Enrollment in other public TVET providers including the Opportunities Industrialization Centers and National Vocational Training Institute (NVTI) centers has also been declining.
- Enrollment in the Community Development Vocational/Technical Institutes and the Integrated Community Centers for Employable Skills (ICCES) has been more or less stagnant over the 2002–11 period (see appendix sections "Community Development Vocational/Technical Institutes" and "The Integrated Community Centers for Employable Skills").

The picture is more complex in terms of demand for different courses: Enrollment has apparently increased for some trade areas (especially those related to construction, information technology (IT), and electrical trades) and decreased for others (such as carpentry, dressmaking, and to a lesser degree hairdressing).

Although public TVET enrollment figures suggest a falling social demand for TVET, this is not necessarily representative of the sector as a whole, given that most TVET is private, delivered through informal apprenticeships and private vocational institutes. There appears to be a strong social demand for apprenticeships in particular, and the estimated 445 private vocational training institutes (VTIs) train about 73,000 youth at any one time, almost twice the number as those trained by public VTIs (see chapter 3). Nonetheless, evidence is emerging that enrollment in many of these private VTIs may also be stagnating, which suggests that social demand for private TVET is also declining. We should also consider that public TVET enrollment gives an indication only of the social demand for *current* TVET offerings and does not also indicate latent demand for other types of TVET skills that might not be currently offered by providers.

Whereas enrollment in formal training courses in recent has declined, or at least stagnated (see chapter 3), evidence from the Ghana Living Standard Surveys (GLSSs) indicates that the share of the population who have attended a TVET program increased over the period from 1991/02 to 2005/06 (World Bank 2008a). The two sets of data are not necessarily contradictory; TVET participation may have increased during the 1990s, and declined or stagnated since the mid-2000s. Further analysis is required to fully understand the historical trends.

In addition to public and private TVET institutions, there is the much larger informal, or traditional, apprenticeship system, which trains in excess of 440,000 youth at any one time. According to the living standards surveys of 1991/92 and 2005/06, the proportion of youth 20–30 years of age who have had apprenticeship training increased over the period (World Bank 2008a).

Even if enrollment in private VTIs is stagnating, clearly the large informal training sector is an indication that parents, and youth themselves in some cases, are willing and able to pay for private TVET, formal or informal. This is a clear indication of social demand for skills training.

Factors Affecting Social Demand

First, the social demand for TVET is constrained among certain disadvantaged and marginalized groups as a result of a series of factors that restrict their access to TVET (discussed in chapter 3). Here, we shall highlight the apparent link between initial general educational achievements at the basic education level and subsequent access to quality TVET opportunities. On the one hand, we note that most formal TVET providers, public and private, have minimum educational entry requirements (usually a complete JHS level of schooling with a minimum threshold aggregate score). Furthermore, even with informal apprenticeships, the evidence is very clear that the majority (75 percent) of those now entering informal apprenticeships are actually JHS completers (Palmer 2007a; Monk, Sandefur, and Teal 2008; World Bank 2008a), and some apprenticeships appear to require higher levels of education completion than others (see appendix section "Informal Apprenticeship Training"). On the other hand, we note that large numbers of poorer children and youth do not meet these minimum requirements, either because of low levels of learning, or because they leave school early or never attend school; we shall briefly examine each of these issues in turn:

- *Low levels of learning, leading to low Basic Education Certificate Examination aggregate scores:* National education assessment results show that 90 percent of children in primary grade 3 in deprived districts are not proficient in either math or English (World Bank 2012a; see also World Bank 2011b).
- *Not being in school for the right amount of time or not entering school at all:* Surveys show that about one million children and adolescents (6–16 years of age) are out of school in Ghana (school year ending in 2011): 567,000 primary age children and 422,000 lower-secondary age children (UNESCO 2012c). These numbers include those who started school but then dropped out, those who are expected to start school but are older than the usual age for their grade level, as well as those who are expected never to go to school.

Inequitable access to basic education (see also CREATE 2011), therefore, contributes to inequitable access to TVET and hence contributes to suppressing social demand for TVET among certain groups. This is especially the case in the three northern regions where basic education access and achievement can be very low (World Bank 2012a), impeding access to—and social demand for—TVET in this area.

Second, social demand for TVET in Ghana is suppressed because of the low public prestige value given to TVET and associated occupations; it is seen as an area where academically weak students and dropouts go (Bortei-Doku Aryeetey, Doh, and Andoh 2011). For those who do decide to take up TVET, either through choice—or lack of it (if it is their only option for post–basic education and training)—the perceived and actual quality of skills training that the public and private providers offer is likely to affect the social demand for different types of training. Given a choice, families are more likely to enroll their children in better-quality VTIs.[6] The result is an unofficial hierarchy of VTIs: parents prefer to send their children to TTIs; if this proves impossible, NVTIs are given second priority, followed by community development institutes, and youth leadership and skills training centers. Of all the publicly funded VTIs, Integrated Community Center for Employable Skills, MoELR (ICCES) are generally the least sought after.

A third factor influencing the social demand for training relates to the perceived and actual relevance or usefulness of the training offered to the labor market. Do the posttraining employment and income opportunities for TVET graduates encourage others to enroll? Indeed, TVET may have a role to play in influencing the preferred type of work (wage or self-employment). However, graduate pay is inadequate, jobs are scarce, and support for the creation of MSEs is insufficient. As a result, TVET remains less popular than general education,[7] regarded by many as a better preparation for the available formal employment opportunities.[8]

A fourth factor influencing social demand for training relates to subsequent opportunities to progress to further education and training following that initial training. If training is perceived as a dead-end option, with little or no further chance to progress vertically (to higher levels of education and training) or horizontally (to different types of education and training at similar levels), it will lessen the popularity of the initial training.

Although low levels of learning achievement at the basic education level, as well as low or no attendance at this level, will obviously affect individuals' chances of accessing SHS, for those who do attend school and pass the Basic Education Certificate Examination, there remains a preference for general over technical/vocational post–basic education options for the two last reasons noted above. This is clear in enrollment numbers. Although formal TVET numbers have somewhat stagnated, between 2002/03 and 2009/10 enrollment in SHSs increased from 301,120 to 537,332 students (GoG 2004d, 2011a),[9] clearly underlining the social demand for general education. It will be interesting to track student demand for the vocational, technical, and agricultural SHS streams, to establish the degree of continuity in the nature of demand, reflected in the strong historical preference for the academic, general education stream.

Incentives to Stimulate Social Demand

For the formal public TVET sector, there are no government incentives, such as targeted reductions in training fees or conditional cash transfers, that might encourage parents to send their children for training, or that might encourage more equitable access. This contrasts with the government policy for general basic education, which has been made fee free, through the implementation of capitation grants to all schools, and for which school meal programs in targeted schools further stimulate demand. This said, clearly an unfinished educational agenda remains at the basic education level—with about one million children out of school and low levels of learning. Thus, a strong rationale can clearly still be presented for incentivizing and encouraging increased access to and (according to the original objectives) improving learning outcomes at this level. For the reasons noted above, this might also help to stimulate social demand for TVET (though the other issues related to social prestige and relevance of TVET still need to be addressed). Last, it should also be noted that no government incentives stimulate demand for, or promote equitable access to, the private TVET sector either (for private VTIs or informal apprenticeships). Obviously, improving the quality and relevance of TVET provision would be the most effective way to stimulate demand for it, but room still can be found for other measures to stimulate social demand, especially to help achieve equity objectives.

Economic Demand for TVET

This section starts by briefly reviewing the current labor market context; it then furthers the discussion of formal industry's and informal MSEs' skill needs (including the potential skills needs for oil and other emerging sectors); and it reviews the returns on informal apprenticeships.

Labor Market Overview

Ghana's labor market is segmented; the formal and informal economic sectors were estimated at 18 and 82 percent of the total labor active population, respectively (GSS 2008 in Gondwe and Walenkamp 2011).[10] Two-thirds of those in the informal sector are employed in agricultural activities, and the majority of new jobs are informal (World Bank 2008a). Mobility from the low-skill, low-income informal segment of Ghana's labor market to the higher-skill, higher-wage formal segment of the labor market is not easy.

The overall structure of Ghana's economy, with an overreliance on primary products (for example, agriculture, timber, gold) and a large informal economy, has changed little since independence in 1957.

The key productive sectors of Ghana's economy are agriculture (34.3 percent of GDP in 2007 and employing 56 percent of the labor force), services (31 percent of GDP in 2007 and employing 29 percent of the labor force), and industry (26 percent of GDP in 2007 and employing 15 percent of the labor force) (GoG 2005).[11]

The official total unemployment rate is less than 4 percent, while the unemployment rate among 15–24-year-old youth ranges from 9 percent in rural areas to 23 percent in urban areas (GSS 2008). But the official unemployment rates mask the reality of Ghana's unemployment and underemployment situation; the official definition excludes those that are available for work but are not actively seeking for one in the formal economy.

Since the early 1990s, the most interesting development in Ghana's labor force has been the rapid growth in rural self-employment. Formal wage employment has also increased at a faster rate than the growth of the overall labor force, but it is the lowest paying jobs that have seen the most significant increase (Nsowah-Nuamah, Teal, and Awoonor-Williams 2010).

The significance of education has shifted from being an entry point into public employment to being an entry point into the lower paying small enterprise sector (Nsowah-Nuamah, Teal, and Awoonor-Williams 2010).

Despite the rapid increases in primary and basic education in the last decade or longer, the overall skill level of Ghana's labor force remains relatively low. For example, 62 percent of the total employed population either dropped out of primary or lower secondary school or have no formal schooling, and only 9 percent of the total employed population have education to the senior secondary level or higher (GSS 2008 in Gondwe and Walenkamp 2011).

The Private Sector's Demand for Skills
The demand for skills among the private sector appears to be low in Ghana (see below). This might be both because of methodological issues—regarding how skills demand is assessed—and perhaps a result of the low-skills equilibrium in which segments of the economy find themselves.

Many Ghanaian enterprises (but not all, and not in all sectors) appear to have adapted to the low-skills level in the country by adopting low-level technologies, which in turn means relatively few high-skill job opportunities. Poaching externalities mean a lack of incentive for enterprises to invest in training for their employees when they fear that these employees might be hired away or "poached" by another firm. This helps keep skill levels low. Obviously the private sector in Ghana is not a homogeneous block; this low-skill equilibrium that most of the private sector appears to be in coexists with skills surplus and skills shortages in other parts of the private sector.

The bulk of Ghana's private sector is made up of informal MSEs. Evidence suggests that low-skill levels are not felt as a major constraint and training is not seen as a priority, and hence there is a low demand for upgrading skills from these groups (see below). Most Ghanaian informal MSEs operate in low-income domestic markets where purchasing power is low; as a result, predominant demand is for low-cost items, which—in many cases—also tend to be of low quality. The inability of many customers to buy higher-quality items suppresses demand among enterprises to up-skill to meet such a need. Moreover, those individuals who are learning on the job (for example, through informal apprenticeships) usually acquire skills only to produce cheap, low-quality items and find themselves trapped in a low-skills, low-productivity vicious cycle.

According to the 2007 World Bank Enterprise Survey, skills were not considered to be a constraint by many company managers.[12] It is interesting that the "inadequately educated workforce" option was not selected among the top 10 constraints by the managers of the Ghanaian firms surveyed.[13] The survey results show that the overwhelming majority of Ghanaian firms (about 95 percent on average), regardless of their size, do not perceive the skill level of the workforce as a major constraint: Only 6 percent of small firms, 3 percent of medium firms, and 1 percent of large firms selected this option—results that are very different from the Sub-Saharan Africa and world average (see figure 2.1).

Figure 2.1 Firms Identifying Labor Skill Levels as a Major Constraint, by Size: Ghana, 2007, and Sub-Saharan Africa and World, 2006 or Most Recent Year

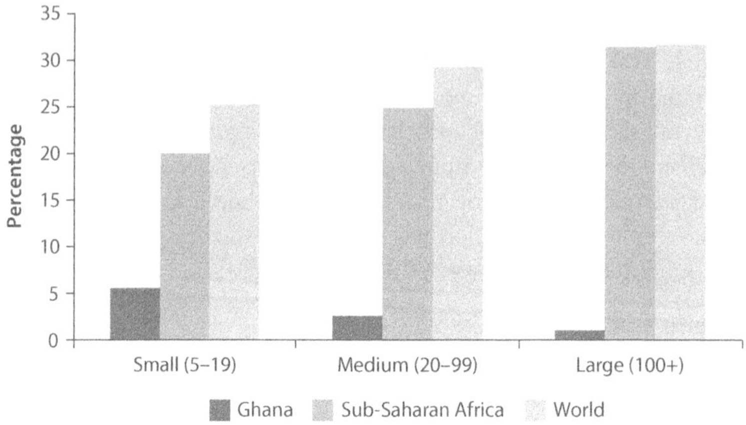

Source: www.enterprisesurveys.org.

According to the World Economic Forum Global Competitiveness Report, between 2011 and 2013, 3–6 percent of Ghanaian businesses asked considered an "inadequately educated workforce" to be their most problematic factor for doing business; this compared to a Sub-Saharan Africa average of about 7 percent (2011/12) (World Economic Forum 2011, 2012). In Ghana, the top five most cited business challenges were access to financing (18 percent), taxation (12 percent), corruption (12 percent), poor work ethic in national labor force (11 percent), and an inadequate supply of infrastructure (9 percent) (World Economic Forum 2012). In 2011/12, the same top five challenges were cited (World Economic Forum 2011).

Furthermore, according to the Association of Ghana Industries (AGI) Business Barometer, none of the top 10 challenges cited by Ghanaian businesses include education or skill constraints. For small and medium enterprises, the top three challenges relate to power supply and credit (table 2.1).

An analysis of 2002 company data found similar results: only 0 percent, 2 percent, and 6 percent of micro, small, and large firms, respectively, identified the lack of the workforce's skills as a problem (Teal 2007).

The 2007 World Bank Enterprise Survey figures for Ghana are significantly lower than those for most Sub-Saharan Africa countries; in fact, Ghana has the fourth lowest percentage of firms in Sub-Saharan Africa that say that an inadequately educated workforce is a major constraint (see figure 2.2). On the face of it, Ghanaian firms' economic demand for skills appears to be low, and companies appear satisfied with workers' skills according to this survey.

The results of these surveys for Ghana have led some analysts to suggest that "there is an adequate or excess supply of the skills required in the labor market for the types of firms and jobs that are emerging in its economy, that is, nonfarm

Table 2.1 AGI Business Barometer, Top Challenges, by Enterprise Size

	Challenges		
Size	1st	2nd	3rd
SMEs	Poor power supply	Access to credit	Cost of credit
Large	Poor power supply	Depreciation of the cedi	Competition from imported goods
African giants	Poor power supply	High level of taxation	Inflation

Source: AGI 2013.
Note: SMEs = small and medium enterprises.

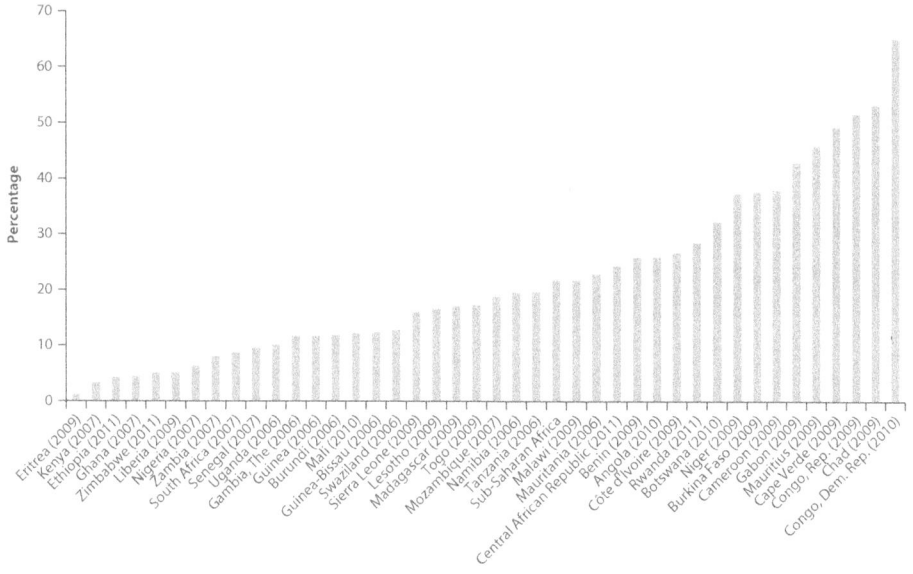

Figure 2.2 Portion of Firms Identifying Labor Skill Levels as a Major Constraint: Ghana, 2007, Compared with Other Sub-Saharan Africa Countries, 2006 or Most Recent Year

Source: www.enterprisesurveys.org.

self-employment and small-scale firms" (Fasih 2008, 43). However, in the light of the inadequacy of the supply of skills in terms of relevance and quality (see chapter 3), it is clear that a more careful interpretation of these data is required to understand the apparent inadequate economic demand for skills. For example, it is not clear what types or levels of skills respondents where referring to when responding to the surveys. Neither is it clear which skills are rewarded by the private sector and which ones are not. The skills concept can be very broad, including everything from foundation skills (the 3Rs: reading, writing, and arithmetic), through core and soft skills, to technical, vocational, and entrepreneurial skills, among others. In fact, the survey simply asked firms whether an "inadequately educated workforce" was an obstacle to their operations.[14]

On the other hand, the World Bank Enterprise Survey methodology used was the same for all countries, meaning that the results are comparable, and underlines the relatively low priority given to skills by Ghanaian firms, when compared to almost all other countries surveyed.

Although the causes of this situation require further investigation, some hypotheses have been formulated:

1. The apparent low economic demand for skills may actually be a manifestation of Ghanaian firms' constructive reaction to the weakness of education and skills training supply. In recognizing that the supply of skills is poor, firms respond by providing significant enterprise-based training to compensate.
2. The small size, low capital intensity, and low productivity of Ghanaian firms may account for the low level of firms' concern about some issues, such as workers' skills (World Bank 2008a).
3. Most of the demand for products and services produced by informal MSEs comes from low-income groups in the domestic market. This may reduce the demand for skills training, given that the market cannot afford better quality goods and services (Johanson and Adams 2004, 135; Palmer 2007a).

However, these arguments could apply to other developing countries as well, and yet they appear not to. In the World Bank Enterprise Surveys, Malawi was the country with the highest proportion of firms citing skill levels as a constraint (50 percent, compared with less than 5 percent for Ghana); for small firms, the respective figures were 26 percent and 6 percent. This is surprising, given that Malawi, like Ghana, is a country with a large informal economy dominated by micro and small enterprises.

To complicate matters further, other surveys have produced opposite results. An analysis of firms' training needs in the Greater Accra area, conducted by a team of consultants for the (now defunct) Ghana Industrial Skills Development Center (GISDC) in late 2005, seems to contradict the World Bank Enterprise Survey findings (GISDC 2005).[15] The firms interviewed by the GISDC were involved in processing industries (including food, beverages, and other commodities), ranging from large multinationals to small and medium enterprises (SMEs).[16] The center noted that labor skill levels appeared to be a serious constraint and concluded that

> Each company experienced serious difficulties in maintaining their plant due to the lack of suitably skilled staff. In many cases these difficulties resulted in excessive downtime and loss of production. In some cases companies had to bring in expertise from Europe at considerable expense to solve problems. In other cases, companies were unable to expand their business due to a reluctance to modernize their equipment because of a lack of suitable maintenance skills. (GISDC 2005, 13)

As part of this training needs analysis, three main areas of skills and knowledge shortages were identified:

1. Skills for the installation, commissioning, maintenance, and repair of modern automated electro-mechanical plants, including for the use of programmable logic controllers, electrical motor installations, electronics, pneumatics, hydraulics, pumps, fans, compressors, and associated control systems
2. Fundamental common engineering skills and the associated underpinning knowledge, including bench and pipe fitting and metal machining, welding and material joining, and the fundamentals of mechanical, electrical, and electronic technology
3. Soft skills, including in problem solving; team working; effective communication, health, safety, and environmental awareness, and information and communication technologies (ICTs).

A small survey of seven industries, four industry associations and support agencies, and six informal sector associations in the Greater Accra area was conducted (Ahorbo 2009b). It also revealed that employers experience great difficulty in finding the right quality of technically skilled workers. Industries are reluctant to recruit people who have acquired their skills through informal apprenticeship training; they focus on candidates who can read, write, communicate, work with other people, solve problems, show initiative, plan and manage their own workload, and work with minimum supervision. In addition, there is demand for multiskilled people who are also prepared to continue to learn.

At the technical operation level, the skills required are related to general plant maintenance (mechanical and electrical) and process engineering. These include skills in instrumentation and controls, refrigeration and air conditioning, communication and technical reporting, leadership, and team working. In the mines, the skills in demand are related to bench and pipe fitting and machining, electrical installation, repair and maintenance activities (including the use of programmable logic controllers), and welding and metal fabricating. In most industries, the soft skills in such areas as communications, leadership, and teamwork form aspects of the in-house training conducted for employees.

In the Ghana Employers Association's 2006 Skills Gap Survey, which sampled 90 employers, the largest share of employers, 47 percent, reported computer literacy or IT skills as lacking among existing employees, followed by teamwork skills, cited by 43 percent of employers. Thirty percent of employers indicated that employees lacked technical or practical skills (see figure 2.3).

Are Skills a Constraint in Ghana or Not?
The Ghana Skills Development Initiative Project, financed by German Society for International Cooperation (GIZ), the German Society for International Cooperation, has found that the master craftspeople and informal sector trade associations they are cooperating with articulate a clear need for skills improvement.[17]

Figure 2.3 Skills Lacking in Existing Employees

Skill	Percentage
Computer and information technology	46.7
Teamwork	43.3
Career planning and development	40.0
Customer relation	40.0
Management	40.0
Problem solving/analytical	36.7
Technical or practical	30.0
Literacy	16.7
Numeracy	10.0

Source: GEA 2006.

Although these findings appear to be contradictory, they may in fact be the result of the different methodologies used, or the type of skills respondents, interviewers, and analysts had in mind at the time of the various surveys. For instance, the World Bank Enterprise Survey aimed to assess the workforce's skill levels, but asked enterprise managers only if their workforce was "inadequately educated." The GISDC training needs assessment, on the other hand, was much more specific: It asked enterprise managers to identify shortfalls for a series of skill categories including technical knowledge, practical and technical skills, communication skills, problem-solving skills, team-working skills, numeracy skills, behavioral skills, IT skills, and other areas. Clearly, surveys need to be much more specific about the type and level of skills being evaluated. Failure to do so may lead to results that could be misinterpreted by policy makers.

According to two key members of Ghana's Council for TVET (COTVET), the true economic benefits of technical and vocational skills are not fully appreciated. As a result, Ghanaian firms tend to underestimate the constraints related to the lack of skills and actual demand is therefore artificially low. As a result, COTVET argues, it is necessary to stimulate the demand for technical and vocational skills.[18]

COTVET also indicated the need for skills needs' assessments to be conducted, especially for the key economic sectors (see more below). Indeed, the absence of such assessments to help identify the critical mass of skills and the expertise required for the structural transformation of the economy is a concern. However, some small-scale attempts have been made, such as the GISDC analysis noted earlier.

Skill Demand and Supply in Selected Sectors

Sector-level assessments completed for high-potential sectors (ICT, construction, oil and gas, hospitality/tourism, horticulture, livestock) in 2010 suggests that these sectors cannot grow to full potential without expansion of the skills pool (World Bank 2010d–h).[19] Below we summarize the key issues arising from these studies on ICT, construction, hospitality and tourism, and oil and gas, as well as discussing the informal sector.

ICT Sector

The ICT sector in Ghana is facing a supply shortage due to low availability of ICT-trained personnel, high labor costs, and inadequate industry readiness of graduates. Supply-side bottlenecks are inhibiting demand across the ICT space, in both core (IT, telecom, IT-enabled services) and allied (noncore such as banking and insurance) sectors. The core sector is small and does not employ a sizeable number of personnel. Noncore/allied sectors such as banking, insurance, and the public sector are rapidly absorbing ICT-trained people in technical, technomanagerial, and support positions. These allied sectors are growing fast in Ghana and adopting technology into their mainstream business models. Software and IT companies spend $4,000–12,000 per employee to train them to productive levels and provide them with internationally recognized industry certification. This constitutes a huge financial burden, discourages intake of new talent, and shrinks the demand for labor and skills. Furthermore, because the pool of well-trained IT professionals is small (fewer than 1,000 graduates per year with an IT-related higher education degree), small IT firms lose their trained employees to larger corporations such as banks and telecoms, which further discourages them from hiring and training more talent. Addressing the supply-side bottlenecks through encouraging professional training, certification, infrastructure for teacher training, and increasing capacity for entrepreneurship is recommended. Simultaneously, building linkages with the global and regional markets needs to be a priority for Ghana in the ICT space, and the case study proposes some solutions for this.

Construction Sector

The construction sector story from a skills-development perspective is one of a supply-side bottleneck. The strong 10–12 percent growth (by employment) in the Ghanian construction industry, predominantly in the informal market, is not matched by an increase in number of skilled construction personnel because of insufficient infrastructure and low institutional capacity to match the growing need for sophisticated construction skills needed for new, modern projects. This is pronounced in the segment of artisans/tradesmen who form the bedrock of the Ghanian construction industry, and whose deficit is in the range of 60,000–70,000 workers. In the Ghanian construction industry, one finds both a quantity and productivity issue, and although the informal sector makes up for some of the deficit, it exacerbates the productivity issue because of inefficient and ineffective training practices.

Hospitality/Tourism Sector

Although the hospitality/tourism sector is growing rapidly and has tremendous potential to absorb personnel, productivity improvements have not kept pace with the increasing demand. Compared with construction, where the problem is in terms of both quantity and quality of labor, in hospitality/tourism the challenges are primarily around quality. The two main sources of low productivity are poor ICT skills (due to training programs with outdated ICT curricula and limited field experience) and high variation in the soft-skill quotient of the workers. This has much to do with the nature of the industry. The hospitality/tourism sector is fairly fragmented with primarily SMEs and a few large hotels. To attain efficiency in distribution, customer acquisition, and services, these firms are adopting ICT and e-business in a big way. However, the industry-polytechnic linkage is weak, the ICT curriculum is outdated, and the teachers are from Europe and North America and not familiar with ICT usage in local industry. All these severely impact the productivity of personnel. At the same time, the industry is also heavily dependent on human capital, where soft skills are very important. However, polytechnics find it hard to train students within a span of six months to a year. Some of these traits, such as "being solution-oriented, having a positive and proactive attitude, and a patient and calm demeanor in the face of challenging requests," are not easy to train people to acquire. The main reforms are taking a critical look at the current ICT curricula and including more field work, as well as creating agreements with larger hotels to provide operational orientations for staff, especially for soft skills.

Oil and Gas Sector

In mid-2007, Ghana's then president John Kufuor announced a significant oil discovery off the west coast, where production began in December 2010. Oil revenues are expected to be about $1 billion a year in the years ahead (OBG 2011); in 2012 oil revenue amounted to about $540 million, and this was expected to rise in 2013 (GoG 2013a). As of 2012/13, Ghana is primarily operating in the upstream part of the oil and gas value chain (exploration, drilling, and production), and many of the jobs created require higher levels or specialized skills for which Ghana cannot meet the demand. However, even when all the oil fields are online, and taking into account the requirements to hire local staff, Ghana is looking at creating only 10,000 jobs in the next five years. Ghana's exposure in midstream (transport, trading) and downstream (refining, storage, distribution to final customer) is low for various reasons such as inadequate infrastructure capacity and lack of fabrication and service capabilities. Since most oil and gas (O&G) companies are doing vertical integration (upstream, midstream, and downstream), they are also looking for graduates who are flexible across sectors and able to cater to different parts of the value chain. To play more in downstream sectors, some policy reforms are needed to produce more skills of a relevant quality.[20]

Furthermore, additional assessment is needed to appraise the needs for both extraction and processing skills, and those required by related industries, such as pharmaceuticals, solvents, fertilizers, pesticides, and plastics.

Some implications for Ghana's O&G industry can also be derived from the experience of other countries:

1. The number of formal employment opportunities that the O&G industry will create should not be overestimated, because the industry is capital inten-

sive by nature. Nonetheless, employment opportunities for both less skilled and more skilled workers will arise.
2. Global industries such as the O&G industry understand the value of training and do not need to be convinced to conduct enterprise-based training.
3. Many O&G companies like to offer entry-level workers in-service training. In Australia, for example, the extensive, high-quality formal and informal training delivered within the industry has essentially been conducted in isolation from the formal TVET sector (Figgis and Standen 2005).
4. The increasing complexity of operations and the sophisticated nature of technology means that employers expect a higher level of skills and adaptability of new recruits, including the ability to work with computers and other sophisticated equipment. Companies also like new recruits to have problem-solving skills and good communication and teamwork skills.
5. O&G sector employers are more interested to know about potential employees' specific competencies than their general qualification level. As a result, competency-based training is important.

Informal Sector
In Ghana, where the majority of the workforce is engaged in informal economic activities, training should be driven by the very different demands of both the formal and informal sectors. COTVET does not have any informal sector board representatives, but inviting participation from this immense sector would help the council become better attuned to the demand for training from the informal economy.

Given that workers' pay is typically thought of as a reflection of demand for their skills, it is interesting that individuals who followed informal apprenticeships typically earn even less than those with no training (Monk, Sandefur, and Teal 2008). A World Bank study (2008a) claims this to be the same for those with an apprenticeship and different levels of education. In other words, someone with either primary or secondary school education and an apprenticeship earns less than someone with either primary or secondary schooling alone. Meanwhile, Monk, Sandefur, and Teal (2008) claim that the returns to doing an apprenticeship decline with level of formal schooling. However, the World Bank (2008a, 72) cautions about self-selection behind this effect. And there are other reasons why policy makers should interpret Monk et al.'s findings with caution. Economic returns are very likely to vary according to location, type of trade, and the quality of the teaching received by apprentices. Claims about returns to informal apprenticeship, of unspecified type, quality, or context, are no more helpful to policy makers than the unqualified generalization about four years of schooling making a difference to agricultural productivity (see King, Palmer, and Hayman 2005 and King and Palmer 2006 for a discussion).[21]

Master craftspeoples' skill needs relate to managerial, technical, and pedagogical areas.[22] Apprentices' skill needs include foundational skills (literacy and numeracy), basic theoretical trade knowledge, and entrepreneurial and customer service skills.

The informal apprenticeship system has been running for decades without structured syllabuses or course outlines (see appendix section "Informal Apprenticeship Training"). Few formalized schemes are used to assess the skills acquired by apprentices, meaning that the quality of the training provided remains uncertain.[23] Often apprentices' skills are acknowledged by a testimonial given to them by their master, but this has limited currency or portability outside the locality in which that master is known. One of the well-known disadvantages of informal apprenticeships is that the training apprentices receive is limited to what their master knows (or has the ability to teach). This in turn is generally determined by what master craftspeople have themselves been taught through the informal apprenticeship system, watching their own masters work, with little or no academic explanations or theoretical backing.

Training of master craftspeople and their apprentices by a third party is usually approached on an ad hoc basis. Typically, when it does occur, training for master craftspeople (and apprentices) is organized by informal sector associations when their members are confronted with technical problems or challenges that require upgrading of skills. Such training is often sponsored by nongovernmental organizations (NGOs) or donors.

Concluding Comments

This review of TVET demand in Ghana illustrates several of the market and nonmarket imperfections outlined in the conceptual framework elaborated in chapter 1.

In recent years, enrollment in formal public and private TVET institutes has either stagnated or declined. This appears to be because of the poor quality of training programs and, more to the point, because the training is not seen as leading to (formal) jobs. This is both a cause of, and a consequence of, the existence of a low-skills equilibrium in a large part of Ghana's private sector. The labor market continues to signal to people that formal academic education results in higher wages, and, although true, the number of such formal jobs is limited and support for the creation of MSEs is insufficient. Meanwhile, this signaling causes demand for places at general SHSs to continue to increase sharply. This is also illustrative of the information inadequacies that are prevalent.

Demand for TVET is also affected by labor market segmentation and barriers to vertical mobility. Ghana's labor market is segmented; the formal and informal economic sectors are estimated at 18 and 82 percent of the total labor active population, respectively. Mobility from the low-skill, low-income informal segment of Ghana's labor market to the higher-skill, higher-wage formal segment of the labor market is not easy.

The demand for TVET by the private sector is generally low. Ghanaian formal enterprises appear to have adapted to the low skills level in the country by adopting low-level technologies, which in turn means that there are relatively few high-skill job opportunities. Meanwhile, the bulk of Ghana's private sector is made up of informal MSEs, and evidence suggests that training is not seen as a priority or the lack of skills as a major constraint; hence there is a low demand for upgrading skills from these groups.

The two most significant nonmarket imperfections with regard to demand include (1) the inadequate information on skill needs that is provided to both the private sector and to young people and (2) the lack of synchronization between TVET reform programs and policies that promote better utilization of skills.

Notes

1. For a conceptual framework related to the supply and demand analysis, see Fasih (2008).
2. A paragraph briefly addressed the potential demand for training (see World Bank 2008a, 60–61).
3. Basic education includes two years of preschool, six years of primary, and three years of JHS.
4. This trend ignores the artificial enrollment increase that is seen in 2011/12 data (see chapter 3).
5. Private communication, February 18, 2008.
6. The same point has been made with reference to general academic schooling (Fasih 2008).
7. Of course, in many countries—including high-income countries—TVET also remains less popular than general education.
8. It has been noted that in this sense general education is more "vocational" than vocational education and training proper, in that it may be seen as a better pathway to gainful employment (Foster 1965a, b).
9. Enrollment in SHS was even higher in 2010/11, at about 730,000 (GoG 2011a). However, this figure is not used above because it contains large number of students who have been retained in the SHS system during the two to three years when the government implemented a four-year SHS program. And it is therefore not representative of recent trends in SHS enrollment, which have shown year-on-year increases of approximately between 20,000 and 40,000 students.
10. See also World Bank (2012b, ch. 5) for more on Ghana's labor market, including on the extent of informality.
11. See *CIA World Fact Book* (2009), https://www.cia.gov/library/publications/the-world-factbook/geos/gh.html.
12. The 2007 World Bank Enterprise Survey in Ghana, quoted in World Bank (2008a), asked firms about their top 10 constraints. The 15 options were access to finance (availability and cost); access to land; business licensing and permits; corruption; the courts; crime, theft, and disorder; customs and trade regulations; electricity; the inadequately educated workforce; labor regulations; political instability; practices of competitors in the informal sector; tax administration; tax rates; and the transport of goods, supplies, and inputs (see www.enterprisesurveys.org).
13. The two main constraints identified by Ghanaian firms in 2007 were electricity (49 percent of firms) and access to finance (33 percent of firms). It is not surprising that electricity was the most frequently cited constraint because there were serious electrical shortages in 2007 at the time of the survey.

14. Commenting on the World Bank Investment Climate Surveys, which show that firms in more than a fifth of recently surveyed developing countries rate workers' inadequate skills as a major or severe constraint to their operations, the United Kingdom's Department for International Development (DFID) notes that it appears that the skills most widely demanded by businesses appear to be those acquired in two to three years of good quality secondary education (DFID 2008, 6). Teal (2007), with similar findings, measures the workforce's skills according to the average number of years of education and the extent of its general, and firm-specific, work experience. However, using years of education as a measure of skills tells us nothing about the type of education (general or vocational), its quality, or indeed the type of skills being measured (cognitive, noncognitive, soft, core skills, and so on). Likewise, using work experience as a measure of skills does not specify the type of skills being referred to. It can be argued, therefore, that the questions related to skills in these surveys are too vague to be of significant policy use; indeed, they may result in misleading findings.
15. See appendix B on the GISDC.
16. These companies included Guinness, Fan Milk, Tex Styles Ghana, Euro Metal, Tema Oil Refinery, Unilever, Coca-Cola, Accra Brewery, Wienco, and Nestlé.
17. GIZ official, private communication, March 3, 2013.
18. Personal meeting with the executive director and chairman of COTVET, December 3, 2008.
19. See appendix A for the full case studies on the ICT, construction, hospitality/tourism, and oil and gas sectors.
20. This paragraph was written largely by consultant Priyam Saraf. See the appendix section, "Oil and Gas Sector."
21. The research about schooling and agricultural productivity concluded that schooling had a positive impact only on productivity, where the farming took place in a "modern" context (with access to fertilizers, machinery, and so on). In the absence of this enabling environment, schooling was shown to have little or no impact.
22. See Amankrah (2007) for a discussion of informal apprenticeship trades with market potential.
23. The NVTI conducts annual proficiency tests for about 7,000 informal apprentices (see appendix section "National Vocational Training Institute (NVTI) (MoELR)"). In addition to this, some of the larger informal sector associations operate their own informal skills testing, resulting in certificates being issued by the associations that are recognized by their members nationwide (Haan and Serrière 2002).

CHAPTER 3

TVET Supply, Performance, and Assessment

This chapter on technical and vocational education and training (TVET) supply complements the discussion in an earlier World Bank report, "Ghana Job Creation and Skills Development" (2008a, see esp. pp. 60–66), providing a considerably more detailed analysis of the variety of TVET providers, distinguishing between different types of public and private institutes. This distinction should be useful to policy makers.

The Suppliers of Technical and Vocational Education and Training in Ghana

A wide variety of formal training providers are found in Ghana, but information is lacking about most of them, with the exception of the Ministry of Education technical training institutes (MoE TTIs). The large number of other providers tends to be overlooked. Although this report's appendixes provide ample detail on each of the main TVET providers (for the 2002–13 period), this chapter aims to provide a more general overview of the scope of pretertiary[1] TVET supply, through formal public TVET providers, private institutions, and private enterprise-based training, including informal apprenticeships (see table 3.1).

The analysis draws out thematic issues related to the following: (1) the coverage and location of training, (2) access (the number of institutes, youth targeted, entry requirements) and enrollment (by gender), (3) equity, (4) staffing (the number and quality of staff, availability of in-service training), (5) the training environment (tools, equipment, curricula, course duration), (6) the labor market relevance of training (staff and trainee industrial attachments and other links to enterprises, posttraining support, career guidance), and (7) institutional autonomy and the availability of data (on access, efficiency, quality, outcomes, tracer studies, and impact assessments).

Table 3.1 Main Public and Private TVET Providers, by Backer, 2012/13

Public TVET Providers	Provider
Technical training institutes	Ministry of Education/Ghana Education Service
National Vocational Training Institute centers	Ministry of Employment and Labor Relations
Integrated community centers for employable skills	
Opportunities industrialization centers	
Social welfare centers	
Youth leadership and skills training centers	National Youth Authority, under the Ministry of Youth and Sports
Community development vocational/technical institutes	Ministry of Local Government and Rural Development
Ghana Regional Appropriate Technology Industrial Service Foundation	Ministry of Trade and Industry
Farming institutes	Ministry of Food and Agriculture
Roads and transport training center	Ministry of Roads and Highways
Private TVET Providers	*Provider*
Private vocational training institutes	Private
Private formal enterprise-based training	Private
Private informal apprenticeship training	Private

Note: See appendixes for more details.

Formal Public TVET Providers

The Ghanaian government still acts as a large provider of skills in the country. Public TVET institutions offer intermediate, advanced, and technical skills training:

- The Ministry of Education Technical and Vocational Education (TVE), referred to in this report as "school-based," is handled through TTIs by the Ghana Education Service (GES), which operates all public schools and institutes.[2]
- The Ministry of Employment and Labor Relations[3] TVET is provided through vocational training institutes, including NVTIs, ICCESs, Social Welfare Centers, and OICs.
- Up to five other ministries offer sector-specific training programs. These include the Ministry of Youth and Sports (MoYS), the Ministry of Local Government and Rural Development (MoLGRD), the Ministry of Food and Agriculture (MoFA), the Ministry of Transportation (MoT), and the Ministry of Trade and Industry (MoTI).

Ghana's public sector training market remains highly uncompetitive, and government policies have, over the years, helped to create and maintain a supply-driven training system, within which uncompetitive providers operate and, crucially, are not incentivized to behave any other way.

Table 3.2 Coverage and Location of Public TVET Institutes, by Type, 2012

TVET Type	Coverage	Location
Technical training institutes	All regions	Urban
National vocational training institute centers	All regions	Mainly urban
Integrated community centers for employable skills	All regions	Mainly rural
Opportunities industrialization centers	Three regions	Urban
Community development vocational/technical institutes	All regions	Urban and rural
Social welfare centers	All regions	Mainly urban
Youth leadership and skills training centers	All regions	Rural
Ghana Regional Appropriate Technology Industrial Service	All regions	Urban and rural

Note: See appendixes for more details.

Coverage and Location

Public institutional TVET providers can be found in all 10 regions of the country, with the exception of OICs, found only in three. Most tend to be located in urban areas, with the exception of the Integrated Community Centers for Employable Skills and the Youth Leadership and Skills Training Centers, which are predominantly rural (see table 3.2). Especially in rural areas, public training providers are often geographically dispersed, and this reduces competition among providers and therefore reduces quality.

Access and Enrollment

There are more than 200 public TVET institutes, including 45 under the MoE, 116 under the MoELR, and the remainder under different other ministries. The MoE's technical training institutes accounted for over 70 percent of total public enrollment in public TVET institutes in 2011–13, being far larger than other public training institutes. The average number of trainees in a TTI is 818, compared with 278 in the OICs, 257 in the NVTIs, 128 in the Community Development Vocational/Technical Institutes, and up to 80 in the Youth Leadership and Skills Training Centers and the ICCES (see table 3.3).

Reporting on pubic TVET enrollment data by the MoE tells only part of the story. According to the MoE's Education Management Information System (EMIS) (GoG 2012a), public enrollment in TVET increased sharply between 2010/11 and 2011/12 by over 30 percent, and it suggests that this is in part because of the absorption of some private Vocational Training Institutes (VTIs) into the public system. It is true that some private VTIs have been absorbed by the MoE TTIs, but over this period (2010/11 to 2011/12) this accounted for only an additional two to three thousand students (in 2012/13, a further nine private vocational institutes were absorbed by the MoE to become TTIs). A much more significant factor for this increase was the extension of the second-cycle duration to four years. For the MoE TTIs, the switch from three years second-cycle duration to four years was short lived (only for those students *starting* in the years 2007–09; it has since reverted back to three years), but this had the effect of increasing enrollment by about a third. The three-year time lag until these students reached

Table 3.3 **TVET Enrollment of Full-Time Students, by Type of Institute and Gender, Latest Year**

	Year	Number of institutions	Trainees-center ratio	National enrollment	Female (%)	Enrollment trend[a]
Technical training institutes	2011/12	36	812:1	29,218	17	Stagnant 2001–10
National vocational training institute centers	2012/13	45	818:1	36,830	26	Recent decline
Integrated community centers for employable skills	2011/12	36	257:1	9,500[b]	30[b]	Decline or stagnant
Opportunities industrialization centers	2011/12	59	76:1	4,465[b]	55	Recent decline
Community development vocational/technical institutes		3	278:1	835	68	Stagnant 2001–10
Social welfare centers	2011/12	24	128:1	3,070	53	—
Youth leadership and skills training centers	2010/11	18	131:1	2,350[b]	36	Slight increase
Ghana Regional Appropriate Technology Industrial Service	2011/12	11	71:1	1,948	—	Recent decline
	2010	12	27:1	245		
Total		208	—	47,393	34	Stagnant/decline

Sources: Personal communication direct from above providers (May 2012). See also appendix B and GoG 2013b.
Note: — = not available.
a. This trend ignores the artificial enrollment increase experienced 2011/12 (see below).
b. Estimate.

their fourth year explains why there was a sudden enrollment increase in 2011/12. But it is an artificial increase; it simply shows the same students staying in the system longer, rather than more students actually entering. It does not indicate an increase in demand for public TVET. Since the second cycle has now reverted back to three-year duration, it can be expected that future years' data for total public enrollment will decline again and stabilize at a much lower level.[4]

In 2012/13, total enrollment in public TVET institutes of full-time students was approximately 47,000 trainees. Factoring out this artificial enrollment increase, all the data from the public TVET providers themselves clearly show that enrollment levels over the last several years are either stagnant or in slight decline. For example, over the period 2001/02 to 2009/10, technical training institute (TTI) enrollment has remained largely stagnant at around 20,000 students (appendix B); NVTI enrollment dropped by close to 10 percent over two years, from 7,297 to 6,710 (appendix B); ICCES enrollment dropped by almost 40 percent (2008–11) (appendix B); and, over the period 2001/02 to 2011/12, enrollment in the Community Development Vocational/Technical Institutes has been more or less stagnant, with a slight decline in the most recent year (appendix B). Although the decline in enrollment suggests a decline in access to, and demand for, TVET, the Ghana Living Standard Surveys (GLSSs) show that even though TVET reaches only a small share of the population, this share did actually increase over the 1991/92 to 2005/06 period (World Bank 2008a). It is not clear why there is this apparent paradox, because it is not possible to tell from the GLSS survey what type of TVET has managed to increase enrollments and whether enrollment increases are concentrated in private or new forms of public provisions.[5]

Information on training efficiency (measured by dropout and completion rates) is not routinely collected by the majority of training providers. Based on the available evidence from Integrated Community Centers for Employable Skills, 10–30 percent of trainees drop out annually, which implies completion rates for four-year courses ranging between 24 and 65 percent.

Entry Requirements

Most formal public and private TVET providers target lower secondary school graduates and often set a minimum aggregate Basic Education Certificate Examination score as an entry requirement. However, the ICCES centers and the Community Development Vocational/Technical Institutes appear to be the most accessible of all the public TVET institutes; they admit junior high school (JHS) dropouts, youth with weak JHS aggregates, and sometimes young people with even less schooling. Some nonprofit private vocational training institutes are also more lenient (Palmer 2007a).

Equity

Ghana's TVET system tends to exclude the poor. The share of individuals having followed a TVET course rises with families' level of wealth. For example, the share of individuals from the highest income quintile having technical or vocational training is seven times that of those from the poorest quintile (World Bank 2008a). The reasons appear to be the following:[6]

1. *Educational entry requirements* set by most formal TVET providers, public and private, are often not met by poorer pupils; incomplete basic education and very low learning outcomes inhibit access to formal TVET.
2. The *mainly urban location of formal training institutions* makes for difficult access by inhabitants of rural communities, who tend to be poorer. Only the public ICCES and some nongovernmental organization (NGO) training centers are located in more rural areas.
3. Most formal TVET training courses are preemployment *courses of long duration* (two to four years). The resulting opportunity costs of not working are too high for poorer families to support. In some communities, opportunities exist for petty trading or other activities that do not require any vocational or technical skills, and provide immediate income, even if it is low.
4. The *direct cost of formal training* (tuition fees, contributions to parent-teacher associations, fees for practical class supplies, uniforms, books, and so on) may not be affordable to the poor, leading to their exclusion, especially from for-profit VTIs or TTIs.
5. *Few VTIs offer scholarships*, though some have informal arrangements to facilitate fee payment, such as extended payment terms or ad hoc support from staff. Other options of financial support are equally scarce.
6. *Public spending has not reacted to market inequalities* that inhibit the access of marginalized groups to TVET. In fact, much public spending on TVET is not targeted at the poor but is captured by those who are less in need, thus widening inequalities. For example, the World Bank (2010b) estimates that only 19 percent of the public spending for MoE vocational education reaches the poor. The hardest public TVET provider for young people to enter (the TTIs) is the most subsidized provider with the lowest fees; TTI training fees are on average about one-tenth of those in the other public TVET providers (see appendix B).

Most public TVET enrollment is male: In the TTIs and NVTIs that account for the highest enrollment; only 17 percent and 26 percent of trainees are female, respectively. However, the Community Development Vocational/Technical Institutes and the OICs attract greater proportions of female trainees, at 68 percent and 55 percent, respectively. Sociocultural and traditional pressures steer women to traditionally female trades in both the formal TVET system and the informal apprenticeship system, giving them fewer opportunities to access more dynamic and emerging areas of study such as electronics, information and communication technology (ICT), and auto mechanics. Overall, female trainees account for approximately 34 percent of the total (table 3.3).

Staffing

The training, qualification, and upgrading of instructors is of obvious importance to public and private TVET institutions. The 2008 EMIS survey (GoG 2008c) found a significantly higher proportion of trained instructors in public institutes (63 percent) than in private ones (46 percent).[7]

In-service training provided by public TVET institutions is infrequent (see table 3.4). Meanwhile, EMIS data show that, on average, public and private providers train their staff about the same; between 2009/10 and 2010/11 4 to 5 of every 10 instructors in both public and private TVET institutes indicated that they "hardly ever" received training (GoG 2011b). Most departments and agencies responsible for TVET provision cite the lack of funding as the main cause.

Given that most public TVET staffing decisions are taken at the head office level, it can be difficult for training institute managers to hold their staff to account for performance, or offer them incentives.

Staffing regulations are not linked to incentives that would drive improvements in industry-related skills, for example, linking participation in industrial attachments to career progression and salary increases. Instead, promotion and salary enhancement comes from getting higher and higher academic-related qualifications.

Training Environment

Training quality is to a large extent driven by the public funding policies for government TVET institutions (see chapter 5).

Table 3.4 TVET Staff and In-Service Training, by Type of Institute and Gender, Most Recent Year

	Teaching staff	Female (%)	In-service training	Data year
Technical training institutes	2,019	18	Limited	2011/12
National vocational training institute centers	—	—	—	
Integrated community centers for employable skills	About 700[a]	33	Limited	2011/12
Opportunities industrialization centers	50	—	None	
Community development vocational/technical institutes	186	84	On an ad hoc basis	2011/12
Social welfare centers	177	52	Limited	2010
Youth leadership and skills training centers	103	39	Nonexistent before 2010; limited since	2011/12
Ghana Regional Appropriate Technology Industrial Service	9, plus training experts	—	None	2009

Source: Unless otherwise stated, data from private communication with training providers listed above, May 2012.
Note: See the appendixes for details. — = not available.
a. Estimate.

Table 3.5 Public TVET Training Environment, by Type of Institute, 2012

	Quality of equipment and tools	Trainee-teacher ratio
Technical training institutes	Some large machinery, mainly outdated; some new equipment	13:1
National vocational training institute centers	Low quality	—
Integrated community centers for employable skills	Low quality, outdated	7:1[a]
Opportunities industrialization centers	Mostly outdated and obsolete	17:1
Community development vocational/technical institutes	Low quality, outdated; some new equipment expected 2012	17:1
Social welfare centers	Mostly low quality	13:1
Youth leadership and skills training centers	Low quality	19:1
Ghana Regional Appropriate Technology Industrial Service	Good	27:1

Source: See appendixes.
Note: — = not available.
a. Estimate.

Many TVET institutes have infrastructure, whether public or private, that is dilapidated, and equipment and tools are often outdated or simply lacking (see table 3.5). According to 2005/06 EMIS data, only 12 percent of public and 29 percent of private training centers described themselves as "well equipped." In contrast, 37 percent of public and 12 percent of private institutions described their facilities as "poorly equipped" or with "no equipment" (GoG 2006f). Furthermore, 2010/11 EMIS data showed that 20 percent of public and private institutes' classrooms needed major repairs (GoG 2011b).

Equipment in most TTIs is usually obsolete and bears little resemblance to what is commonly used in industry: Equipment is generally more than 20 years old; indeed, much of the equipment at Accra Technical Training Center and Tema Technical Institute dates back to the Soviet support of the mid-1960s. In 2011, a Ghana-Austria TVET Project rehabilitated and equipped some existing workshops at the Takoradi Technical Institute, St Paul Technical Institute, Kukurantumi (SPATS), and Tema Technical Institute. Moreover, in 2012, the Development of Skills for Industry Project funded by the African Development Bank will provide support to 10 TTIs. Community Development Vocational/Technical Institutes are expecting to receive new equipment, tools, and infrastructure upgrades under the African Development Bank (2009–13) Gender Responsive Skills and Community Development Project. Many of the ICCES lack even such basics as tools, books, and materials.[8] Public TVET institutes typically have no regular budgetary allocation for the development, improvement, and rehabilitation of infrastructure, or for tools and equipment. Where the latter do exist, the amounts are woefully inadequate.

As a result, the general quality of training is poor. The quality of graduates depends on the core strength areas of the institution attended to a great extent. However, the generally inadequate preparation of new TVET graduates means that companies generally need to retrain them.

In terms of other non–trade-specific courses provided by formal TVET providers, many have traditionally offered subjects such as math and English. Under the New Education Reform (NER) project, the government indicated that core examinable subjects should be taught in all second-cycle institutions (including formal TVET providers), including math, ICT, general science, social studies, and English. Part of the rationale for this was to improve vertical mobility of trainees, because these core subjects will facilitate access to a polytechnic, for example. However, so far only the MoE TTIs have been able to fully adopt all these subject areas. NVTI teaches English, math, entrepreneurial studies, and ICT as examinable subjects (but not science or social studies).

Labor Market Relevance

The global labor market relevance of TVET in Ghana is generally poor. Curricula tend to be excessively theoretical; instructors with marketable and up-to-date skills are difficult to attract and retain, and they are not encouraged to acquire the required practical experience through industrial attachments. Other market links such as industry liaison officers, training for the informal sector, short courses, and posttraining support are almost absent. Even the market relevance of privately offered TVET is questionable. Industrial attachments are almost standard practice for students,[9] however, despite some shortcomings, and trainees gain further experience by carrying out contracts for external clients.

TVET training curricula tend to be very theoretical and oriented toward formal employment. No training needs assessments are conducted, and courses remain predominantly supply driven. Preemployment training courses are usually long, and few are competency based. Employers and existing enterprise owners have virtually no input into the determination of the trade areas of courses or the design of their content.

The inflexibility of TVET instructors' posts, partly due to their protection by labor unions, means that it is difficult for formal public training institutes to react quickly to changes in economic demand and provide new courses or change teaching approaches as required (Botchie and Ahadzie 2004; Levine 2008). It is difficult to dismiss instructors whose skills are outdated or who cannot adapt, and the limited availability of in-service training and industrial attachment positions for staff means that retraining instructors is neither quick nor straightforward. As a result, supply-side pressure may exist to offer courses for which instructors are available, even when labor market demand for certain trade areas or skills sets is dwindling. Furthermore, as salaries in public and most private TVET institutes cannot compete with those of industry, it is difficult to attract and retain instructors with up-to-date, marketable skills.

Opportunities for industrial attachments for staff are scarce, especially in rural areas, and few instructors other than TTI staff are offered any support to benefit from them. There are no financial incentives; indeed, instructors are expected to prefinance their attachments and await later reimbursement. There is no career incentive either, because the promotion system does not take the industrial experience acquired into account. As a result instructors have low motivation to gain practical experience. Furthermore, attachments are usually available only with larger formal companies, meaning that instructors' understanding of the informal economy and micro- and small-enterprise business issues is poorer still.

Finally, in other ways the labor market relevance of TVET ranges from inexistent to weak:

- *Industry liaison officers* are found only in TTIs, but they are not effective in their work.
- *Short courses* are not common: only the Ghana Regional Appropriate Technology Industrial Service (GRATIS) and some of the TTIs offer them.
- *Training for the informal sector* is only regularly offered by a few public TVET providers. The NVTI, for example, provides short courses for master craftspeople, OIC has a project to train informal apprentices, and GRATIS undertakes the regular training of a variety of informal sector workers. Between 2003 and 2005, the government Skills Training and Entrepreneurship Program (STEP) program provided short-duration training to the unemployed in partnership with public TVET institutions.
- *Posttraining support* (such as start-up tools or capital) is virtually inexistent. At best, graduates may obtain some informal advice from their instructors about which government and nongovernmental organizations might be able to offer them guidance. Some support is offered by private VTIs, especially those receiving external funding.

It might be expected that private for-profit VTIs provide better quality and more relevant training than their public (or nonprofit grant-funded private) counterparts. Obeying market pressures, for-profit VTIs would have to close if the public perceived their quality to be low or the relevance of the training offered to be minimal. Indeed, the decline in enrollment in many private VTIs may reflect precisely this. Although some private VTIs clearly do attempt to engage with the labor market through industrial attachments and the provision of services directly to the public, enabling them to meet the needs of the labor market, it is difficult to establish their number (see appendix section "Private Vocational Training Institutes").

On the upside, work placements are fairly common for trainees. Only ICCES, social welfare centers, and some private VTI trainees do not carry out practical industry attachments, although even they are due to in their third and fourth years of training, as part of the latest reforms. The success of these placements varies however, because of the challenges faced: (1) opportunities are limited, especially for the more rural VTIs, (2) industries and enterprises are offered no incentive to offer trainees the experience, and (3) the sustenance stipend is inadequate, and trainees often face accommodation and transport problems as a result.

Market contracts are also undertaken to a varying degree by all TVET providers (carpentry trainees manufacture furniture to order, for example), representing a necessary source of income for private institutes, and raising training providers' awareness of market needs.

Institutional Autonomy and Data Availability

In most cases, the autonomy of public TVET institutions is limited. Typically, decisions on budgets, the hiring, dismissal, and transfer of staff, course choices, and fee levels are made at the head office level. Training institutes' directors are usually allowed to take the initiative to undertake contracts and other activities, and they are entitled to determine the use of the income generated and the training fees collected.

Almost all data on formal TVET provision relate exclusively to supply-side monitoring (number of institutes, staff, and enrollment); for example, as reported in the annual "Report on Basic Statistics and Planning Parameters for Technical and Vocational Education in Ghana" (for example, see GoG 2007a, 2008c, 2009a, 2011b). Apart from gender disaggregation, no other equity indictors are available. Little or no data are available for (1) the quality of training, (2) efficiency (including dropout and completion rates), (3) financing of the system, or (4) training outcomes (such as the share of graduates finding a job, or if and how they use the skills acquired).[10]

Private Institution TVET Providers

In addition to public skills provision, a considerable range of private for-profit and nonprofit institution-based preemployment training is found. In general, private for-profit VTIs are located in urban and metropolitan areas, faith-associated VTIs are in both urban and rural areas, and nonprofit VTIs run by NGOs are usually found in rural areas.

The number of nongovernmental TVET institutes is not precisely known. A 2008 EMIS report (GoG 2008c) noted that there were 629 public and private TVET institutions in its database, while the 2011 EMIS report put the figure at 700 institutions (GoG 2011b), implying the existence of between 430 and 500 private providers based on the data above. This figure is similar to those of both the January version of Ghana's 2004 "Draft TVET Policy Framework" (GoG 2004c) and a policy research report that mentions the existence of 450, registered and unregistered (Botchie and Ahadzie 2004). On the other hand, a report from NVTI in 2010 states that there were 345 private VTIs registered with the institute (NVTI 2010), which suggests that up to 150 private VTIs operate unregistered nationwide.

Total enrollment in private VTIs is not known exactly either: since 2006/07, EMIS has been collecting some basic data on private TVET institutes, but the

Table 3.6 Private TVET Institutes Covered by EMIS Sample, 2006/07 to 2010/11

	2006/07	2007/08	2008/09	2009/10	2010/11
Enrollment	20,957	23,452	25,929	24,547	29,307
Number of institutes in sample	129	143	163	154	169
Average enrollment/institute	162	164	159	159	173

Sources: 2006/07 data from GoG 2008c; 2007/08 and 2008/09 data from GoG 2009a; and 2009/10 and 2010/11 data from GoG 2011b.

sample is only partial, covering between 130 and 170 of the approximately 430–500 number of registered and unregistered private VTIs (table 3.6). Nonetheless, the average enrollment per institute suggests that enrollment levels are largely static. Apart from a few VTIs that receive external grants, evidence from a small survey of 10 private VTIs in the Greater Accra area suggests that enrollment may actually be declining (Ahorbo 2009a).

If we assume that 20 percent of the unregistered VTIs have closed, we might estimate that the total number of private registered and unregistered VTIs is 445 (345 registered with NVTI and an estimated 100 unregistered and active VTIs). Taking an average enrollment per institute of 164 trainees (the per institute average for the period 2006–11), an estimate of the total national enrollment in private TVET institutes for 2010/11 might be 73,000.

Another type of private institution-based provider was the Ghana Industrial Skills Development Center (GISDC) at Tema, a public-private partnership between the Dutch and Ghanaian governments and Ghanaian private companies, which offered short competency-based training courses to Ghanaian industry (see appendix section "The Ghana Industrial Skills Development Center (GISDC)"). However, for all its promise, the GISDC collapsed after only a couple of years of operation; it failed to attract enough industry investors, courses were too expensive, staff salaries too high, and ultimately the GISDC ran out of funds to operate.

Enterprise-Based TVET Providers

Informal Apprenticeship Training

The largest provider of skills training remains the informal apprenticeship system; there are about four informal apprentices for every trainee in formal public and private training centers combined.[11] The informal apprenticeship system provides training to more than 440,000 youth (15–24 years old) at any one time (GLSS 2005/06 data in Nsowah-Nuamah, Teal, and Awoonor-Williams 2010).[12] The fact that so many young Ghanaians are being trained at no cost to the state is a major factor in approaching a sustainable TVET system.

Informal apprenticeships are offered throughout Ghana, although they tend to be concentrated in regional and district capitals and larger rural communities. In more rural locations, master craftspeople tend to practice their trade skills only on a part-time basis, farming being the main activity, and so are less likely to take on apprentices.

Although widespread, and more accessible than formal TVET provision, informal apprenticeships have well-known disadvantages (see appendix section "Informal Apprenticeship Training"). Informal apprenticeships offer largely uncompetitive training, mainly because of the uncompetitive nature of the informal enterprises within which the training takes place. This said, a slight degree of competition is found between types of informal apprenticeship, as evidenced by the different levels of education of apprentices in the different trades (see appendix section "Informal Apprenticeship Training"). Informal apprenticeships are gender biased, like formal TVET training, with female trainees being attracted to the traditionally female trade areas.

Informal apprenticeships remain the most accessible option of skills acquisition for the poor. Unlike formal TVET, there are no entry requirements, such as having completed basic education, although most apprentices have done so, often performing poorly at the Basic Education Certificate Examination. Training fees are often lower, and the terms of payment are more flexible than for formal training. Apprentices can also usually arrange a payment schedule according to their personal circumstances. Some are trained and pay in installments, some pay after the training, and others are trained for free by relatives and friends. A further arrangement is for trainees to work for their masters for a number of years after completing their apprenticeship, effectively repaying the master craftspeople in kind. This generally means that the poor take longer to complete their training. Many apprentices do, however, usually receive "chop money" from their masters, thus reducing the burden on their family. Apart from this food stipend, trainees do not earn anything during their training (Palmer, Akabzaa, and Casely-Hayford 2009).

Anecdotal evidence from 2012 suggests that some apprenticeship trade areas have become less popular, including carpentry and tailoring. The large influx of Chinese-made plastic furniture, tables, and ceiling sheets as well as ready-made garments has undoubtedly had an impact on the demand for carpenters and tailors in Ghana and could explain the drop in interest.

Several attempts have been made to support informal apprenticeship training in Ghana (see appendix section "Informal Apprenticeship Training" for details), but no intervention has yet had any systemic and sustainable impact. The latest government attempt is via the National Apprenticeship Program (NAP) (appendix B). The NAP has been some 10 years in the pipeline and today has become something very different from what was originally envisaged in the 2002 President's Committee Report (GoG 2002). At that time it was suggested to formalize and regulate certain aspects of the largely private apprenticeship system (for example, registration of apprenticeship providers, training content, duration of training programs, and certification). The NAP was designed to develop competency-based training (CBT) material for various trade areas, provide CBT to master craftspeople, and provide start-up kits to apprentices. However, after nine years of delay, the NAP was launched in 2011 at a very low scale; state-funded program serves only 1 percent of the nearly half million youth in informal apprenticeship. Or, to put it another way, each year some 120,000 youth leave basic education without access to post–basic education programs (World Bank 2011a); the NAP reaches only 4 percent of this number.

Formal Industry Training

Industry training is also offered in the formal wage sector of the economy, which is small in Ghana, accounting for approximately 18 percent of employment according to the Ghana Statistical Service (GSS) (GSS 2008 in Gondwe and Walenkamp 2011).

A 2007 enterprise survey conducted by the World Bank found that firms of all sizes offer formal training, although medium-sized and especially large firms

Figure 3.1 Firms Offering Formal Training, by Size (Number of Employees), Ghana, 2007, and Sub-Saharan Africa and World, 2006 or Most Recent Year

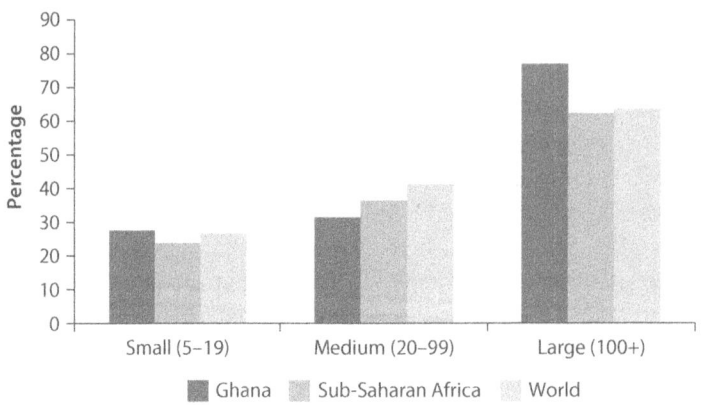

Source: www.enterprisesurveys.org.

are more likely to do so than small firms (figure 3.1). Indeed, 77 percent of large firms in Ghana offer enterprise-based training, significantly more than the Sub-Saharan Africa and world averages of 62 and 64 percent, respectively. The same survey found that foreign-owned firms were more likely to train their staff than nationally owned firms, and exporting firms offered more training than their nonexporting counterparts.[13]

A small survey (Ahorbo 2009b) of seven industries, four industry associations, and various support agencies in the Greater Accra area found that, in general, industries acknowledge a skills mismatch and that formal TVET institute graduates are inadequately trained. It is in an effort to narrow this gap that some industries have established training workshops where new recruits undergo intensive training before assuming their responsibilities.

The majority of new recruits in medium-sized to large industries start working as apprentices, even if they recently graduated from a formal TVET institute. They are generally given one or two years of in-house training to strengthen their foundation skills (for example, science and mathematics) and build their technical trade knowledge and skills (for example, plumbing, electrical wiring, welding, and machining) to enable them to handle multiple tasks.

Industries are particularly interested in technicians with knowledge and skills in one or more trades other than the one in which they specialize. In an effort to help TVET instructors be abreast of the current technologies and manufacturing processes, attachment programs are organized by some industries for instructors during school vacations. Technical training is offered to employees as and when the need arises, for instance, when new equipment or manufacturing processes are introduced; and health, safety, and environment compliance training is offered regularly. Some companies also encourage their employees to devote time to their personal development, fully bearing the cost when the courses selected are relevant to the employees' work.

Concluding Comments

This review of TVET supply, performance, and assessment in Ghana illustrates several of the market and nonmarket imperfections outlined in the conceptual framework elaborated in chapter 1.

We have shown that a training market imperfection exists in Ghana. The formal TVET providers remain largely supply driven and uncompetitive, despite all the rhetoric about "demand-driven" approaches. Such institutes are typically very unresponsive to changes in demand; they lack the autonomy, the capacity, and the incentives to behave differently. In many rural parts of Ghana, public training providers are usually so geographically dispersed that there is simply no competition among similar providers. This is very much the case for the Integrated Community Centers for Employable Skills and the Youth Leadership and Skills Training Centers, which are predominantly rural.

By far the largest provider of skills training in Ghana, the private informal apprenticeship system, remains largely uncompetitive—on account on the uncompetitive nature of most MSEs in Ghana. Moreover, though numerous attempts have been made to improve the private informal apprenticeship system—since the mid-1990s to date—no systemic improvements have been achieved, only a series of time-bound and geographically or subsector-limited projects.

We have also noted many examples of the inequalities of TVET provision. Ghana's TVET system tends to exclude the poor. The share of individuals having followed a TVET course rises with families' level of wealth. For example, the share of individuals from the highest income quintile enrolled in technical or vocational training is seven times that of those from the poorest quintile. The mainly urban location of formal training institutions makes for difficult access for the typically poorer rural communities. The inequalities inherent in access to (and the learning outcomes of) basic education in Ghana result, as we suggest above, in inequalities of access into formal (and informal) TVET. The three northern regions suffer the most disadvantages—both in terms of educational inequalities at the basic education level, and in geographical inequalities in the distribution of skill-training opportunities.

Notes

1. Readers interested in the tertiary level are advised to see the recent study on higher education and TVET in Ghana by Gondwe and Walenkamp (2011).
2. School-based TVE programs are also provided by the MoE through senior high schools (secondary technical schools), where students may take elective courses in technical and/or vocational subjects (including building, metalwork, auto mechanics, electricity, textiles, art, and so on), leading to a West African Examination Council certificate. In addition, students take the five core courses (math, English, social studies, science, and ICT). However, it is not possible to consider this TTIs branch of TVET in this analysis, because data on secondary technical schools are not disaggregated from the general secondary school stream.

3. Formerly known as the Ministry of Employment and Social Welfare.
4. The situation varies a little depending on the public provider. Outside the MoE there is confusion about the official duration of second-cycle TVET training, with many providers still providing the four years as per the reform. For example, the Youth Leadership and Skills Training Institutes used to have a two-year training duration, but increased it to four years to align with the NVTI (see appendix section "The Youth Leadership and Skills Training Institutes of the National Youth Authority"). Meanwhile, the NVTI itself increased its training duration from three to four years (see appendix section "National Vocational Training Institute (NVTI) (MoELR)"). As a result, their enrollment increased significantly because the same students were staying longer in the system.
5. The various forms of public and private TVET provisions are detailed in part 2 of the analysis.
6. This section on equity is inspired mainly by Palmer, Akabzaa, and Casely-Hayford (2009).
7. TVET instructors are considered to be trained if they have obtained the Technician II certificate or above.
8. Although this statement is accurate in general, several centers in Ashanti Region are in a slightly better position because they have received some support from NGOs over the last 5–10 years to improve workshop equipment and introduce computer equipment.
9. Except for the social welfare centers and for the Integrated Community Centers for Employable Skills.
10. Also, critically, no real data on impact, for example, using control groups.
11. See appendix section "Informal Apprenticeship Training" for further discussion on informal apprenticeship training. See also a summary of skills development in Ghana's informal sector in World Bank (2012b).
12. In total, approximately 730,000 adults (15–64 years of age) were engaged in apprenticeship in Ghana in 2005/06 (World Bank 2012b), meaning that there are approximately 290,000 apprentices who are older than 24 years (or 40 percent of all apprentices); many apprentices are known to start late because they often try other avenues of education and training first, before coming to apprenticeships.
13. www.enterprisesurveys.org.

CHAPTER 4

TVET Coordination

Introduction

One of the most serious nonmarket imperfections regarding technical and vocational education and training (TVET) is that of coordination of providers, qualifications, strategies, polices, legislation, and development partner support. This chapter examines various coordination issues related to TVET and the new education reform. TVET is delivered by a plethora of entities: some eight ministries, private for-profit and nonprofit institutes, and nongovernmental organizations (NGOs) and through informal apprenticeships (see chapter 3). According to the Japanese International Cooperation Agency, the TVET system in Ghana is so fragmented and shared among so many different ministries and state agencies that "not even the government have a full-clear picture of the situation" (GoJ 2004, 3). Interviews conducted as part of this report very much suggest that major information gaps still existed as of May 2012, which means that Council for TVET (COTVET) still does not have a complete understanding of the situation.

Earlier governments have attempted—and ultimately failed—to coordinate Ghana's TVET sector. Previous attempts included (1) the establishment of the National Vocational Training Institute (NVTI) in 1970, which was initially mandated to coordinate all aspects of vocational training nationwide (GoG 1970), and (2) following the NVTI's failure at coordination, the creation of a National Coordinating Committee for Technical and Vocational Education and Training (NACVET) in 1990 to coordinate a national TVET system, including both formal and informal providers. NACVET also ultimately failed in this coordination function. This failure can be attributed to several factors. First, it became diverted from coordination functions to become another training *provider*, through its network of NVTI centers. Second, NACVET was never able to reconcile the rivalries between the ministries of education and employment. Third, NACVET was never established by an act of parliament and so had no formal, legal mandate. Last, NACVET had little capacity and almost no technical and managerial experience in the area of vocational training. NACVET effectively ended its days as an entity that set secretarial examinations and examinations for farm institutes.

Following the recommendations of the 2002 Anamuah-Mensah report and the 2004 White Paper, in 2006 the government set up a technical committee to facilitate the establishment of COTVET. Parliament passed the bill on July 27, 2006, leading to the COTVET Act (718) in September of that year. COTVET is mandated to develop strategic policies for Ghana's TVET sector, covering the broad spectrum of pretertiary and tertiary education, formal and informal (GoG 2006e).

COTVET has been slow to establish its governance capacities. It took a year from the COTVET Act to set up the first 15-member COTVET board (which became effective in November 2007). Once set up, it was hindered in its activities during its entire first year by the absence of a secretariat. In addition to the delays in setting this up, it took a full year for the board to appoint an executive director, who started work in November 2008. By this time, the change in the government as a result of the elections in January 2009 led to the dissolution of the first COTVET board. The second COTVET board was then active from mid-2009 for two years and then was itself dissolved in July 2011 by the Minister of Education. It then took a further six months to set up the third board (established January 2012), which ended up having an acting board chairperson from the Ministry of Education (MoE) instead of a board chair from the private sector (because the private sector nominee apparently declined to be chairperson on the day they were to be sworn in).

This instability of the COTVET board has not helped COTVET to establish itself on firm footings, and as of May 2012, the Secretariat still required technical capacity building to improve in-house expertise on TVET.

Moreover, COTVET remains under the MoE and is still regarded by many as an MoE (and not cross-ministerial, let alone extra-ministerial) entity.[1] The current situation (May 2012) is complicated further because of tensions between COTVET and NVTI regarding the mandate of the latter being superseded by the former. Two areas of contention (see below) relate to (1) apprenticeship coordination and (2) certification.

In spite of these challenges, COTVET has still managed to set up five standing committees and further subcommittees. The standing committees are the National TVET Qualifications Committee (NTVETQC), the Industrial and Training Advisory Committee (ITAC), the Training Quality Assurance Committee (TQAC), the National Apprenticeship Committee (NAC), and the Skills Development Fund (SDF) Committee.

The coordination challenge has many different dimensions that COTVET would do well to confront. These include, but are not necessarily limited to, the following:

- The coordination of TVET supply to labor market demands for skills
- Government strategies and development plans that relate to TVET in whole or in part, as well as development partner support
- TVET qualifications and quality assurance
- The coordination of the TVET-related committees, which exist under various ministries, with the new COTVET board and committees
- The legal framework for TVET

The first three of these dimensions of the coordination challenge are dealt with in greater detail below, given their strategic importance for the sector.

The Coordination of TVET Supply and Demand

Supply

The COTVET act mandates COTVET to coordinate and formulate policies for both pretertiary and tertiary TVET. However, the tertiary institutions (universities and polytechnics) have their own act that gives authority to their respective councils/boards to direct their policies. Some in COTVET would like to see a change to the COTVET act so that COTVET focuses on pretertiary TVET.[2]

COTVET has made some initial steps toward coordination of the supply side of TVET, such as setting up the National TVET Qualifications Committee (NTVETQC) and the Training Quality Assurance Committee (TQAC). The former is working toward coordinating qualifications (see below), while the latter will be responsible for accrediting providers.

However, not much coordination or even engagement is still seen among public TVET providers; many staff members complain that they never have a chance to engage with their colleagues in other departments in the same ministry (for example, Integrated Community Center for Employable Skills [ICCES], Social Welfare, NVTI under Ministry of Employment and Labor Relations [MoELR]), let alone with colleagues in other ministries.[3]

Meanwhile, COTVET's National Apprenticeship Committee and its National Apprenticeship Program are attempting to engage with informal apprenticeship. However, instead of developing policies that would impact on the wider informal apprenticeship system, they have developed a small, state-funded, and short (one-year) "national" apprenticeship program that affects only 1 percent of youth in informal apprenticeships (see the appendix section, "National Apprenticeship Program," for a discussion).

Demand

According to one senior official working with COTVET, as of May 2012 "industry has not been involved in a dynamic way" with COTVET's operations.[4] COTVET's Industrial Training Advisory Committee (ITAC) and its subcommittees are responsible for the development of national occupational standards, which are meant to link the demand for skills from employers with the effective delivery of those skills by providers.

Adapting TVET supply to labor market demand will require a responsive feedback mechanism that communicates information on the evolving nature of the skills demanded by the economy to training providers. Given that information is so scarce in Ghana, especially on the demand side, the establishment of a TVET–labor market information system would be an effective first step toward coordinating supply and demand.

The TVET–labor market information system has to start collecting more demand-side data related to TVET (market studies, future skills need studies, tracers); as of May 2012, TVET indicators and data are all supply-side focused: number of schools/VTIs, number of staff, number of students, expenditure on technical and vocational education (TVE), and so on.

At the level of the training provider, there is a very weak supply-demand relationship. The lack of autonomy to be able to set up new courses, the general lack of any business representatives on institution boards, the almost complete absence of real tracer studies (let alone impact studies with control groups), as well as the lack of other government regulations and incentives contribute to this supply-demand failure (see chapter 3 for more discussion).

Coordination of Government Strategies, Plans, and Development Partner Support

Government Strategies and Plans

At the policy level, one finds insufficient coordination, which has led to the development of parallel agendas, plans, programs, and committees.

The fragmentation of TVET provision (see also chapter 3) is mirrored by a fragmentation of TVET policies and strategies among—and within—the main TVET-delivering ministries. So, for example, the NVTI (under MoELR) has a strategy, Opportunities Industrialization Center (OIC) (MoELR) has a strategy, ICCES (MoELR) has never really had a strategy, and meanwhile the MoELR itself does not have an overall TVET strategy. The MoE TTIs and their secondary technical schools are linked to the Education Strategic Plan. Meanwhile, COTVET is busy setting up new committees and frameworks. Moreover, some confusion still exists about the mandates of various entities, and some existing legislation is contradictory. A case in point is the state of affairs between the NVTI and COTVET when it comes to informal apprenticeship. On the one hand, the NVTI has its National Apprenticeship Council, which is backed by Legislative Instrument Apprentice Regulation LI 1151 of 1978, to "oversee all matters concerning apprenticeship in the country."[5] On the other hand, in April 2010, the COTVET Board set up a National Apprenticeship Committee "to formulate and supervise the implementation of a national apprenticeship policy" (COTVET 2010: 9). COTVET's National Apprenticeship Strategy (COTVET 2010) makes no reference to the NVTI National Apprenticeship Council.

We have already noted the dual-track policy-making process of the New Education Reform (NER) and the Education Strategic Plan (ESP) (see chapter 1), as well as the fragmentation of policies and strategies of TVET-providing ministries, but we should also highlight that numerous other strategies, plans, programs, or policies exist that relate, in whole or in part, to TVET.[6] Little attention has been given to the obvious synergies and interlinkages that exist between these agendas.

For example, the National Development Planning Commission (NDPC) (2010a) "Medium-Term National Development Policy Framework" for 2010–13 outlines the general strategies proposed for TVET, without going in to any detail. It simply states that, regarding TVET, policy interventions include the construction and rehabilitation/upgrading of facilities in all public Technical and Vocational Institutes in each District across the country; repositioning TVET in education and human resource development; and strengthening linkages with industry ... re-organiz[ing] and expan[ding] the current national apprenticeship program; providing opportunities for trainers in Technical and Vocational Institutes to undertake further studies in pedagogy; developing competency-based curriculum for TVET; strengthening career guidance and counseling services; supporting TVET institutions in generating funds internally; and exploring other funding sources to support other TVET institutions not under the Ministry of Education. (NDPC 2010a, 76–77)

It also notes that a key policy measure is to "empower ... COTVET to provide a more skills competency-based technical and vocational education" (NDPC 2010b, 20).

Very significant resources are still being spent by the government on TVET activities that are not coordinated with COTVET and largely operate independently of the main TVET-delivering ministries, departments, and agencies. The 2003–05 Skills Training and Entrepreneurship Program (STEP) was an example of such a program (see appendix B). From the STEP, the National Youth Employment Program (NYEP)[7] emerged, which contained a module related to TVET; in 2007, the NYEP had a budget that was five times the total budget of the Ministry of Employment and Labor Relations (World Bank 2010b). A more recent case is the Local Enterprise and Skills Development Program (LESDEP; appendix B), which has been granted a budget of Gh₵96 million for 2011/12 (about $50 million); this is more than the entire Skills Development Fund budget ($45 million) (World Bank 2011a; see also chapter 5).

Development Partner Support

Development partner and NGO support to TVET in Ghana has traditionally been highly fragmented. For the most part, development partner and NGO support has consisted of a series of specific projects without any overall framework for coordination. Although, in many cases, this support has improved the quality in individual training institutions, it has not had an impact on the national TVET system—partly because that support has targeted individual beneficiary institutions and also because TVET is spread across numerous different ministries. The usual scenario saw development partners set up bilateral partnerships with different ministries (most often MoE), for example:

- The Vocational Skills and Informal Sector support project (VSP) (1995–2001) saw the World Bank partner with the MoE (World Bank 1995).
- The vocational-technical resource centers (1999 to mid-2000s) saw the Netherlands partner with the MoE.
- The NVTI Centers Support Project (1996–98) saw the Department for International Development (DFID) partner with NVTI (MoELR).
- The Education Sector Project (2004–10) saw the World Bank partner with the MoE (World Bank 2004).

Since 2010, positive signs have indicated that development partners are starting to align behind COTVET. Indeed, the majority of the new programs have COTVET as their key partner, including the following:

- The World Bank's Ghana Skills and Technology Development Project (World Bank 2011a)
- Danida's Enterprise Development Program (Danida 2009)
- The German government through German Society for International Cooperation (GIZ 2011) and KfW (PLANCO Consulting 2011)
- The African Development Bank (ADF 2012)[8]

Meanwhile, NGOs continue to provide uncoordinated support to TVET mainly through bilateral relationships between an individual NGO and an individual school or training center.

TVET Quality Assurance and Qualifications

Quality Assurance

Historically, there has been no coordinated approach regarding quality assurance for either formal or informal TVET providers. In 2010/11, COTVET established a Training Quality Assurance Committee (TQAC) that is responsible for ensuring that training providers and qualification awarding agencies maintained satisfactory standards in the delivery of training and the award of qualifications. In 2012, a Legislative Instrument (LI 2195) was passed (GoG 2012b) that outlines the regulations and criteria for the registration and accreditation of TVET providers (with "TVET providers" defined as institutional training providers, workplace training providers, and informal sector training providers). The LI specifies that these TVET providers "shall not operate unless registered by the Council [COTVET]" (GoG 2012b: clause 1). To be registered and accredited, that provider must meet certain minimum standards. What is not clear is how the quality assurance function of TQAC will extend to the massive informal apprenticeship system. The LI clearly identifies "informal sector training providers" as being required to register with COTVET in order to provide training, but quite how this would be enforced is not known.

Qualifications

Before the arrival of COTVET, Ghana had developed various qualification-awarding organizations—which, as of May 2012, still existed—and include, among others the Ghana Education Service (GES) of the MoE (which conducts the Technical and Commercial Examinations), the NVTI (which conducts Proficiency, Grade II, Grade I, and the National Craftsmen Certificate Examination), and the National Board for Professional and Technical Examinations (which conducts the Higher National Diploma examinations in collaboration with the polytechnics) (CPTC 2006, 51–52).

Table 4.1 National TVET Qualifications Framework

Level	Qualification	Required entry background
1	National Proficiency I	From no formal education to some basic education but less than Basic Education Certificate of Education
2	National Proficiency II	Proficiency I
3	National Certificate I	Basic Education Certificate of Education or Proficiency II
4	National Certificate II	West African Secondary School Completion Exam or Certificate I
5	Higher national diploma	West African Secondary School Completion Exam or Certificate II
6	Bachelor of technology	West African Secondary School Completion Exam or higher national diploma
7	Master of technology	Bachelor of technology
8	Doctor of technology	Master of technology

Sources: COTVET 2012a, b and GoG 2012b.

In 2010/11, COTVET set up a National TVET Qualifications Committee (NTVETQC), which is responsible for coordinating the certification and qualifications offered. The NTVETQC has designed a National TVET qualifications framework (NTVETQF) (table 4.1.), which will ultimately replace other existing frameworks.

LI 2195 also gives COTVET more power with regard to qualifications and awards. It contains clauses related to registration and accreditation of awarding bodies; policies, criteria, regulation, and procedures for the operation of the national TVET qualifications framework; and regulations for the NTVETQF (COTVET 2012a; GoG 2012b).

Despite the fact that COTVET is now mandated by its establishing law to set up a unified TVET qualifications structure, as noted above other TVET qualifications are still being offered in several ministries, departments, and agencies, which draw on earlier laws to justify their positions. In the words of one senior government official, "some organizations are trying to hang on to functions that should now be performed by COTVET."[9] However, NVTI and other TVET awarding bodies are required by the 2012 LI (GoG 2012b) to register with COTVET.

In the case of NVTI, it clearly makes sense to separate its training function from its certification-awarding function, because having one organization carry out both functions would appear to carry an inherent conflict of interest. However, NVTI's testing department brings the organization significant revenues, a factor that may make NVTI reluctant to see such a change.

Indeed, there is meant to be a phase-in period during which time both the old (for example NVTI, GES) certificates will be offered (to those students already on those programs) in addition to the new certificates (offered to those starting on the new programs). However, significant confusion exists among the public TVET providers (though not so much the Ministry of Education Technical Training Institutes [MoE TTIs]) about how and when this phase-in is meant to take place.

Concluding Comments

The establishment of COTVET represents a hopeful shift toward better TVET coordination in Ghana. Since its establishment, it has been making moves in the right direction with the establishment of a competitive Skills Development Fund, a National TVET Qualifications Committee, a Training Quality Assurance Committee, and plans to draft a national skills strategy. The Legislative Instrument (LI 2195) passed in 2012 also represents a positive step forward.

Nonetheless, the market and nonmarket imperfections outlined in this study present serious challenges. The training market in Ghana is highly fragmented; the public system is spread over multiple ministries, while the private system—made up of the massive informal apprenticeship system as well as formal private providers—is not incentivized to coordinate. Ghana has a history of failed attempts to coordinate TVET, dating back to the 1970s with the establishment of the NVTI, initially mandated to coordinate all aspects of vocational training nationwide, and then (in the 1990s) with the failed National Coordinating Committee for Technical and Vocational Education and Training. In 2006, a new TVET coordinating body was set up, the Council for TVET, which was backed by an Act of Parliament. However, COTVET remains under the MoE and is still regarded by many as an MoE (not cross-ministerial, let alone extra-ministerial) entity. It does not yet have sufficient power (or say in how the majority of all public financial resources are allocated to TVET) to be able to significantly influence TVET nationwide. At the strategy and policy level insufficient coordination still exists, which has led to the development of parallel agendas, plans, programs, and committees.

Since 2010 there have been positive signs that development partners are starting to align themselves behind COTVET. Indeed, the majority of the new programs have COTVET as their key partner. This is a significant and positive change from the past, seeing that DP and NGO support to TVET in Ghana has traditionally been highly fragmented.

Notes

1. Senior official working with COTVET, private communication May 3, 2012. The MoELR is one ministry that is said not to be happy with the placement of COTVET under the MoE.
2. Senior government official, private communication, May 2, 2012.
3. Interviews, May 2012.
4. Senior government official, private communication, May 3, 2012.
5. www.nvtighana.org.
6. These include (or have included), for example: the NDPC (2008) medium-long term national development plan and then the NDPC (2010a) "Medium-Term National Development Policy Framework," the National Employment Strategy, the skills component of the National Trade Sector Support Program (2006–10), the Private Sector Development Strategy II, the National Youth Policy, and the Ghana Industrial Policy 2010.

7. The NYEP aimed to promote job creation for young people (18–35 years of age). Launched in October 2006, the program was designed around different modules offering various work and training opportunities (see World Bank 2010b). In 2012, the NYEP was transformed into a permanent agency called the Ghana Youth Employment and Entrepreneurial Development Agency (GYEEDA).
8. The African Development Bank also has a bilateral project agreement with the Ministry of Gender, Children and Social Protection (formerly the Ministry of Women and Children's Affairs), the Gender Responsive Skills and Community Development Project. http://www.afdb.org/documents/document/ghana-gender-responsive-skills-and-community-development-project-gpn-8206/
9. Private communication, May 2, 2012.

CHAPTER 5

TVET Financing

This chapter examines various key technical and vocational education and training (TVET) funding issues. First, it examines the suggestions that have been put forward for over 10 years regarding the identification of sustainable sources of systemic TVET funding. Second, it summarizes the main financing approaches used by TVET providers (public and private, institute and enterprise based). Third, it highlights some general cross-cutting issues concerning TVET financing. Some TVET funding recommendations are presented in chapter 6.

Systemic TVET Financing

At the systemic level, identification of sustainable sources of funding for TVET requires urgent attention. Over the decade 2002–12, numerous proposals were made about how the reform of the TVET sector might be sustainably financed; although no agreement has been reached on a national financing framework, progress has been made in the setting up of a Skills Development Fund (SDF) (see below).

The proposals made during the 2008 Education Sector Annual Review (GoG 2008b) and in the 2007 report of the TVET subcommittee of the National Education Reform Implementation Committee (NERIC) (GoG 2007d) were very similar to those made in the latest August 2004 version of the TVET policy framework (GoG 2004b, ch. 12). This in turn overlapped with the TVET financing recommendations formulated in the 2002 Anamuah-Mensah Report (GoG 2002). Table 5.1 summarizes and compares the respective recommendations over the period 2002–08.

However, some of the core financing suggestions made in these documents were rejected by the Ministry of Finance in 2004 (GoG 2004b, annex). The rejected suggestions include the following: (1) that the government increase the annual budgetary TVET allocation, (2) that the Ghana Education Trust Fund (GETFund) be used to finance TVET, (3) that a percentage of district assemblies' common funds be allocated to supplement district level TVET activities,

Table 5.1 TVET Funding Recommendations, 2002–08

Anamuah-Mensah Report (2002)	TVET Policy Framework (2004)	NERIC Report—TVET Section (2007)	Education Sector Annual Review (2008)
Establish a Skills Development Fund			
With the support of agencies such as the Association of Ghana Industries, Ghana Employers Association, Trade Union Congress, the Chamber of Mines, and the Chamber of Commerce and Industry	With contributions from member industries and businesses (1 percent of payroll), labor unions, and trade associations (0.5 percent of their membership fees)	Yes	With a payroll tax of 1 percent for both public and private industries, and contributions from trade unions of 0.5 percent of their annual membership fees
Allocate/increase the Ghana Education Trust Fund's (GETFund) contribution to TVET			
10 percent for the rehabilitation of existing infrastructure and the establishment of new institutes	"A categorical percentage"	"A specific percentage"	Increase to 10 percent of funds allocated from GETFund
Allocate share of District Assemblies Common Fund to TVET			
Minimum 5 percent	"A categorical percentage"	"A specific percentage"	5 percent
Increase ministries, departments, and agencies' budget funding of TVET			
"Considerably"	Yes	MoE (7.5 percent, for TTIs), MoELR (20 percent, for NVTI), MoFA (5 percent, for agricultural VTIs), create a budget line for national apprenticeships	"Progressively"
Mobilize resources for TVET from development partners			
From donors	From nongovernmental organizations and external agencies	From donors	From development partners
Promote training institute income-generating activities			
And create endowment funds	From custom jobs or production units	And through production units	Assist providers to develop strategic plans
Promote private sector donation appeals			
For equipment and consumables	For resources	Not mentioned	Not mentioned
Increase household contributions to training costs			
For part of consumables and other expenditures	Yes	Not mentioned, but implied	Not mentioned but implied
Establish a Ghana TVET Patrons' Fund			
Not mentioned	To mobilize foreign revenues	To obtain revenues from remittances, foreign institutions, and philanthropists	Not mentioned
Student loan scheme			
Not mentioned	Loans to students to be funded with the Ghana TVET Patrons' Fund	Create a student loan scheme for pretertiary TVET	Not mentioned

table continues next page

Table 5.1 TVET Funding Recommendations, 2002–08 *(continued)*

Anamuah-Mensah Report (2002)	TVET Policy Framework (2004)	NERIC Report—TVET Section (2007)	Education Sector Annual Review (2008)
Loans to private TVET institutes			
Not mentioned	Not mentioned	Give registered and accredited private institutes access to soft loans	Not mentioned
Public subsidies for private institutes			
Not mentioned	Not mentioned	Subsidize registered and accredited private institutes through a 50% salary grant	Not mentioned
Public subsidies for private apprenticeship training			
Not mentioned	Not mentioned	Not mentioned	—

Source: World Bank.
Note: MoE = Ministry of Education; MoELR = Ministry of Employment and Labor Relations; MoFA = Ministry of Food and Agriculture; NERIC = National Education Reform Implementation Committee; TVET = Technical and Vocational Education and Training; VTI = Vocational Training Institute; — = not available.

and (4) that there be established a Skills Development Fund (based on industry levies) and a Ghana patrons' fund. Having been rejected in 2004, it is not clear why the same recommendations were made again in 2007 and 2008 without first initiating a dialogue with the Ministry of Finance.

Although no progress was made in identifying sustainable sources of financing for TVET over the 2004–08 period, a process was initiated in mid-2008 and again in January 2009 to establish a Skills Development Fund (set up initially by donors). Two Danida-funded consultants initiated a dialogue with key TVET stakeholders, including industry representatives. The initial intention, agreed on by Council for TVET (COTVET), was for development partners (the World Bank and Danida) to finance the creation of the SDF mechanism and then provide the initial capital (the World Bank in 2009 and Danida in 2010). The intention was that a levy on industry could be instated to recapitalize the SDF on a sustainable basis. This is an ongoing process, discussed in greater detail below.

Apart from the establishment of the SDF (which is almost entirely donor financed, without any agreement on an industry levy to finance it), in the decade since the 2002 Anamuah-Mensah Report, little overall progress has been achieved. In the period 2009–12, no really significant new suggestions have been made on TVET financing approaches.

Skills Development Fund (SDF)

One of the most positive TVET developments in recent years has been the establishment of a Skills Development Fund, which was launched in September 2010. The objective of the SDF is to finance technical and vocational skills (and technology development) programs in prioritized economic sectors through a demand-driven mechanism that is managed by COTVET (World Bank 2011a).

SDF Resource Mobilization

The World Bank and Danida initially capitalized the SDF. However, in the long term, a Ghanaian SDF will be sustainable only if financed by a levy on industry and enterprises in general, as in many Sub-Saharan African countries and elsewhere (Johanson and Adams 2004). The levy could take the form of a payroll tax for both public and private sector entities. Although some may not consider it fair to impose such a levy until the quality and relevance of the training provided by the TVET system is significantly improved, the skills system needs strong buy-in from the private sector to improve quality and relevance. Such private sector buy-in may be both in the form of financial support but also (and perhaps more importantly) in terms of advice on how to make training more relevant. If the private sector is paying into a skills levy (or represented on the board of a levy-grant mechanism), it will have greater incentive to get more involved in reforming and strengthening the TVET system.

For the levy to be successful in Ghana, employers need to be incentivized to participate (for example, via tax credits), and they need to feel like they have a real say in where the funds are allocated. The levy should ideally not be limited to formal (and larger) private companies, but also aim to include micro and small enterprises (MSEs) and the government. As the largest formal employer, government contributions would be significant. For industry to be willing to contribute, the fund has to be seen to be independent of government control and be led by representatives of private enterprises along with employee and employer groups, associations, and unions. It should be kept in mind that the capacity and resources of these groups can sometimes be limited, so capacity-building efforts would be required to help them inform clients and eventually to become more involved both in TVET services and in TVET financing.

Including SMEs in the levy would be a challenge, but it is important to get their buy-in because they make up the bulk of the private sector. International experience shows that it can be challenging to include SMEs in such a levy system. However, because the majority of private enterprises in Ghana are SMEs, and skills upgrading is known to happen less often in SMEs compared to large enterprises in Ghana (see chapter 3), this should be an important consideration for fund sustainability. It is clear that the Ghanaian Skills Development Fund recognizes the need to reach out to informal sector enterprises—as evidenced by the specific funding window for them, as noted below. A strong need is seen for SMEs to upgrade their skills, and seeking levy contributions from them toward training could be a mechanism to encourage them to do so. However, some countries that operate sector training funds exempt enterprises whose revenue is less than a specified amount from paying levies, though these enterprises are still eligible to access grants from the fund. Ghana may opt for this model. Ghana's well-developed informal sector associations may serve as a useful conduit through which to secure levy payments from SMEs. It should be noted, though, many kinds of challenges and unintended effects may result from such an approach. More analysis is needed on involving SMEs, and particularly microenterprises, in a future levy to finance the Ghanaian SDF.

COTVET is making efforts to get a law for contributions by employers, employees, and others for sustainable technical and vocational skills development funding in the country (COTVET 2012a). In the short term, until legislation can be connected to an industry levy, the World Bank and Danida have agreed to provide initial seed funds. The World Bank, at the request of the government, restructured its Education Sector Project to make funds available in 2009. Danida allocated approximately Gh₵10 million for the SDF through the Support to Private Sector Development Program (2010–14; Danida 2009). Significant support to the SDF was also included in the World Bank (International Development Association; IDA) Ghana Skills and Technology Development Project (2011–15; World Bank 2011a). The government of Ghana contributed via GETFund.

In late 2008, several COTVET board members voiced concerns about the sustainability of an SDF that was set up by donors. As a result, COTVET and development partners have been working closely to ensure that the fund is country led (by COTVET). However, as of May 2012, some concern remained about the inadequacy of GoG contributions to SDF. One senior government official commented that the SDF "to a large extent dependent on donor funds";[1] this is clearly seen in the contributions of each of the actors: World Bank ($35 million), Danida ($10 million), and the government of Ghana (zero). Meanwhile, it is also clear that the government is still allocating large sums of money outside of the SDF mechanism; for example, none of the funding for the Local Enterprise and Skills Development Program (see appendix section "Local Enterprise and Skills Development Program") in 2011/12 ($50 million) went through the SDF.

Now that the SDF has been established, it is starting to be used as a mechanism to harmonize and coordinate development partner funding; several donors (World Bank, Danida) are channeling their funds directly into the SDF. Several others are actively engaging with COTVET and the SDF management to see how they can channel funds through the SDF; the German KfW is planning a training voucher system for the informal sector (to start 2013/14), and the African Development Bank wants the SDF to come up with a competitive grant scheme to encourage training providers to establish production units to produce goods and services to sell on the market to generate revenues.[2]

The SDF board and COTVET are responsible for ensuring that donor-funded activities (especially those outside the SDF) complement, and do not duplicate, each other. This is in line with the Paris declaration on aid effectiveness, as well as the Accra Agenda for Action and the Busan Declaration.[3]

SDF Resource Allocation

In 2008, before the SDF was established by COTVET in 2010, employers and industry groups voiced concerns about how they would access funding from the fund and appeared wary of the government on this issue. This is further reason for industry and employers' groups to be centrally involved in the management of the fund, and for the SDF to have a governing and oversight structure that is largely independent of the government.

Table 5.2 Skills Development Fund Applications and Approvals

SDF Support Window	Call 1 (2011)			Call 2 (2012)			Call 3 (2013)		
	Applications Received	Grants Approved	Value of Grants $	Applications Received	Grants Approved	Value of Grants $	Applications Received	Grants Approved	Value of Grants $
Formal sector training	23	1	0.59	65	12	3.60	56	32	6.11
Informal sector training	79	3	0.30	182	47	3.42	292	120	9.75
Training innovation	23	1	0.40	118	6	2.59	55	9	5.76
Technology partnership	8	0	—	50	4	0.53	30	5	2.36
Technology center	12	1	0.23	13	4	5.17	16	2	0.69
Total grants	**145**	**6**	**1.52**	**428**	**73**	**15.31**	**449**	**168**	**24.67**

Source: COTVET Skills Development Fund Secretariat.

At its founding, the SDF had three funding windows aimed at technical and vocational skills development (COTVET 2009). Window 1 focuses on technical and vocational skills for formal sector medium and large enterprises. Window 2 focuses on skills for MSEs in the informal sector. Window 3 focuses on innovative training approaches. In addition, for the Ghana Skills and Technology Development Project, the SDF opened a fourth window to support technology upgrading by enterprises and linkages between industry and technology providers (World Bank 2011a).

The SDF issued its first call for proposals in September 2011, and 483 proposals were received. In mid-May 2012, the proposals were still being reviewed. Analyses of the responses received are detailed in table 5.2.

From a review of the proposals it is apparent that greater communication is required to get applicants to better understand the focus and objectives of the SDF. For example, a large proportion of the proposals received under window 3 (training innovations) were requests from training providers to finance, for example, new hostels, classrooms, and workshops. After the initial screening, only 16 of the 216 applications got to the second round.[4] The second call for proposals was planned for July 2012.

Financing COTVET Itself

A related concern is that of identifying broader financing for COTVET and its cross-cutting activities. COTVET is (2012/13) financed through World Bank and Danida support as well as GoG funding. GoG budgetary support is regarded as inadequate, and COTVET has had to rely more on development partners to fund its programs; concern has been expessed that the cessation of support from the development partners would curtail COTVET's programs (COTVET 2012a).

This approach is obviously not ideal, given that COTVET as an entity represents multiple institutions, some of which are extra-ministerial bodies. Being both an official dependency of the Ministry of Education (MoE) and funded by the MoE will likely contribute to COTVET being seen as an MoE entity, which was one of the reasons for the failure of COTVET's predecessor, National Coordinating Committee for Technical and Vocational Education and Training (NACVET). Ideally, a sustainable funding mechanism would be created, including an SDF funded by an industry levy, so that COTVET can have greater autonomy.

TVET Financing Modalities

Financing School-Based TVE

The MoE runs two types of TVE programs, both school based: the first, usually the only one reported on, are the technical training institutes (TTIs) (under the TVE division of the Ghana Education Service [GES]); the second are the secondary technical schools: senior high schools offering students a main focus on technical and/or vocational subjects, including building, metalwork, automechanics, electrical work, textiles, art, and other subjects.

Between 2003 and 2010 budget expenditure for the public TTIs as a percentage of the total resource envelope for education under the MoE has remained about 1 percent (GoG 2008a, 2011a).

TTIs receive a government grant to cover staff/personnel emoluments, administrative activities, service activities, and investment activities. Personnel emoluments are paid directly to staff. Training fees, which are standardized nationwide, are charged and retained by individual TTIs. Some TTIs also engage in income-generating activities and receive a limited amount of funding from nongovernmental organizations (NGOs) on an ad hoc basis. For example, at the Accra Technical Training Center (ATTC), the government grant accounts for approximately 70 percent of the center's income, ATTC training fees for 10 percent, and income-generating activities (internally generated funds) for the remaining 20 percent. For TTIs that do not engage in income-generating activities, the government grant may account for up to 90 percent of income.[5]

Turning to resource allocation, funds are transferred from the GES headquarters to TTIs through the district directorates. The current financing mechanism means that schools with reduced enrollment obtain less funds. No official mechanism exists to offer financial incentives to better performing departments or staff. Some TTIs, like the ATTC, do, however, offer ad hoc incentives to better performing personnel.

Unit costs are routinely quoted in the MoE "Preliminary Education Sector Performance Reports." For example, the 2011 report (GoG 2011a) notes that the recurrent unit cost for TTIs was around Gh₵194 in 2006, increasing to about Gh₵650 in 2009 (see table 5.3) as a result of escalating salaries. It is important to note, however, that these figures are subject to serious data limitations.[6]

However, these unit costs do not take internally generated funds into account, such as training fees, parent-teacher association fees, or the proceeds of other

Table 5.3 Technical Training Institutes' Actual Unit Costs, 2006–09

Ghana Cedis

		2006	2007	2008	2008
Technical training institute	Per capita	196	172	379	885
	Unit cost	194	171	305	650

Source: GoG 2011a.
Note: The per capita cost is the total expenditure on that level of education divided by public enrollment at that level. The unit cost is the recurrent expenditure divided by public enrollment at that level.

income-generating activities. Moreover, they do not account for the recurrent cost associated with the depreciation of the equipment required for training, which can be very expensive and should be included. The unit costs quoted must therefore be considered in the light of these limitations, until further work allows them to be calculated with more precision.

The Financing of Public Vocational Training Institutes (VTIs)

Financing varies for the different public non-Ministry of Education Vocational Training Institutes (MoE VTIs), including the Community Development Vocational/ Technical Institutes, National Vocational Training Institute (NVTI) centers, the Integrated Community Center for Employable Skills (ICCES), the Opportunities Industrialization Center—Ghana (OICG), the social welfare centers, and the Youth Leadership and Skills Training Institutes (see table 5.4 on the financing of ICCES). However, some common threads can be noted, as highlighted below.

Public VTI staff salaries are covered by the government. Many public institutes also receive a grant to cover the costs of administration and service and investment activities (those that don't receive such a grant include ICCES, the social welfare centers, and the Community Development VTIs). At the national level, the NVTI directorate, unlike public VTI directorates, also generates sizeable income from trade-testing fees and the training of master craftspeople, which account for about 25 percent of the NVTI national budget (see appendix section "National Vocational Training Institute (NVTI) (MoELR)").

All public VTIs charge training fees, which are retained by them. The institutes use them without interference from the head or regional offices. Fee structures vary according to the type of institute:

- Community Development Vocational/Technical Institutes' training fees range from Gh₵4 per year in Bongo, one of the poorest districts, to Gh₵180 per year in Madina district, where fee levels are determined by the parent-teacher association and the board of governors.
- Training fees for most NVTI centers range from Gh₵150 to Gh₵250 per year, although catering courses can cost up to Gh₵350 per year; however, the nine NVTIs in the three northern regions charge only Gh₵15 per year.
- Training fees at the ICCES are set by individual institutions and depend on the estimated ability of members of the local community to pay; annual ICCES fees are about Gh₵150.

Table 5.4 ICCES Financing Modalities and Implications

Modalities	Implications
ICCES centers' instructors are paid directly by the ICCES head office; individual centers and regional offices have no control over staff payments.	Individual staff often feel more accountable to the ICCES directorate than their center's manager or regional coordinator.
Individual ICCES centers and regional coordinators have no idea of the national ICCES budget; the ICCES directorate is not accountable.	Centers are not told how funds are spent, only that there are never enough. This lack of transparency creates ill will toward the ICCES directorate.
ICCES centers receive nothing from the ICCES directorate or from the central government for training materials, equipment, textbooks, or infrastructure (although some district assemblies offer ad hoc support).	Centers do not feel obliged to report on their financial position to the regional or head office since they receive virtually no support (other than the salaries paid direct to staff).
ICCES centers have a high level of financial autonomy; they keep all training fees and internally generated funds, reach bilateral funding agreements with NGOs and district assemblies, and can hire additional teachers. (The government of Ghana covers the salaries of about five instructors per center, which is insufficient.)	There are virtually no financial accountability mechanisms; the ICCES directorate has little data on ICCES centers' financing, and centers are not required to submit financial reports.
No incentives are offered to ICCES staff or centers for better performance, and salaries are lower than for Ghana Education Service instructors.	This saps instructors' morale, especially as most ICCES centers are in rural locations that instructors find unattractive.
Since approximately 2010, Regional Coordinators have not been given grants to cover administrative and monitoring costs. Instead, they have been told to seek funds from the centers in their regions.	Except where the regional coordinator has managed to secure support from a nongovernmental organization (as is the case of Ashanti region), it is likely that the work of many regional coordinators has been adversely affected. It is not realistic to expect individual centers to finance the running costs of the regional office.

Source: Authors' interviews with numerous ICCES staff and personal experience working with the ICCES system over the last decade.
Note: ICCES = Integrated Community Center for Employable Skills.

Most public VTIs also engage in some form of income-generating activity at the institutional level to obtain additional income for training and administrative activities. Activities might include vegetable farming, sewing of uniforms, operation of canteens, hair salons, sale of cold water, goat rearing, or contracts to build doors and windows.

Most public VTIs seek additional support from NGOs, but such relationships, when established, are usually ad hoc bilateral arrangements between a given VTI and an NGO, rather than being organized by the directorate. Social Welfare Centers and the OICGs are an exception to this: They have, respectively, established a partnership with United Nations Educational, Scientific, and Cultural Organization (UNESCO) to provide tool kits and with a German faith-based organization to undertake an apprenticeship upgrading program.

Very few data are available on the financing of public VTIs: unit costs are not calculated, and many individual public VTIs do not routinely send financial reports to their regional or head offices.

The Financing of Private VTIs

Perhaps unsurprisingly, the main source of income for private institutes is the school fees collected from students (Ahorbo 2009a). However, the unpredictability of the fees affects the operation of many private VTIs. Private TVET delivery is comparatively expensive because of the demand for instructors with practical trade experience, making it crucial to find a reliable and sustainable source of financing. Some nonprofit private VTIs receive donations from foreign institutions, but these are a secondary source of revenue.

Salaries generally represent over 50 percent of expenditures, reaching 90 percent in some cases (private TVET providers that are supported by private donors tend to spend more on salaries than the school fees collected). Spending on training and learning materials is generally as low as 1–3 percent of total income.

Generally, private VTIs survive the challenges of low enrollment and high operating costs by passing their operational costs on to their students in order to turn resulting surpluses into a profit. This is reflected in the low share of income spent on training and learning materials (which students often have to purchase themselves), low salaries, and other related costs.

From this analysis, three approaches to the reliable financing of private TVET providers can be proposed:

- *Income-generating activities* that relate to the general activities of institutes in their core areas, which could serve two good purposes: (1) providing reliable income to the school and (2) offering students the opportunity to gain practical experience
- *Public subsidies*, effectively passing on part of the financial burden to the government, providing institutes with some relief (this may take the form of targeted scholarships, vouchers, loan subsidies, or direct grants)
- *Making available funds from a skills development fund*, which has a sustainable financing stream with contributions from the government and businesses. As noted above, the current SDF does not have any private sector contributions, though private VTIs are fully able to apply for funds (for example, window 3 on training innovations is especially relevant to private VTIs).

Financing Informal Apprenticeship Training

Informal apprenticeship training costs are borne by apprentices and their families with no input from the government or communities. Unlike preemployment training, there is no need for a training center or special tools or equipment. No tradition is in place of *systemic* government support, control, or supervision in Ghana to date.[7] There is, however, a history of sustainability. Often many different types of fees are related to informal apprenticeship training:

- In many cases, training fees include both commitment and graduation fees, paid at the start and at the end of training.[8]
- Some master craftspeople ask for contributions in kind, commonly a crate of minerals (soft drinks) or malt (nonalcoholic malt drink), a bottle of spirits, cigarettes, or a goat.[9]
- Apprentices usually have to provide certain items before commencing training. For instance, carpentry apprentices usually have to bring some basic tools (hammer, chisel, measuring tape), and dressmaking apprentices need to provide their own machine, scissors, and measuring tape.[10]

On the other hand, master craftspeople often provide apprentices with a small daily stipend to cover their food, known as "chop money" (Breyer 2007; Palmer 2007a).[11]

Breyer carried out some detailed work on the costing of informal apprenticeship training in urban areas, mainly in Accra. In 2007, the average commitment fee, usually charged at the start of training, was $85 (ranging from $22 to $336); the average graduation fee, charged at the end of training, was $93 (ranging from $11 to $440). The sum of the different fees (the commitment fee, contributions in kind, and the graduation fee) is $160 on average, ranging from $22 to $616. In addition to this, the average cost of a toolbox in 2006 was $45 (ranging from $6 to $224), varying considerably among different trades.

Apprenticeship fees are generally lower in rural areas and are likely to be lower in urban areas other than Accra. Palmer's (2007a) study of rural apprenticeships asked about the total fees paid by apprentices and did not disaggregate the commitment fee and the graduation fee. This study, based on 2005 data for the rural Ashanti region, estimated the average total fee to be $42, ranging from $13 to $173.

Two attempts are currently being made to improve informal apprenticeships: the government-funded National Apprenticeship Program (NAP) (appendix B) and the GIZ-funded Ghana Skills Development Initiative (GSDI) (see appendix section "Informal Apprenticeship Training"). Neither program is proposing a large outreach. The NAP reaches about 1 percent of the apprenticeship population per annum, while the GSDI is proposing to reach about three to five thousand apprentices and masters over a five-year period. The latter is introducing a systemic approach by implementing standards and structures for a bigger rollout after piloting. Selected training providers and informal sector trade associations are expected to profit from intensive capacity-building measures in 2013.[12]

Financing Formal Enterprise-Based Training

The cost of on-the-job training of employees is fully borne by companies when it is relevant to their work. For example, Anglogold Ashanti estimates that it spent about $427 to train each formal apprentice in 2006, rising to $519 per apprentice in 2007. Fan Milk Limited estimated that the unit cost of training a staff member was approximately $265. The Coca-Cola Bottling Company estimated the cost of training new employees graduated from TVET institutes to be approximately $135 (Ahorbo 2009b).

Outcomes and Issues

Poor Data Availability

Formal institute-based TVET provision is usually more expensive than general education, but planners have very little information on the actual costs of training. All MoE unit costs for TVET refer exclusively to the TTIs and do not consider all recurrent costs. Very little other unit cost data for TVET providers are available. No disaggregation is made of the cost of secondary schools between technical and nontechnical. Unit costs for secondary technical schools are assumed to be the same as for general senior secondary education, which implies that the investment in secondary technical schools is also below requirements. It is advisable to disaggregate secondary school spending to obtain unit costs for secondary technical schools. Public VTIs such as OICG, ICCES, and NVTI do not compute unit costs, and, the data on average unit costs at private VTIs are scarce. The cost of informal apprenticeships is slightly better known, because of recent research in this area.

The Ineffective Funding Model

The public financing approach and (lack of) incentives used to support TVET in Ghana help to create and perpetuate a supply-driven, low-quality skills system. Public financing incentives are lacking for training providers to deliver better services, for employees to improve their skills and employability, and for employers to train more. In many cases, government financing approaches end up distorting markets.

TVET public financing is not based on any transparent funding mechanisms. Once an institution begins to receive funding, subsequent allocations are guaranteed. Funding is based on inputs (the number of students and teachers) irrespective of the institute's performance, outputs (the percentage of students graduating or achieving a specified minimum standard), or outcomes (the percentage of graduates finding employment or becoming self-employed within six months of graduating). The same levels of finance are allocated to poorly performing institutes with high dropout rates as to those that maintain a high quality of teaching and performance. The current public financing mechanism has created long chains of accountability between the providers (TTI, NVTI, and so on) and the clients (the youth and their parents). Salaries of teachers and instructors in the public providers are paid by the government, not directly by parents, and teachers know that they will get paid regardless of how many students pass their exams or gain adequate practical competencies. As well, they are not easily fired for underperforming, coming to class late, or not coming at all for extended periods.[13]

Planners' lack of consideration of performance, outputs, and outcomes in deciding how much to allocate to a particular TVET institute, combined with the lack of incentives for TVET institutes' effective use of available resources, results in training providers having insufficient interest in their finances. Training providers have no financial incentive to meet labor market needs or to improve their performance.

To make a more performance-based system work, it will be necessary to improve TTIs' and VTIs' management capacities and to hold managers accountable for results (World Bank 2008a, 77).

Both public and private TVET institutions should be able to compete for public financing. Providing beneficiaries with training vouchers could stimulate competition among TVET providers, improving training quality (World Bank 2008a). Vouchers are more effective where beneficiaries have a real choice of providers and are therefore less effective in rural areas where TVET institutes are more dispersed.

Where public funding has been used to support private informal apprenticeships (as with the NAP), it does so in a way that risks substituting for private financing; in other words, the government ends up paying for something that the private sector would have normally paid for; the government is financing a one-year informal apprenticeship, with apprentices themselves paying nothing, where normally they would have financed the training.

Where public funding has been used to support short duration skills training in Ghana, as was the case of the Skills Training and Entrepreneurship Program (2003–05) (see appendix B) or, more recently, the Local Enterprise and Skills Development Program (LESDEP) (appendix B), it is often done so in an inefficient way; for example, the targeting is inadequate, so the program benefits are captured by better-off segments of society, or the program is not well designed and functions in parallel to the existing TVET programs.

Equity Implications of Current TVET Financing
Is public finance for technical and vocational skills development used strategically to promote social equity?

As noted in chapter 3, the poor have considerably lower access to skills training in Ghana, be it institute based or enterprise based; fees and other contributions by private households constitute obstacles to participation.

Much public spending on TVET is not targeted at the poor and is captured by those who are less in need, thus widening inequalities. For example, the World Bank (2010b) estimates that only 19 percent of the public spending for MoE vocational education reaches the poor. The public TVET provider that is the most difficult for young people to enter (the TTIs) is the most subsidized provider with the lowest fees; TTI training fees are on average about one-tenth of those in the other public TVET providers (see appendix B).

The majority of public TVET providers do not offer scholarships to poor youth; those that do, do so on a very small scale and ad hoc manner. In some public VTIs (for example, ICCES and OICG until recently), training center managers often offer poor students very flexible payment arrangements, but this has often resulted in large fee arrears because many such students default on fee payments and complete their training owing training fees for multiple years.

Other kinds of public subsidies for TVET are often used inefficiently. For example, where subsidized (or free at point of use) short-term training is introduced (sometimes with the offer of some free or subsidized equipment), these can result in trainees dropping out of longer term training they might currently be in (and paying for); this was the case with the 2003–05 Skills Training and Entrepreneurship Program in Ghana (see appendix B). Another example of inefficient use of public subsidies is the financing of the NAP (appendix B); the selection process for NAP apprentices does not favor the socially disadvantaged, but simply has a blanket prerequisite that participants should have completed JHS, a condition that tends to favor the more privileged.

Targeted allowances and stipends may improve access, but it may be difficult to create a transparent mechanism to identify those who should, and should not, qualify.

Diversified Sustainable Sources of TVET Financing

As noted above, identifying diversified and sustainable sources of systemic funding for TVET has proved to be problematic. Ghana's planners recognize that TVET is expensive (compared with general education) and that it therefore cannot be fully funded by the government (GoG 2008b). Indeed, as chapter 3 underlined, most TVET is delivered and financed privately, especially through the informal apprenticeship system. Although most TVET provision in Ghana is private, the public TVET system remains seriously underfunded, and expenditure trends do not indicate that TVET is an education priority (GoG 2008b, 2012a). It is clear to all stakeholders that a diverse funding portfolio is required, including both public and private sources. The Skills Development Fund mechanism is promising. But for it to be sustainable, international good practice indicates there needs to be agreement on an industry levy.

A divergence appears to exist between government (and political) rhetoric concerning the importance of TVET and actual financial support to the subsector. The government's political commitment to the TVET strategy (both the New Patriotic Party government 2001–08 and the National Democratic Congress government since 2009) has not so far translated into appropriate fiscal commitments for the future. TVET in Ghana competes with other high-priority sectors and social strategies.

Concluding Comments

This review of TVET financing in Ghana illustrates several of the market and nonmarket imperfections outlined in the conceptual framework elaborated earlier (chapter 1). An overriding issue is that at the level of the institution, public TVET funding in Ghana is based on enrollment numbers and historical allocations, with no official mechanism to offer financial incentives to better performing departments or staff. In addition, current policy undermines equity in several ways.

Although public TVET institutions are allowed to charge and retain student fees, many, especially those in rural or poorer urban areas (but not technical training institutes and NVTIs), have significant problems with student fee collection. As a result, although the government financing model assumes 100 percent on-time fee collection, the realities on the ground dictate that institutional heads are often left with a choice of excluding (most often) poorer students for nonfee payment, or else letting the institution run up large fee arrears, which results in declining quality. No public funds are available that can be borrowed by institutions to bridge periods of nonfee payment.

Public spending has not reacted to market inequalities that inhibit the access of marginalized groups to TVET. In fact, much public spending on TVET is not targeted at the poor and is captured by those who are less in need, thus widening inequalities. For example, the World Bank (2010b) estimates that only 19 percent of the public spending for MoE vocational education reaches the poor. The hardest public TVET provider for young people to enter (the TTIs) is the most subsidized provider with the lowest fees; TTI training fees are on average about one-tenth of those in the other public TVET providers.

For the formal public TVET sector, few government incentives exist, such as targeted reductions in training fees, scholarships, or conditional cash transfers, that might encourage parents to send their children for training, or that might encourage more equitable access. The majority of public TVET providers do not offer scholarships to poor youth; those that do, do so on a very small scale and ad hoc manner. Similarly, no government support is available for the formal private TVET sector, and where public funding has been used to support private informal apprenticeships (as with the NAP), it does so in a way that risks substituting for private financing.

Large inefficiencies remain in the systemic financing approaches used. Very significant resources are still being spent by the government on TVET activities that are not coordinated with COTVET and largely operate independently of the main TVET-delivering ministries, departments, and agencies. Despite the establishment in 2010 of a Skills Development Fund, meant to stimulate sectoral improvements, the government is still allocating large sums of money outside the SDF mechanism; for example, none of the funding for Local Enterprise and Skills Development Program (LESDEP) in 2011/12 ($50 million) went through the SDF.

Where public funding has been used to support short duration skills training in Ghana, as was the case of the Skills Training and Entrepreneurship Program (2003–05) or, more recently, the LESDEP, it is often done so in an inefficient way; for example, the targeting is inadequate, so the program benefits are captured by better-off segments of society, or the program is not well designed and functions in parallel to the existing TVET programs.

Notes

1. Private communication, May 2, 2012.
2. Private communication, SDF manager, May 3, 2012.
3. The Accra Agenda for Action, adopted on September 4, 2008, reflects the international commitment to support the reforms needed to accelerate the effective use of development assistance and will help to ensure the achievement of the Millennium Development Goals by 2015. The agenda is the result of an extensive process of consultation and negotiations among countries and development partners, focusing the aid effectiveness agenda on the main technical, institutional, and political challenges to the full implementation of the Paris principles. The Busan aid effectiveness meeting at the end of December 2011 helped to bring new actors into the "tent" (emerging donors, private sector, civil society, fragile states). The Busan Outcome Document reaffirmed the Paris principles but did not agree on a new system to measure progress.
4. Private communication, SDF manager, May 3, 2012.

5. Proceeds from internally generated funds are approximately 5 percent for short courses for industry, 10 percent for custom projects, and 5 percent for the hiring out of premises (figures from former and current ATTC principals, November 19 and April 15, 2008).
6. Since then, particularly in 2012, as a result of a public employment reform called the Single Spine Salary System, salaries in public institutions increased twofold.
7. Several projects, such as the World Bank–funded Vocational Skills and Informal Sector Support Project (World Bank 2001), have attempted to improve the informal apprenticeship system, but these have had little systemic or sustained impact (see appendix section "Informal Apprenticeship Training" for further discussion).
8. According to Breyer's urban survey, 65 percent of master craftspeople charged a graduation fee, while 97 percent charged a commitment fee (Breyer 2007).
9. Breyer's survey found that 75 percent of small or microenterprises solicited this type of contribution in kind (Breyer 2007).
10. Surveys found that 81 percent of apprentices were asked to bring their own set of tools (Breyer 2007; Palmer 2007a).
11. In Breyer's urban survey, 75 percent of master craftspeople paid their apprentices chop money. Palmer found that 52 percent of rural master craftspeople paid their apprentices chop money on average. However, 75 percent of male apprentices were paid this stipend (in the trade areas of carpentry, masonry, and mechanics), compared with only 20–25 percent of female apprentices (in dressmaking and hairdressing).
12. GSDI official, private communication, March 3, 2013.
13. In contrast, private training providers tend to have relatively shorter chains of accountability; parents pay school fees to the school, and teachers and principals aim to deliver a good service and be seen to deliver good outcomes (high proportions of students getting high marks, or going to higher education and training). If they don't, parents are quite free to take their money to another private school.

CHAPTER 6

Policy Recommendations

TVET Policy Development and Governance

A national technical and vocational skills development strategy is in preparation under the auspices of Council for TVET (COTVET). To best contribute to Ghana's development goals, the strategy should be responsive to the challenges stemming from social demand (equity, employment), be relevant to private sector and labor market demand, be informed by market and nonmarket failures, be in harmony with the national economic development priorities (diversification, shared sustainable growth), and be effective in terms of incentivizing the training providers to align with these expectations. The national skills strategy should aim to complement, and be complemented by, reforms that are under way in related sectors (such as private sector development and employment, the informal economy, information and communication technology [ICT], and agriculture).[1] Good practice indicates that skills training is more effective if explicitly linked to post-training support agencies (for example, governmental, nongovernmental organization [NGO] and private providers of credit, business advice, or job information).

Consideration should be given to changing the focus of the government's role. That role could be more effective if less directly involved in training provision and more involved in promoting coordination, and providing incentives, standards, accreditation, quality assurance, and information. Any government intervention should aim to be cognizant of current market offerings, and of the risks of creating undesirable market distortions. The government should seek to effectively address the market failures, such as inequality, while minimizing its role as a market participant. For example, if the government helps build up a functioning qualification system as the cornerstone of quality assurance, the quality assurance system should be independent of government control, because it would be difficult for the government to both provide and control technical and vocational education and training (TVET).

The national qualification system under construction would do well to focus on training and skills that are effective in improving the chances of youth to find employment, and in improving individual earnings, enterprise growth, and productivity. Furthermore, the qualification framework needs to be developed in sync with the competency-based training system that is being gradually introduced in Ghana. This system focuses less on the inputs, courses attained, and years passed and more on the skills and competencies acquired. Also, a key cornerstone of the national qualifications framework is the recognition of prior learning that effectively integrates apprenticeship and other informal and nonformal types of training into one qualification framework.

For COTVET to be effective it would need to be vested with real authority and not merely be a consultative agency; it must be allowed to make decisions and ultimately control—or have significant influence over—the allocation of TVET resources. As it stands, the bulk of all TVET resources are outside of COTVET's control and authority; for example, all the public ministries providing TVET control their own budgets, and the GoG also heavily finances TVET-related activities through programs such as Local Enterprise and Skills Development Program (LESDEP) (appendix B). It would be wise to learn the lessons of why National Coordinating Committee for Technical and Vocational Education and Training (NACVET) failed; part of the reason was because it did not have sufficient power. It is a very positive development that COTVET is now coordinating and managing external support to TVET from development partners; this could usefully be extended to support from NGOs, so that COTVET serves as the counterpart agency for all external assistance, ending a tradition of bilateral agreements between development partners and ministries, agencies, or departments. COTVET may opt to hand over operational responsibilities to a specific agency or department for the implementation of training.

In parallel with the strategic agenda, COTVET needs to continue to strengthen its own capacity to handle its coordination and monitoring functions and to develop policies to stimulate both demand and supply. A key capacity is COTVET's ability to coordinate across sectors, government agencies, and various types of providers, including by developing (1) standards for training services and a qualification framework, (2) monitoring and information systems, and (3) development partner and NGO support.

COTVET will only be as strong as its staff and as the staff of key stake-holding organizations that it interacts with; efforts are also needed, therefore, to strengthen the capacity of key TVET stakeholders, both government and nongovernmental, so that they can better contribute to TVET policy development within the COTVET framework. The Ministry of Employment and Labor Relations (MoELR) is particularly in need of capacity building in the area of TVET policy formulation and the provision of intermediary services. Capacity-building efforts are needed at all levels, from agency heads to regional offices, through institutional heads.

A Demand-Driven, Responsive TVET System

Ghana's TVET system will not get transformed into a demand-driven TVET system so long as the demand side of the economy is itself having problems. Incentives linked to stimulating demand are required. We know that the majority of those working in Ghana's labor market work in the informal economy, most often in small-scale, low-productivity agricultural and nonagricultural ventures. And we know that most new jobs are created here, while the formal labor market has a much lower absorptive capacity for labor. The informality of the labor market and the existence of a low-skills equilibrium across many sectors and/or enterprise sizes is persistent. But options exist that could be taken to help move away from this. More effort is needed to stimulate growth in the informal economy, as well as to stimulate demand for higher skill levels. In addition, increased focus should be placed on TVET for the informal economy, and a move away from the notion that *only* formal sector demand should be considered when we talk about TVET being "demand driven."

At the systemic level, a mechanism is required to determine formal and informal sector skills requirements on an ongoing basis. For this to be achieved, collaboration between ministries (especially Ministry of Education [MoE], MoELR, and Ministry of Trade and Industry [MoTI]) and the private sector needs to be strong; ideally, this would be promoted under the coordination of COTVET's Industrial Training Advisory Committee. In order to identify and forecast skills demand, COTVET might consider developing a scarce skills list such as South Africa's (RSA 2007); this list would reflect the skills that are most needed and on which policy makers need to focus acquisition and development efforts. COTVET might also look at the Labor Market Intelligence Reports produced by the Philippines Technical Education and Skills Development Authority. Other countries pursue this approach and publish separate reports on the current and future skills needs of different sectors (see Figgis and Standen 2005; Government of Australia 2005).

Decentralization plays a key role in making training decisions more relevant to the market. TVET development and expansion can be successful only in a decentralized context where districts and institutions take the lead. This will require capacity-building efforts at the institutional and district levels, as well as capacity building of informal trade associations. Formal public institutions could be run under strategic leadership, with a clear outcome focus and effective management, adopting the best aspects of private institute management. Public TVET institute managers would need to be given increased autonomy (to set fees, hire and dismiss staff, determine curricula content, and choose training materials and pedagogy).

The performance of both public and private institutions (and their managers) could be promoted through specific incentives. TVET institute boards could be reformed to include local private sector representatives. In this way the schools and centers could be more in touch with market demand and be better placed to seek private sector support (financial or in kind). Private sector representatives' participation could be encouraged through tax concessions. To adjust to this reorientation, public and private TVET institutes' managements require ongoing capacity building to better read local market demand for skills and organize resources accordingly. In this regard, it is positive that the TVET subcommittee report of the National Education Reform Implementation Committee (NERIC) proposes that institutional management and leadership be strengthened (GoG 2007d); however, such capacity building could usefully be extended to private providers also (World Bank 2008a).

The government and COTVET would do well do revisit the design of the National Apprenticeship Program, which appears to have been built more on good intentions and less on evidence-based experience of past programs. It contains several elements (for example, a one-year duration, government taking over fee payment, and the offering of stipends to apprentices) that have either not worked in the past, have been shown to reduce the quality of apprenticeship leavers, or have proven to be unsustainable (appendix B). Lessons from Ghana (and more widely from West Africa) suggest several approaches to improve informal apprenticeships, making them more responsive to changing demands, provide literacy and second-chance education programs for master craftspeople and apprentices, improve access to technology for master craftspeople, offer further technical and pedagogical training for master craftspeople, and improve training quality through certification and workplace monitoring.

Equity Considerations

Equity considerations should be given significantly more attention from the enterprise and institutional level to the strategic level. The inequitable access to education, to TVET, and to employment strongly suggests that it would be useful to increase targeting of the poor to help them to "catch up." The low levels of proficiency in literacy and numeracy at the basic education level have implications for the supply of young people entering TVET. Ghana cannot hope to develop a competitively skilled post–basic education workforce when the inputs into this skills system lack basic capacities.

The education reform goal to increase access requires a carefully designed scholarship scheme for TVET that does not exclude private financing. Such a scholarship scheme could promote access especially for the poor, and for women to enter trades that are not traditionally female. Experience in implementing scholarship schemes has shown that it can be very difficult to achieve a transparent selection process that does not become politicized or distorted by local power imbalances. But the potential benefits, both in terms of helping many individual needy youth and as a public good, underscore the need for greater efforts to make such a scholarship scheme operational.

A more rigorous social profile of Ghana's youth is required to enable the development and delivery of various types of training (and complementary) interventions. Improving access to and completion of a quality junior high school (JHS) education will help to make access to post-JHS TVET programs more equitable. Policies and initiatives related to reducing direct and opportunity costs of training will also help.

TVET Financing

Some of the many financing proposals that have been made over the last decade should be revisited and translated into action. Without such a step, new TVET policies cannot be implemented.

Alternative (sustainable) sources of revenue are needed for the Skills Development Fund (SDF) (beyond donor contributions); this might be through the establishment of a payroll tax for both public and private sector entities. It would be important that the levies not be diverted to the government treasury and used for general TVET budgetary expenditures, but be managed by the fund itself. Given that 80–90 percent of Ghana's economy is informal, a risk exists that the formal enterprise base (public and private) may not be sufficiently broad to make such a levy sustainable or viable. Planners will want to explore options for involving informal businesses in a levy-grant mechanism.

Beyond the mobilization of resources for Ghana's TVET system, just as important is the issue of developing ways to use these resources effectively and efficiently, and creating incentives to encourage and reward good performance. The issue of resource allocation is not sufficiently discussed: At the 2008 Education Sector Annual Review, the TVET thematic group made recommendations about potential funding sources for TVET, but failed to discuss the mechanisms to enable resources to be used more effectively (GoG 2008b).

Channeling the majority of TVET resources through the Skills Development Fund will make it easier for funding to be allocated in line with both general national socioeconomic priorities and specific priorities identified by COTVET. The allocation mechanism could encourage a demand-driven approach, linked to effective training delivery focusing on market skills requirements. For example, instead of transferring funds directly to training providers, allocations could be made to businesses, employers' organizations, or individuals who would then decide which training provider to use, thus promoting healthy competition among public and private providers. This competitive process would in turn enhance the quality and relevance of training provision in both the public and private sectors.

In addition, a fully capitalized SDF could be used to stimulate innovation and improve performance. Training institutes' financial allocations could be linked to their performance by developing and monitoring benchmarks and indicators. It would be more effective to replace old input-based funding mechanisms with new funding formulas based on inputs, outputs, and outcomes (Johanson and Adams 2004).

A new resource allocation mechanism for TVET would do well to focus above all on one issue: incentives. An effective incentive system will encourage change and responsiveness in Ghana's TVET system, to accomplish the following:

- Public and private institutes meet industry standards and requirements.
- Training staff and departments are rewarded for better performance and their ability to react to changing market demands.
- Private industry is encouraged to participate in the sector's reform (providing trainers and board members, supporting competency-based training development, agreeing to staff and student attachments, and so on).
- Equity objectives are achieved.
- The focus of training shifts from inputs to outcomes.
- Existing resources are used more effectively and efficiently.

Data, Monitoring and Evaluation, and Information Systems

More data are needed on other forms of informal skills acquisition and learning that are taking place in the informal economy in Ghana. This report acknowledges that a great deal of informal learning of skills is taking place, especially in the household, on the job, and via casual labor. It recognizes that small-scale farmers and street vendors constitute a very substantial part of the informal economy, and that learning in these trades does not take place via informal apprenticeship. Further research is needed on the different modes of learning practiced in the informal economy.

The capacity of Ghanaian institutions, governmental and nongovernmental, to conduct TVET research needs to be strengthened. In contrast to the evidence base generated in support of externally supported projects in Ghana, the capacity of national researchers to support policy development is limited.

It is recommended that more (disaggregated) wage data be collected via regular labor force surveys. The analysis of the demand for TVET in the report would have been greatly improved if recent and robust wage data were gathered through a labor force survey; this would reveal what the market is demanding in terms of skills.

The political economy of the TVET reform process is a critical factor but not well understood. We have noted on several occasions in this report the strong influence of politics on TVET policy making and how politicians are sometimes too quick to propose TVET as a solution to youth unemployment. However, a better understanding of the political economy of the reform process is required, and further research in this area would be useful.

The evidence base for TVET reform and policy learning from successful countries need to be enhanced. Policy makers in Ghana would likely benefit considerably from learning more about how other countries have reformed or built up their TVET systems, and how this experience might be relevant or adapted to the Ghanaian context. Equally, Ghana's own history of TVET reform efforts, and lessons learned, needs to be made more accessible and more clearly stated for national policy makers in other countries. It would be beneficial to have a follow-up study on this topic to help inform the Government of Ghana (GoG) TVET strategy.

Strengthening TVET information systems, including the monitoring and evaluation of TVET supply, demand, and financing, is important. In Ghana, key TVET stakeholders (including COTVET, public ministries, public and private training providers, employers, and potential labor market entrants) largely operate without access to useful and timely information to help them make the right decisions at the right time. The TVET information system envisaged in the COTVET 2012–16 Strategic Plan (COTVET 2012b) needs to go beyond the current approach of focusing on inputs.

Since the 2005/06 academic year, the MoE's Education Management Information System (EMIS) project has produced an annual report based on a survey of a nationwide sample of TVET providers: the "Report on Basic Statistics and Planning Parameters for Technical and Vocational Education in Ghana

2007/2008" (see GoG 2008c). Although this is a useful step forward, the reports face a series of shortcomings:

- They focus entirely on TVET inputs (the number of students, institutions, and teachers).
- Although they cover both public and private formal TVET institutes, they do not cover all of these providers; they are based on a sample.
- They do not cover efficiency (dropout, repetition, and survival rates), effectiveness, outputs (the share of trainees who pass examinations), or outcomes (the share of trainees entering wage or self-employment six months after graduating).
- Institutional financing and unit costs are not considered.[2]
- Only some indication of quality is provided (the share of trained teachers, the state of infrastructure).
- No information on enterprise-based training (both training in formal enterprises and informal apprenticeship training) is included.

There is no disaggregation of data for the different public providers (for example, technical training institutes [TTIs], National Vocational Training Institute [NVTI], and Integrated Community Centers for Employable Skill [ICCES]), and there are no data on secondary technical schools.

Notes

1. See also Palmer for a discussion of the types of enabling environments that need to be created through complementary reforms (Palmer 2009b).
2. As noted earlier, unit costs are only calculated for the MoE technical training institutes, and the calculations are not a true reflection of the actual unit costs.

APPENDIX A

Demand for Skills in Selected Economic Sectors

Information and Communication Technologies Sector

A key challenge is that sectors such as banking, which do not provide information and communication technologies (ICTs) as their core business, rapidly absorb the limited supply of ICT-trained personnel.[1]

The broader ICT sector in Ghana can be segmented into two categories: core and allied. Telecommunications, information technology (IT), and information technology–enabled services make up the small but growing "core" category. Banking, finance, insurance, retail, and other verticals are "allied" sectors (see figure A.1) that do not provide ICT but rely heavily on it in conducting their own business. The allied sector is sizeable and growing rapidly.

The core ICT sector in Ghana is small and highly fragmented with the three largest IT firms employing only 30–40 professionals each and earning revenue in the ballpark of $1–1.5 million per year. A total of 25–35 firms in the core sector employ approximately 2,000 IT professionals (World Bank 2010d). The core ICT sector is not a significant employment generator. Within the local core ICT sector, segments such as business process outsourcing, particularly back-end ICT outsourcing, and local content creation are poised to grow faster than other areas (OBG 2012, 161).

However, non-ICT sectors such as banking and the public sector are rapidly absorbing ICT-trained people in technical, techno-managerial, and support positions. IT is increasingly being integrated as business-critical inputs into high growth non-ICT sectors. In Ghana, the percentage of IT professionals in some banks is as high as 10 percent of total staff.

Assessments of demand for skills in the key economic sectors were completed by Anubha Verma and Petra Righetti (information and communication technology), Gerald Kojo Ahorbo and Øystein Førsvoll (oil and gas industry), Divine K. Ahadzie (construction industry), and Victor Antwi (livestock sector). The Council for Technical and Vocational Education and Training (COTVET) provided a sector report on demand for TVET in the hospitality and tourism sectors. Priyam Saraf provided an analysis of demand for skills in the cocoa industry. Priyam Saraf also summarized all the analyses of demand for the selected economic sectors.

Figure A.1 Mapping the ICT Sector

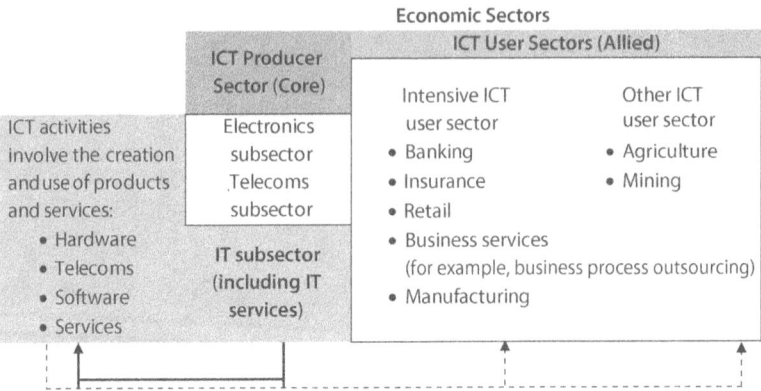

Source: Paterson 2006.
Note: ICT = information and communication technologies; IT = information technology.

This trend of shifting resources from core to allied sectors in ICT is likely to continue as sectors such as banking adopt IT for core services (e-banking), support (internal computer systems), and back office (transaction processing) functions. For instance, 88 percent of banks have adopted automated teller machines (ATMs), 82 percent personal computer banking, 88 percent electronic fund transfer, 76 percent phone banking, and 94 percent branch networking (OBG 2012, 161). As allied sectors become more technology dependent, demand for ICT-trained personnel in these industries is positioned to increase.

Even though the demand from allied sectors is rising, the supply of ICT skills faces bottlenecks of availability, cost, and quality.

Availability: Supply of ICT talent is limited, especially for the high-level skilled personnel (see table A.1). Fewer than 1,000 graduates are produced every year who can do high-level IT tasks (OBG 2012). When ICT personnel are hired

Table A.1 Demand-Supply Gap for ICT Skills in Ghana's Labor Market

ICT subcategory	Level of skill	Size (2009)	Estimated supply (2009)	Jobs profiles
IT jobs	High (BSc or BE in computers or IT)	2,000 (in core IT) 800 (in banks) 225 (in telecom) 3,025 (total)	970	Software programmers Database professionals Networking professionals Project managers
	Low (diplomas, certificates)	>10,000	4,500	Hardware installers IT support staff
Telecom jobs	High (core telecom degrees)	2,775	258	Telecom engineers Network engineers Project managers
	Low (diplomas, certificates)	15,000	100	Installation and maintenance staff
ITES jobs	Business process outsourcing	2,500	—	

Source: World Bank 2010d.
Note: BE = Bachelor of engineering; BSc = Bachelor of Science; ICT = information and communication technologies; IT = information technology; ITES = information technology–enabled services; — = not available.

Table A.2 Firm Cost for Training ICT Personnel in Ghana

ICT subsector	Enterprise-based training (and retraining) in Ghana, average cost (per new employee), $ per year
Information technology (software and IT services)	12,000
Business process outsourcing	4,000
Telecom	10,000–12,000

Source: World Bank 2010d.

in the core ICT sectors, they gain skills in creating IT products and services that enhance the competitiveness of the Ghanaian ICT industry. However, core sectors have to compete aggressively with banking, finance, and other allied verticals for personnel and are not faring well because of their inability to match the high salaries offered in banking and other sectors.

Cost: Limited supply is driving up labor costs. Compared to the Arab Republic of Egypt, India, and Mauritius, Ghana's labor costs in ICT are higher. An average entry-level BPO salary is $5,369 per year in Ghana, while it is $4,237 in Egypt, $3,911 in India, and $4,281 in Mauritius.

Quality: Even with the high cost, graduates are not found to be "industry ready." Firms have to invest significantly in in-service training, which further raises the cost of hiring ICT personnel (see table A.2). The problem with professional training centers is that they have low requirements for admittance and provide largely technical competencies. This leads to a deficit in skills related to critical thinking, communication, writing, and problem solving. Many students in these centers opt for "minimum certification," which provides them with the basic diploma to qualify for ICT jobs. There is a gap between "quality" and "industry-ready" graduates in ICT labor markets in Ghana.

Such supply-side bottlenecks are inhibiting business at domestic and global levels. To begin, the domestic ICT market is small at $40 million (2010 figure). The high cost of ICT personnel is creating a shortage situation. Ghanaian firms do not have strong regional and global linkages. Their exposure to global standards, certification, personnel training programs, and innovative practices is limited. Even though the regional market for IT in West Africa is lucrative,[2] Ghanaian firms have not tapped it sufficiently. The global addressable market for IT services is large at $200 billion (ibid.). Responses from ICT firms in Ghana suggest that high cost of labor and training is driving low capacities at firms, and this in turn has impeded the sector's growth at multiple levels.

Addressing supply-side issues is a priority for Ghana to exploit both domestic and international demand. Ghana has to develop a high-quality, low-cost, professional talent pool that can make the sector competitive along international standards.

To accomplish this, three action items are suggested:

1. Build an apex institution for ICT skills development based on a public-private partnership (PPP) approach, which would perform skills assessment and benchmarking, professional training and certification, and teacher training—all to raise quantity and quality of graduates.

2. Initiate an "Incubators and Pre-incubator" program to spur entrepreneurship and help build a critical mass of ICT-based enterprises that are innovative, skills driven, and linked to domestic and global markets.
3. Set up an ICT Observatory to act as an information and outreach hub for ICT sector issues (including skills issues), hosted possibly within the industry association (Ghana Association of Software and IT Services Companies).

Construction Sector

Demand for skills in general in the construction sector is only partially met, especially for artisans and tradespeople.[3]

The Ghanaian construction industry is picking up after experiencing the impact of the global financial crisis. Despite issues such as tightening liquidity, crowding out due to foreign firms, and high cost of inputs, the Ghanian construction industry contributes about 8 or 9 percent of overall gross domestic product (GDP) and is becoming more important as big-ticket projects are moving forward, and international and private sector involvement grows (OBG 2012, 164–68).

Employment in the Ghanian construction industry is expected to grow at about 10–12 percent annually (World Bank 2010e). However, provision of skilled labor in construction has not been able to keep up with industry-level growth because of supply-side constraints. Insufficient technical training infrastructure, especially for artisans and tradesmen, and low institutional capacity to cater to the growing need for sophistication in construction skills are acting as supply-side choke points.

At present, about 350,000 people are employed in the Ghanian construction industry, and 70–80 percent of these are in the informal sector (World Bank 2010e). Accounting for growth, employment in the sector is estimated to generate approximately $400–500 million in the next 10 years. This implies approximately 1,000,000 employment opportunities by 2020, of which approximately 250,000 would be skilled (artisans and tradesmen). Much of the Ghanian construction industry's growth comes from opportunities in Ghana's residential market, followed by nonresidential demand for skills, which is driven by the expansion of commercial and retail shopping, heavy engineering (especially road works), and multistory and high-rise buildings. This translates into strong demand for skills such as bricklaying, plastering, plumbing, roofing, steel-frame flooring, steep roofing, and architectural assistants at all levels.

However, the strong growth of 10–12 percent in construction-related employment is currently not being met by a sufficient quantity, or quality, of high-skilled labor. Estimates show a shortfall of approximately 100 graduates per year for each of the construction-related disciplines (figure A.2). Similarly, middle-level manpower is also in deficit of 350 persons per year for each discipline, a deficit that rises to 700 for building technology and civil engineering.

Much of this is attributed to the limited capacity of existing technical training institutes in terms of small class sizes, insufficient teaching and administrative personnel, and outdated curriculum. With the limited capacity of its construction departments, the Kwame Nkrumah University of Science and Technology,

Figure A.2 Supply of Skilled Labor in the Ghana Construction Industry, 2000–10

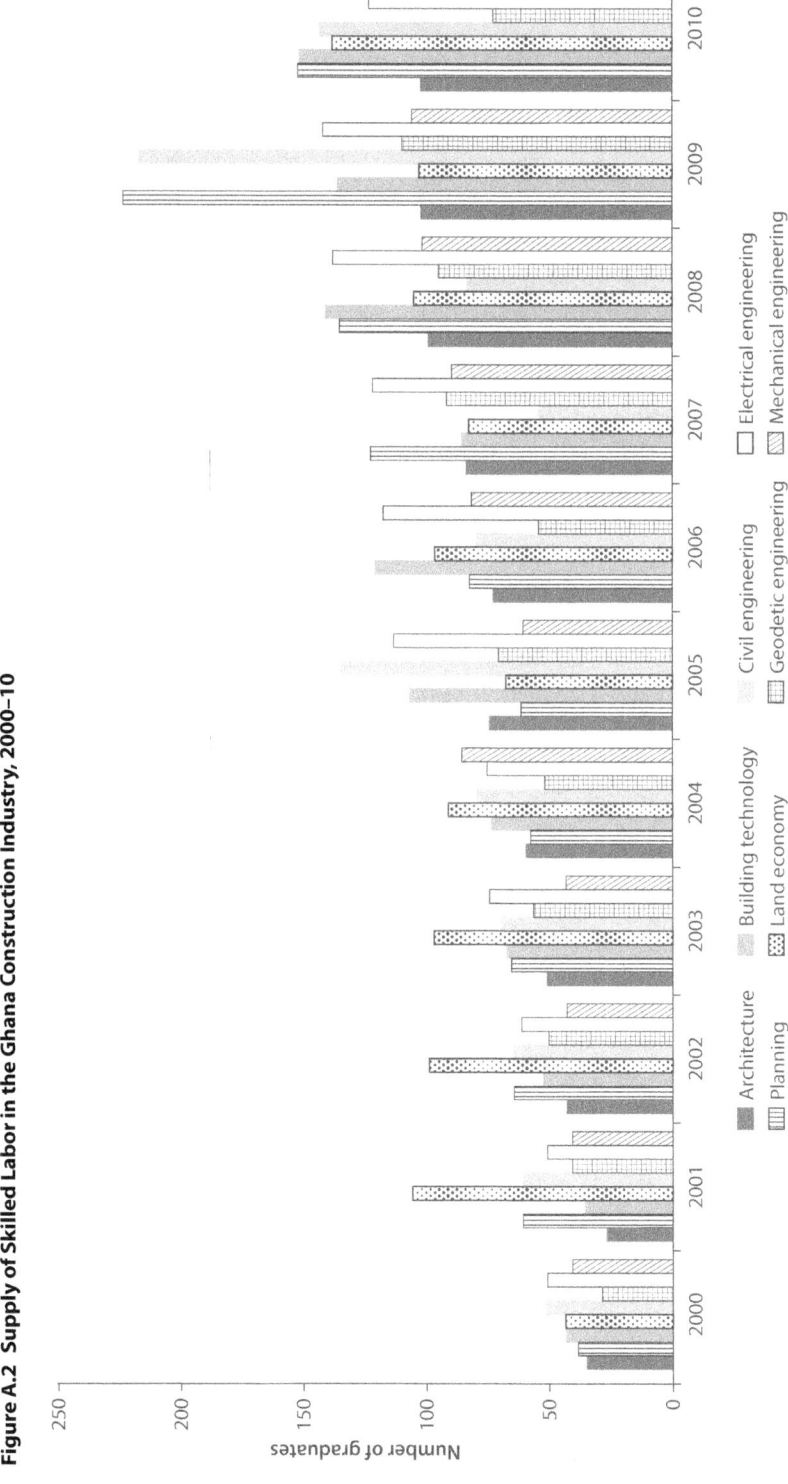

Source: Kwame Nkrumah University of Science and Technology 2010 in World Bank 2010e.

the only university currently offering comprehensive construction related courses, is unable to increase enrollment to meet the supply.

The supply shortage is particularly pronounced for the category of artisans and tradesmen. In 2010 the projection for well-trained and qualified artisans and tradesmen was short by approximately 60,000 (ibid.). The apprenticeship system is unable to substitute as a channel for good quality and sufficient skilled labor. Although part of the 60,000 deficit is being taken care of by microenterprises, these artisans and tradesmen demonstrate a lower level of productivity and problem-solving skills. The productivity issue in the Ghanian construction industry is of concern, with an average of 7.44–16.78 person days/m^2 for building a finished structure as compared with an average of 2.33 in Britain, 3.28 in Ireland, and 1.53 in the United States (ibid.).

Low productivity for the large segment of artisans and tradesmen who form the bedrock of the Ghanian construction industry is attributed to ineffective and inefficient training. In operational terms, this means that Ghanaian artisans and tradesmen are more likely to spend a large part of their working hours, often 40–50 percent, in nonproductive tasks or multiple iterations of the same activity.

Low institutional capacity in training potential artisans and tradesmen is even more debilitating because of the need for sophisticated skills in new construction projects. For instance, currently the 36 technical training institutions in Ghana offer training only in block laying, concrete work, carpentry, and joinery. There are no institutions training potential artisans in other needed skills or in the new frontier skills enumerated in the Ghanian construction industry, including steelwork, plastering, modern concrete technology, brickwork, roof technology, architectural sheet metal construction, electric and mechanical systems, fire systems technology and management, plant, machine and crane technology and handling, advanced welding technology, scaffolding technology, quality awareness and assurance, materials and waste management, and site and organizational management.

Oil and Gas Sector

For the oil and gas sector, diversifying the value chain participation is important. Ghana needs to look beyond the upstream part of the value chain and develop capacity in midstream and downstream segments.[4]

The Jubilee Hills oil field was discovered in Ghana in 2007 and began production in December 2010. According to calculations done by the national oil company, Ghana National Petroleum Corporation, Jubilee's reserves are expected to deliver approximately $800 million in revenue annually, assuming a price of $60 per barrel. This would imply a per capita yield of $75 per Ghanaian in 2017—the year of peak production estimates. Another estimate by the U.S. Congressional Research Service puts the annual revenues at $1 billion, but a per capita total at less than $50 (OBG 2012). Even with varying estimates, the annual income from oil revenues may translate into only 6 percent of government revenue. But the contribution from oil and gas helped Ghana's GDP growth rate more than double in 2011, to approximately 13 percent (ibid.). Oil accounted for about half of this increase, according to the International Monetary Fund.

To provide an effective skills set for the growing demands from the oil and gas industry, it is important to understand the oil and gas value chain. The oil industry has three levels: upstream, midstream, and downstream (figure A.3).

Ghana seems to have focused primarily on developing the upstream part of the value chain. Even with the advent of Jubilee Hills, estimates show that Ghanaians could expect only 10,000 direct jobs in upstream oil and gas in the next five years.[5] These jobs would require skills related to, for example:

- Exploration and associated services
- Drilling services
- Petroleum engineering
- Engineering, surveying design, and support services
- Construction, fabrication, and installation
- Production, operation, and maintenance
- Health, safety, and environment
- Security and personnel services

To convert the growth spurt from oil and gas into significantly higher employment, Ghana needs to diversify value chain participation to employ more youth and tap into opportunities that exist midstream and downstream.[6]

Figure A.3 Typical Petroleum/O&G Value Chain

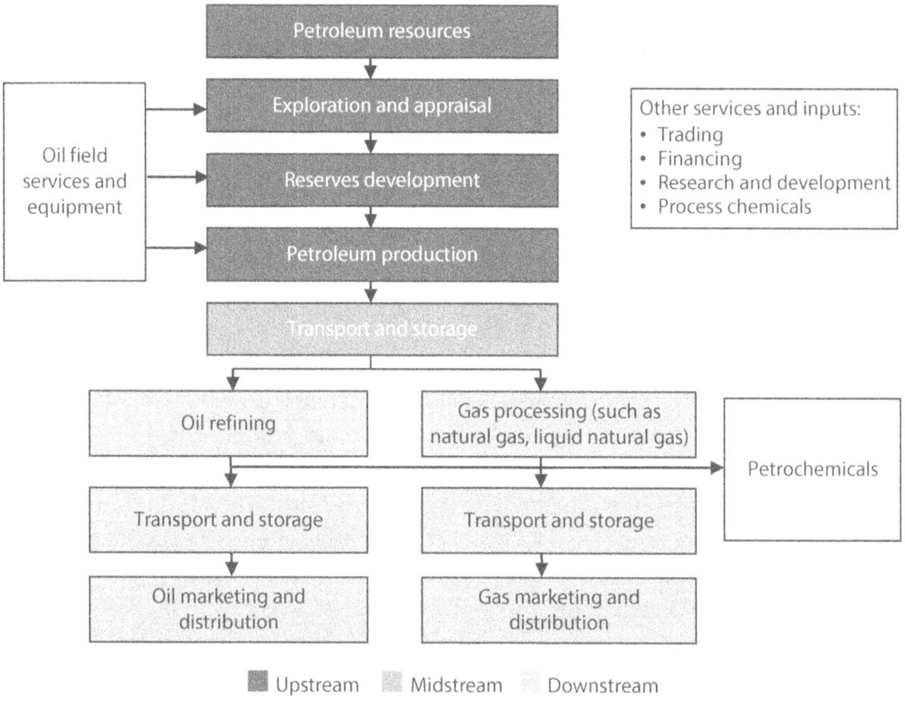

Source: World Bank 2009.

To tap into more downstream opportunities, policy reforms are needed, such as restructuring to deregulate the sector. To achieve local content across the value chain,[7] Ghana has already started forming partnerships with private sector entities. However, lack of domestic manufacturing, fabrication, and service capabilities and lack of adequate water, electricity, and infrastructure to support an expanded refining and manufacturing base are hindering the growth of the downstream sector in Ghanaian oil and gas. Reforms along these lines, including exposing young people to more midstream and downstream opportunities on the supply side, are critical next steps to increase investments, jobs, and skills in this sector.

Livestock Sector

The government should focus on skills training in small ruminants and poultry, rather than in pigs and cattle.[8]

The livestock industry is part of the agricultural sector, which is the largest sector of the Ghanaian economy (ca. 33.6 percent of GDP; ISSER 2009, cited in World Bank 2010g). Agriculture consists of four main subsectors—crops and livestock, cocoa, forestry and logging, and fisheries. The performance of these subsectors played a key role in Ghana's relatively high (over the last decade) GDP growth (7.3 percent in 2008). About 60 percent of the economically active population is engaged directly or indirectly in agricultural activities. The sector has a crucial role in poverty reduction and the growth agenda of the government since the majority of the poor are engaged in agriculture, particularly in food crops and livestock.

However, agriculture is one of the slowest growth sectors. The overall GDP growth of the Ghanaian economy in 2008 was 7.3 percent, but the agricultural sector grew at a far lower rate during this time. Within the slow-growing agricultural sector, the crops and livestock subsector experienced the highest growth rate of 5.8 percent in 2008 (compared with growth in the other main subsectors of 5 percent in cocoa, 3.5 percent in forestry and logging, and 3 percent in fisheries). Crops contributed 59 percent while the livestock industry contributed 6.4 percent of total agricultural GDP. The livestock industry is a very important sector for both growth and employment in Ghana.

Part of the growth in livestock comes from a rising domestic demand for meat (table A.3). Poultry, cattle, pigs, goats and sheep, contributed 32, 19, 17, 17, and 15 percent, respectively, of the total amount of meat produced in 2008.

From a skills development perspective, the government of Ghana should prioritize developing skills and technology in small ruminants (goats and sheep) and poultry, rather than in pigs and cattle, because it is cheaper and easier to produce small ruminants and poultry than pigs and cattle. Moreover, they have a ready market and are easier to dispose of. Even though it seems as if the domestic demand for pigs is very high at 15 percent, it masks a low base effect. The cost of feeding pigs is also relatively higher than that for small ruminants.

Table A.3 Domestic Meat Production, 2004–08

metric tons

	2004	2005	2006	2007	2008	CAGR (%)
Cattle	18,686	18,874	19,140	19,346	19,470	1.03
Sheep	14,004	14,450	14,913	15,390	15,620	2.77
Goats	15,308	15,300	15,588	16,364	16,790	2.34
Pigs	9,979	9,744	16,027	16,498	17,472	15.03
Poultry	22,982	22,709	27,224	29,630	31,853	8.50
Total	**80,959**	**76,582**	**92,893**	**97,229**	**101,205**	**5.74**

Source: Veterinary Services Directorate, Ministry of Food & Agriculture, Accra.
Note: CAGR = compound annual growth rate.

Here is a summary for each subsector within livestock:

- *Small ruminants:* Demand for small ruminants has been increasing over the years, especially in the southern parts of Ghana. The patronage is high with restaurants, and in general during festive occasions. Sheep has significant value for social and religious programs. Goats are in high demand by restaurants, especially in the southern parts of Ghana. Rearing of small ruminants is not that difficult and would not need a lot of space. Their feed could easily be accessed from the locality. Support should be given to people to invest in goat production in the south and sheep production in the north.
- *Poultry:* The poultry industry generates substantial employment and income along its value chain in both the urban and periurban areas. It is the largest source of animal protein produced in the country as well as imported. The egg market is very large, making the poultry industry a very prominent one for investment in skills and technology to support the growth and development of the Ghanaian economy.
- *Pigs:* The pig industry is ranked medium for consideration in skills and technology investment. Its marketing faces some religious and health challenges. Knowledge of good feeding and husbandry practices seems to be lacking. The pig industry, however, has potential to grow and would not require high initial investment. It requires some level of attention in preventing diseases and maintaining the pigs. The cost of feed is relatively high.
- *Cattle:* Cattle are usually owned by households as a form of social security. It takes an average of 36 months to raise cattle from birth to maturity. However, milk production (dairy cattle) and processing has high potential to generate employment and income, especially for youth. Investment in skills and technology for dairy cattle is worth considering for employment and income generation.

Besides direct skills development, support for this sector is urgently needed by providing enabling services such as veterinary services. Ghana is currently facing a severe shortage of veterinarians needed to adequately monitor, prevent, and control infectious diseases of public health and economic importance. Most districts have no public or private sector veterinarians to treat their animals, a situation that threatens the animal industry. Ghana currently requires 800 veterinarians as against the 110 who are in active service.

Areas in which to focus skills development for livestock in Ghana include training to produce small ruminants using less land, thus resulting in more intensive production; training in feed preparation for small ruminants; training in disease control and management and prevention; training in breeding; training in value addition and processing to facilitate preservation and income generation activities along the supply chain; fattening of calves for sale (this would also support downstream investment in processing for the local market); enabling services such as veterinary services (nurses and community animal health workers); and management training for small-to-medium enterprises (SMEs) and microenterprises.

Tourism and Hospitality Sector

Outdated ICT curricula and inadequate soft-skills training limit the productivity of personnel in the rapidly growing Ghanaian tourism and hospitality sector.[9]

The receipts from the tourism and hospitality sector more than doubled between 2005 and 2011, from about $840 million in 2005 to $2.2 billion, contributing an estimated 6.2 percent of GDP (OBG 2011, 2012). Tourist arrivals have grown from about 430,000 in 2005 to approximately 1.1 million in 2011 (ibid.). Tourism and hospitality is currently also the fourth largest foreign exchange earner for Ghana after gold, cocoa, and foreign remittances (Mensah 2011). As the industry has grown, employment of personnel in this sector has also increased. Currently tourism and hospitality accounts for 5.9 percent of total employment in Ghana (ibid.). In 2005, 172,823 people were employed, and by 2010, employment grew by 70 percent to 291,202 (World Bank 2010h).

Ghana's comparative advantage in tourism and hospitality lies in its culture of political stability in the region, passenger airline links with more than 20 capitals in Africa, Europe, the United States, and the Middle East, and a reputation for being friendly and hospitable. In 2008 the United States accounted for 86,000 arrivals, followed by the Ghanaian diaspora at approximately 80,000, with Nigeria and the United Kingdom representing 79,000 and 58,000 passengers, respectively. The real contribution of the business traveler segment is important for Ghana and is approximately 50 percent. This estimate includes unrecorded numbers of Ghanaian residents traveling to and from Accra, as well as business travelers from neighboring African countries (OBG 2011). Largely driven by this segment, the hotels and restaurants sector in Ghana grew by 11.3 percent in 2010 (ibid.), as reported by Renaissance Capital, a Russia-based investment broker. In addition to the business segment, ecotourism is another promising subsector according to the Ghana Tourist Board.

Although these factors spur the demand for tourism and hospitality in Ghana, macrolevel issues are limiting growth: for example, the lack of infrastructure, few world-class hotels, and inadequate health and safety-related services for tourists.

However, even with these challenges, tourism and hospitality remains one of the fastest growing industries in Ghana.

Despite the impressive growth in the sector, skills development in this space is challenged by microlevel limitations in both technical and nontechnical areas. Among these, outdated ICT curriculum and inadequate soft-skills training are two major issues.

The tourism and hospitality industry in Africa, including Ghana, is fragmented, with primarily small and medium enterprises and a few large hotels and tour operators (Dieke 2003). Given the challenges of reaching out to customers or distribution networks, the Ghanaian tourism industry is witnessing a tremendous rise in the adoption of ICT applications and e-business tools that can maximize efficiency, access, and distribution in a diffused and fragmented sector (ibid.). Targeted enterprises include tour operators, travel agents, tourist guide services, airlines, transportation bureaus, restaurants and cafés, hotels and guesthouses, museums, historical sites, and building operators, sports and recreational sport services, nature reserve services, tourism education and training institutions, local tourist offices, and craft industries (European Commission 2005).

A main problem is a lack of graduate students with effective and readily applicable ICT skills and practical work experience and field trips (see figure A.4). Despite the growing use of ICT technologies in the hospitality sector, vocational training institutes have not caught up and updated their curricula.

Several factors hinder the "applicability" of tourism and hospitality skills taught in Ghanaian polytechnics: for example, the lack of practical field experience, teaching staff largely trained abroad and lacking knowledge of ICT usage in the local industry, and training materials derived from European and North American experiences (Appaw-Agbola et al. 2011).

According to Akyeampong and Asiedu (2008), 37 percent of the managers not using computers in their hotels blamed it on their inadequate ICT knowledge, experience, and training. Hotel employees' ICT illiteracy implies that

Figure A.4 COTVET Survey Conducted among Students from Two Polytechnics (Accra and Cape Coast) to Assess Students' Opinions on Their Study Program

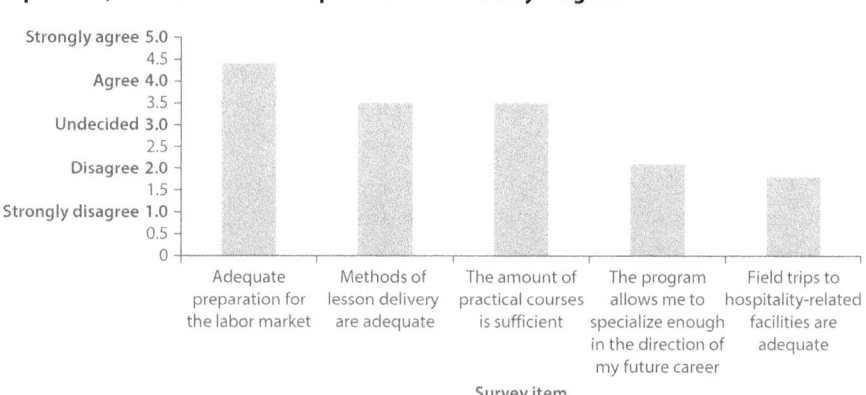

Source: World Bank 2010h, 17.

they are unable to take advantage of the many opportunities for efficiency and improvement.

In another survey conducted by COTVET, small- and medium-enterprise employers in tourism and hospitality frequently mention that soft skills are crucial in the industry (World Bank 2010h). Essential soft skills were found to be the ability to handle pressure and to lead people, a patient and calm nature, a proactive and positive attitude, good listening skills, being good in handling difficult guests, and being solution oriented (ibid.). A well-trained and skilled tourism and hospitality employee is expected to possess these qualities.

However, although the need for soft skills is well understood, technical and vocational training institutes find that these are much more difficult to impart to students than the more technical skills. Many of these are considered to be personality traits, and it is challenging to train someone in these in a span of six months to a year. Tourism and hospitality in Ghana is a sector in which unskilled workers can easily find employment. But easy availability of unskilled labor without readily applicable ICT skills and adequate soft skills hampers the success of the hiring firm. Davidson (1993) explains that "managers and owners of tourist facilities, as well as governments all over the world, realize that the people employed in tourism play a major part in determining the success or failure of the industry." The variation in soft skills among the staffs of hotels in Ghana is significant and can be addressed by improving the quality of in-house training.

It is clear that reform of the training curriculum regarding ICT skills is a priority for enhancing the employability and productivity of personnel in the tourism and hospitality sector. This will require rethinking and reprioritization of existing materials and activities because the time frame for the courses is fixed. It will also demand more interaction between polytechnics and the industry to understand which ICT skills are critical for students and employees to learn.

Notes

1. See World Bank (2010d) for more details.
2. For example, the market for enterprise resource software is worth $700 million a year in Nigeria alone.
3. See World Bank (2010e) for more details.
4. See World Bank (2010f) for more details.
5. http://www.ghananewsagency.org/details/Education/Panelists-advocates-restructuring-of-Ghana-s-educational-system/?ci=9&ai=37830.
6. See http://www.duke.edu/web/soc142/team9/GVC.html.
7. The government of Ghana is committed to deploying a local content and local participation policy in the oil and gas sector, with local participation in all aspects of the oil and gas value chain of at least 90 percent by 2020. With crude from the Jubilee Hills field breaking the surface and ongoing exploration, Ghana is positioning itself to strengthen its existing industry infrastructure and become an energy exporter.
8. See World Bank (2010g) for more details.
9. See World Bank (2010h) for more details.

APPENDIX B

TVET Provision in Ghana

Informal apprenticeship is the largest provider of vocational skills in Ghana, with more than 440,000 Ghanaian youth 15–24 years of age (53 percent female) participating (GLSS 2005/06, the latest year for which household survey was carried out; also in Nsowah-Nuamah et al. 2010).[1] Informal apprenticeships are responsible for 80 percent of all basic skills training, compared with 7 percent from public training institutions and 13 percent from for-profit and nonprofit providers.

Within the public sector, the Technical Training Institutes (TTIs) are the largest providers by enrollment, with some 29,000 trainees in 2011/12, compared with about 7,000 for the National Vocational Training Institute (NVTI) and about 3,500 for the Integrated Community Centers for Employable Skills (ICCES). However, ICCES, which are predominantly rural and typically considered to offer the lowest quality of training, has the largest number of training centers (57), whereas TTIs and NVTI each count 36 centers. The private providers are far more numerous; the total number of registered and nonregistered private VTIs may be around 445.

The Technical Training Institutes

Coverage and Location
Technical Training Institutes (TTIs), under the technical vocational education division of the Ghana Education Service (GES) under the Ministry of Education (MoE), are located in urban areas in all 10 regions of Ghana. In 2007/08, there were 26 institutes. But in the last few years, 10 technical-vocational institutes were taken over by GES and renamed TTIs, bringing the total number to 36 institutes in 2011/12. The majority of the new TTIs were faith-based private VTIs, such as the Don Bosco VTIs in Tema and Brong Ahafo. A further seven private VTIs were expected to be ceded to GES in 2012.

Access and Enrollment
Over the period 2001/02 to 2009/10, enrollment remained largely stagnant at around 20,000 students (table B.1). Technical training is still very much regarded as a second choice (after academic programs). In the words of a senior GES

official: "only a few consciously decide to come to technical institutes. After roaming the length and breadth of the country looking for entry to a grammar [SHS] school, finally they come to technical [TTI]."[2] The reasons for this are many, but the main two relate to the low social image of Technical and Vocational Education and Training (TVET) in Ghana and the expected lower incomes of TVET leavers. Quite simply the reward system does not motivate young people to go into the TTIs; individuals perceive that they can get greater remuneration by pursuing general upper secondary schooling (SHS). No data are available on dropouts or repeaters at the TTIs.

Enrollment data appear to show a large increase in enrollment for the year 2011/12 (table B.1), but this is an artificial peak that has occurred for two reasons:

1. The increase in the number of TTIs (as noted above): Approximately 25 percent of the increase in student enrollment between the years 2009/10 and 2011/12 was due to this factor (about 2,100 of the approximately 8,500 difference in enrollment between these years can be accounted for in this way).[3]
2. The retention of four-year SHS students: The cohorts of students starting in September 2007, 2008, and 2009 were the first—and only—cohorts to go through the four-year SHS program (which was introduced as part of the education reform in 2007). The cohort starting in September 2010 reverted back to the three-year SHS program. As a result, the enrollment figures in 2011/12 are unusually high because of the retention of four-year SHS students (enrollment for 2010/11 is also likely to be high, though the data are not available). Approximately 75 percent of the increase in student enrollment between the years 2009/10 and 2011/12 was due to this factor.[4] It is expected that in 2013/14, there will be a drop again as all the four-year SHS students exit the system.

While there has been some fluctuation over the 2001/02 to 2009/10 period, enrollment targets have not been met in recent years because of the lack of interest in technical vocational courses by lower secondary (JHS) graduates and their parent/guardians (GoG 2007b). The placement of students in technical institutes based on the strict enforcement of the required passing grade in four core subjects and two other electives is creating a downward trend in enrollment (GoG 2008a). The Computerized School Selection and Placement System (CSSPS), which is now used to place students into second cycle institutions including the TTIs, was also cited in the 2006 and 2007 Preliminary Education Sector Performance Reports as the reason for the enrollment stagnation: "Admissions into the TVET Institutes continue to suffer under the CSSPS. JSS graduates still do not consider Technical Education as a first option" (GoG 2007b: 72).

Between 2001/02 and 2007/08 there was a 28 percent increase in the number of females enrolled in TTIs. However, female enrollment growth between 2005/06 and 2007/08 actually declined; part of the reason for this is the continued absence of

Table B.1 Enrollment Data for TVET Institutions under the Ministry of Education, 2001/02 to 2011/12

Enrollment	2001/02	2002/03	2003/04	2004/05	2005/06	2006/07	2007/08	2008/09	2009/10	2011/12
Male	15,603	17,060	15,889	18,440	16,933	—	13,708	—	—	24,243
Female	2,331	2,717	2,783	2,984	3,370	—	2,988	—	—	4,975
Total	**17,934**	**19,777**	**18,672**	**21,424**	**20,303**	**18,432**	**16,696**	**17,280**	**20,694**	**29,218**

Sources: 2001/02 data from GoG 2006a, 89; 2002/03 to 2005/06 data from GoG 2007b, 91; 2006/07 and 2007/08 data from the TVE division of GES (April 2008 and November 2008); 2011/12 data from the TVE division of GES May 2012.
Note: TVET = Technical and Vocational Education and Training; — = not available.

Table B.2 Teaching and Nonteaching Staff, 2007/08 and 2011/12

Year	Staff	Male	Female	Total
2007/08	Teaching	1,033	198	**1,231**
	Nonteaching	638	203	**841**
	Total	**1,671**	**401**	**2,072**
2011/12	Teaching	1,660	359	**2,019**
	Nonteaching	773	345	**1,118**
	Total	**2,433**	**704**	**3,137**

Source: Private communication, TVE division of GES (November 2008 and May 2012).

facilities, such as changing rooms, wash rooms, and boarding facilities (GoG 2007b, 68). Moreover, males still outnumber females in the TTIs by more than 4 to 1.

Staffing

The total number of teaching staff in 2007/08 was 1,231 (16 percent female), while a further 841 nonteaching staff (24 percent female) swelled the ranks on the government payroll (table B.2). The large numbers of nonteaching staff are due to government regulations that result in inefficient allocation of resources; in addition to having their own cooks, matrons, drivers, cleaners, and accountants, many TTIs have their own in-house carpenters, plumbers, and electricians.

By 2011/12, the teaching and nonteaching staff numbers had increased to 2,019 (18 percent female) and 1,118 (31 percent female), respectively. This overall increase in staffing of some 50 percent over the period will largely be due to the increase in number of TTIs as well as the extra number of staff taken on for the four-year cohorts (see above).

The competency of new technical instructors is not regarded highly; a senior government official in the MoE commented that "about 90 percent of all new TTI teachers are young people who have just left school and have no skills."[5] The instructor to trainee ratio is approximately 1:30 for theory and 1:15 for practical classes. Moreover, principals of TTIs get frustrated because disciplining staff for poor performance or lateness is a bureaucratic process; all they can really do is to write an official letter to the district discipline committee. Principals have no autonomy to hire and fire and staff are usually appointed by the ministry and posted to institutes, sometimes without consultation with the relevant principals.

Training Environment

The Anamuah-Mensah Report noted that as of the end of 2002 "[O]nly a few Technical Institutes are in fairly good condition; the rest are in various stages of neglect. Their physical structures are in a terrible state of disrepair, their equipment and curricula are outdated, their teachers and instructors lack relevant work experience and pedagogical skills" (GoG 2002, 79).

In May 2012, a senior GES official commented that the "situation is quite bad ... [most TTIs have] deplorable workshops [that are] poor for skills delivery."[6]

Many of the new TTIs (private VTIs ceded to the Technical and Vocational Education Division of GES [TVED] in the last couple of years) are providing training at a lower level than the established TTIs. For this reason, the TVED is keen to be able to offer Certificate 1 examinations to those students who are not able to reach Certificate 2 level.

Rehabilitation is desperately needed in all TTIs. Equipment is usually very outdated and bears little resemblance to what is currently used in industry; for example, in the Accra Technical Training Center (ATTC) and TemaTech, until very recently, most of the equipment dated back to the mid-1960s (Soviet support to Nkrumah), and other equipment is over 20 years old.[7]

However, rehabilitation of existing TTIs has been ongoing for more than a decade. Between 1999 and 2003, 20 vocational-technical vocational-technical resource centers for technical institutes were completed; however, the vocational-technical resource centers service grant (to repair/maintain the machines) has since ended, leaving individual TTIs to cover the upkeep of equipment—which they cannot afford. In both 2006 and 2007, $1 million was allocated to purchase tools and equipment for the TTIs, and during 2008, 23 out of the 26 TTIs received a school bus. Nonetheless, there is still a massive amount of investment required in the TTIs. Training materials are inadequate in most TTIs because of the low level of budget allocation.

In 2011/2012 a Ghana-Austria TVET Project rehabilitated and equipped some existing workshops at Takoradi Technical Institute, St Paul Technical Institute, Kukurantumi, and Tema Technical Institute.

In 2012 the African Development Bank–funded Development of Skills for Industry Project provided support to 10 TTIs.

The 2006 *Education Sector Performance Report* noted that the curriculum (syllabi, textbooks) in the technical schools was obsolete; they had not seen any revision over the past 30 years (GoG 2006a). Later in 2006 a United Nations Educational, Scientific, and Cultural Organization (UNESCO)/Nigeria collaboration sponsored curriculum for TVET in Nigeria. It was reviewed and adapted to the Ghanaian context in preparation for the competency-based training (CBT) delivery under the new educational reform (GoG 2007b). Since September 2008, 25 TVET elective courses are being offered as part of the curriculum.

CBT was piloted in one TTI (Accra Technical Training Centre) over the period 2007–11 (as part of a Japan International Cooperation Agency TVET project). In 2012 TVED planned to expand CBT to additional TTIs (including the four TTIs supported by the Ghana-Austria TVET project, above) for selected areas (electronics, electrical installation, welding and fabrication, automotive mechanics, mechanical engineering craft, catering, and fashion and designing).

TTI students currently take the GES Certificate 2 examination at the end of three years of training.

Since 2008 TTI students have also been taught and examined in all five-core senior high school (SHS) subjects of English, math, social studies, integrated science, and computer studies, which allow them to progress to the polytechnic level after completion. About 35 percent of the week is now dedicated to these core subjects, which are examined by the National Board for Professional and Technician Examinations.

Under the New Education Reform, it was decided to increase the duration of training in TTIs from three to four years. This took effect with the cohort of students who started in September 2007 (who will graduate in 2011). However, the MoE decided to revert back to the three-year duration from September 2010 entry.

Labor Market Linkages

The TVED Directorate tries to involve industrial experts in curriculum development and review and as examiners. However, there is no systematic engagement to assess industry skill needs. Overall linkages between industry and the TTIs are weak. Poorly functioning staff and trainee industrial attachments, and a few TTIs offering courses for those in industry, are the extent of industry-TTI interaction.

The organization and placement of teachers on industrial attachment has been decentralized to the level of the institution, and both formal and informal industries in the regions are used. In 2006, 50 Technical Teachers were placed on attachment (GoG 2007b). In 2006/07 only nine staff went on attachment.[8] In 2012 the situation regarding industrial attachment has not improved.

Each year, in every TTI, one person from each department is meant to go on industrial attachments for three-to-six weeks during the summer vacation (July–September). However, one senior government official in GES commented in 2008 that staff placements are "not very successful."[9] Meanwhile, a different senior official in GES commented in 2012 that staff placements "have not been working."[10] Staff industrial placements suffer from two main problems:

1. There are inadequate placement opportunities. This problem is more acute in some areas, such as Greater Accra, compared to others.
2. Where opportunities exist, there is no financial motivation for staff to go on attachment, and teachers are expected to prefinance themselves before they are reimbursed. These people on attachment still receive their normal salary, but placements can be problematic if staff have to temporarily reside away from their homes. Although there is usually money from the TVED to pay for transport costs for staff on attachment, no resources cover night allowances for staff staying overnight while on attachment. As a result sometimes teachers refuse to go on industrial attachment—and there is no sanction available to the TVED. As attachments are organized during the long vacation and teachers often do private work during this time, they can be reluc-

tant to participate. No financial incentives are available to motivate staff to do industrial attachment. Furthermore, the promotion system does not take into account industrial experience acquired, further reducing teachers' motivation.

Trainee industrial attachments: Trainees at TTIs are meant to go on attachment with industry, which is organized in one of three ways:

- The individual TTI looks for vacancies in industry. However, although TTIs have an industrial liaison section, it is often "not effective due to lack of mobility" (that is, jobs).[11]
- Industry asks TTIs for a certain number of trainees.
- Trainees have to find their own attachments. This is the most common track.[12] Many of these go on attachment to micro and small enterprises (MSEs) and not the larger industries. Typically, the TTI provides trainees with a letter of introduction.

Formal industry usually accepts trainees only on condition that health insurance is provided by the TTI (or the trainee) and no pay is given to the trainee (though companies might pay for transport).

Three main factors make trainee industrial attachments difficult to organize:

1. Insurance: This remains a problem for those going on attachment to formal industry because trainees are usually only accepted on condition that they have insurance, and many trainees cannot afford this. For trainees going to informal MSEs, insurance is not an issue (MSEs do not request it).
2. There are inadequate placement opportunities: As with staff industrial attachments the catchment area of a particular TTI may provide better or worse opportunities for on-the-job training (OJT) placements.
3. Industry lacks any incentive to take on trainees for attachment. (Incentives should be introduced into the tax system imposed for enterprises.)

A few TTIs offer training programs for industry staff, both block release courses and short courses. The ATTC, for example, has a dual stream system; it trains people through a preemployment stream (like other TTIs) but also has a block-release system where it trains individuals direct from industry.[13] Furthermore, some TTIs offer short courses for those already in industry (box B.1).

Industry view of TTIs:[14] It would appear that some of the industries still take TTI students as trainees and recognize the reputation of some of the better TTIs such as the ATTC and the Kumasi Technical Institute, which have little trouble placing their trainees in industrial attachments. This said, 40 percent of ATTC trainees (preemployment stream) in a typical year do not manage to get attachment with industry.[15] In other TTIs this figure will invariably be higher. Moreover, even ATTC graduates have difficulty being absorbed into the job market after completion of training.

Box B.1 Two-Week Courses for Industry at the Accra Technical Training Centre

The Accra Technical Training Centre (ATTC) has been organizing short two-week courses for industry since 1994. This was set up with the support of the French government at that time, but with no industry investment. Courses include Hydraulics, Industrial Electricals, Pneumatics, Programmable Logic Controller, Refrigeration, Welding, and Meterology.

Courses appear to be quite popular with industry: At any one time between 5 and 18 people from industry are undertaking training. Programmable logic controller training is especially in demand.

The ATTC has developed a basic curriculum package for these courses, which it updates on a rolling basis. In addition, before any industry sends its trainees, the ATTC discusses the specific curriculum with the industry to see how it can be adapted to meet the specific needs of that specific industry.

Courses cost between Gh₵340–560 (approximately the same in U.S. dollars in 2008) and could cater for up to 15 people at any given time.

Takoradi Technical Institute, Kumasi Technical Institute, and St. Paul's Technical Institute also do similar short courses.

Source: Former and current ATTC principal, November 19, 2008, and April 15, 2008.

Formal industry in Ghana appears to be generally of the view that TTIs can provide people with theoretical technical skills but not workplace skills. For example, the human resources manager of a large textile company in Tema commented on TTI graduates: "They have heard about theory but know nothing about practicals. So when they come you have to train them in almost everything … and almost all industries have the same problem."[16] This view was also acknowledged by the vice-principal of one of the TTIs: "industries are not so happy with graduates they get—as they lack some practical experience."[17]

Industry frustration with the public TVET system and the perceived low quality of graduates coming out of the system led a number of industries to back the (now closed) Ghana Industrial Skills Development Centre at Tema (see the "The Ghana Industrial Skills Development Center" section), an institution that was set up separate from any government ministry and allied to the association of Ghana industries.

Institutional autonomy and availability of information: Individual TTIs are able to admit students, engage staff (though according to some principals staff are sometimes posted to TTIs), appoint head of departments, prepare timetables, and disburse budgeted funds. The TVED director needs to approve course expansion and introduction of new courses and is involved in developing curricula and organizing national training programs for staff.

Data on the supply side of the TTIs are quite well kept (number of institutes, staffing, enrollment, budget), but apart from gender disaggregation there are no other equity indictors. Few data are at hand on the quality of training being undertaken and none on the efficiency (including drop out and completion rates) of the system. Outcomes data are also nonexistent (for example, data on the proportion of graduates who found a job after training or those that are using the trade skills).

Funding/Financing

Training fees for TTIs are similar to those at SHS, at only about Gh₵20 ($13 in 2012) a year, which shows the degree of government subsidy at this level. In addition to this, most TTIs charge parent-teacher association fees, which can range from less than Gh₵10 to Gh₵200 a year ($6 to $130 in 2012).[18]

Income and resource mobilization: Between 2003 and 2011 Government of Ghana (GoG) expenditure for the public TTIs as a percentage of the GoG budget for education under the MoE has remained about 1 to 1.5 percent (GoG 2008a, 2011a, 2012a).

TTIs receive a GoG grant that covers personnel emolument of staff, administrative activities, service activities, and investment activities. Personnel emoluments are paid directly to staff. Training fees (standardized nationwide) are charged and retained by individual TTIs. Some TTIs also engage in income-generating activities (see below) and receive a limited amount of funding from nongovernmental organizations (NGOs; on an ad hoc basis). For example, at ATTC the GoG grant accounts for approximately 70 percent of the center's income (box B.2). For other TTIs—that do not engage in income-generating activities—the GoG grant may account for up to 90 percent of a center's income: 70 percent from GoG grants, 10 percent from ATTC training fees, and 20 percent from income-generating activities.[19]

Funds are transferred from the GES headquarters through the district directorates to the TTIs. The current financing mechanism means that schools with reduced enrollment get less funds. There is no official mechanism in place to offer financial incentives to better performing departments or staff. But some TTIs, like the ATTC, do offer ad hoc incentives to better performing staff.

Unit costs are routinely quoted in the MoE *Preliminary Education Sector Performance Reports*. For example, the recurrent unit cost for Technical Training Institutes was around Gh₵194 in 2006, increasing to about Gh₵775 in 2010 (table B.3).

However, these unit costs do not take any account of internally generated funds, such as training fees, parent-teacher association fees, or other

---

Box B.2 ATTC Income, Approximate Breakdown

Government of Ghana grant	70%
ATTC training fees	10%
Income-generating activities	20%
Total	**100%**

Source: Former and current ATTC principal, November 19, 2008, and April 15, 2008.
Note: Internally generated funds: short courses for industry (5 percent), custom projects (10 percent), and income from hiring out premises (5 percent). ATTC = Accra Technical Training Centre.

Table B.3 Unit Costs for Technical Training Institutes Compared with Junior High School and Senior High School, 2006–10

Ghana Cedis

	2006	2007	2008	2009	2010
Junior high school					
Per capita	165	204	275	277	336
Unit cost	156	184	257	260	320
Senior high school					
Per capita	412	525	388	704	603
Unit cost	250	205	281	636	397
Technical training institutes					
Per capita	196	172	379	885	1030
Unit cost	194	171	305	650	775

Sources: GoG 2011a, 2012a.[20]
Note: The per capita cost is the total expenditure on that level of education divided by public enrollment at that level. The unit cost is the recurrent expenditure divided by public enrollment at that level. 2011 data are not shown here because these have been distorted because of reasons outlined in GoG (2012a, 49–54).

income-generating activities. Moreover they take no account of the recurrent cost associated with the depreciation of equipment required for training (such equipment—which can be very expensive—should be included as a recurrent cost). Hence the unit costs quoted need to be understood in this context. Moreover, it should be noted that the unit costs for MoE TVET refer only to the technical training institutes. Unit costs for the technical SHS schools are assumed to be the same as general SHS schools. This also implies that there is underinvestment in secondary technical schools.

Short-Term Priorities

Over the coming few years the priority for the TVED should be on improving the quality and relevance of all its existing institutions. This was a specific recommendation of the Anamuah-Mensah Report, which stated that this should take place "as a matter of urgency" (GoG 2002, 79). Opening up new TTIs should be postponed until all existing TTIs are rehabilitated. Expansion of the TTI network was envisaged as a medium/long term priority in the Anamuah-Mensah Report (GoG 2002, 79, 90). As noted above, however, there have been quite a number of VTIs that have been absorbed by the GES to become TTIs. This will likely stretch resources even more thinly.

It should be a priority to review policies related to making closer links with industry, specifically staff and trainee industrial attachments and TTI board composition. For example, government might look into the feasibility of a scheme whereby trainees going on OJT can be at least partially insured as this would make finding placements easier. There needs to be effective industrial liaison officers in place who have the resources to move about and facilitate linkages with industry. GES recommendations for the composition of TTI boards should be reviewed; currently the recommendations are the same for TTIs as they are for general upper SHSs. Clearly, if TTIs are to have a closer link to industry, there should be more industry representation on TTI boards, and GES recommendations should reflect this.

National Vocational Training Institute

Background

The NVTI was set up in 1970 by an Act (351) of Parliament and was mandated to be responsible for the nationwide coordination of all aspects of vocational training including apprenticeship in both the formal and informal sectors (GoG 1970; NVTI 2002).[21] Today, however, it is also a major provider of classroom-based preemployment technical training.

NVTI was set up under the Ministry of Labor, Social Welfare and Cooperatives, now MoELR, assisted by the International Labor Organization, and it was planned that NVTI should do the following:

- Organize apprenticeship and in-plant training
- Train instructors
- Provide private vocational guidance and career development
- Develop training standards and trade testing
- Initiate continuing study of the country's manpower requirements
- Establish and maintain technical and cultural relations with international organizations that engage in activities related to vocational training.

Under Legislative Instrument (LI) No. 1154 (GoG 1978), the NVTI Department of Apprenticeship was meant to regulate and control all forms of apprenticeship training, formal and informal. The original intention was that the NVTI should provide theoretical top-up training to trainees already in industry. And, although NVTI's original mandate did not include direct preemployment vocational training, by the early 1990s the NVTI shifted much of its focus to this area. NVTI's main programs under its Department of Apprenticeship have been targeted at training formal apprentices at NVTI centers, what the NVTI calls "school-based apprenticeship." This is essentially institutional classroom theoretical instruction combined with on-the-job training through trainee industrial attachments, a method similar to that used by other TVET institutes, such as the Technical Training Institutes. This use of the term "apprenticeship" by the NVTI is therefore confusing.

Meanwhile the NVTI has signally failed to engage with informal apprenticeship training on any scale; according to the Ministry of Employment and Social Welfare (MoESW), the NVTI "has not lived up to this particular mandate" (GoG 2006d, 3).

Coverage and Location

NVTI centers number 37 in total and can be found in all 10 regions.

Access and Enrollment

The total enrollment in NVTI centers was 6,710 trainees in 2007, with females accounting for 26 percent. The average number of trainees per center is 181,

Table B.4 Trainee Enrollment, 2005–07

	2005			2006			2007		
	Number of men	Number of women	Total	Number of men	Number of women	Total	Number of men	Number of women	Total
Enrollment	5,212	2,085	7,297	4,943	1,717	6,660	4,932	1,778	6,710

Source: World Bank.

although this ranges from just 15 to 607 trainees. Between 2005 and 2007 total enrollment fell by just less than 10 percent from 7,297 to 6,710 (table B.4); the NVTI report notes that enrollment "has been plummeting each year" (2008, 21). The majority of trainees have completed lower secondary school, although they may have scored poorly on the Basic Education Certificate Examination. However, trainees are not necessarily those who only fail to gain access to the upper SHSs through poor results on the Basic Education Certificate Examination; many who cannot afford to pay for the cost of SHS education apply for an NVTI.

More recent data from NVTI are not available, but it is known that NVTI increased its training duration from three to four years under the recent reforms. As a result, we might expect the enrollment as of 2011/12 to be approximately 9,500 students.[22]

Staffing
The NVTI as a whole employs a massive 769 employees, split between the 37 training centers, nine coordinating regional offices, and the Head Office in Accra.

Training Environment
Under the new education reform, the training duration increased from three to four years.

Training is offered in examinable trade areas (for example, catering, dressmaking, hairdressing, block-laying and concrete work, and others) following the NVTI curriculum, leading to Certificates 1 and 2 and the old NVTI trade certificates (NVTI is still offering its own NVTI certification, but it is also allowing students to sit for the new Certificate 1 and 2 tests under the National TVET Qualifications Framework [NTVETQF]). In addition, English, math, entrepreneurial studies, and ICT are also examinable.

In 2011 the Ministry of Communications and the Ghana Investment Fund for Electronic Communications established Information and Communications Technology Centers at all NVTI Institutes across the country. Each of the centers was supplied with 20 computers and accessories as well as overhead projectors, scanners, air conditioners, and one-year internet service.

NVTI Links to Industry
Originally the NVTI had close links with industry; trainees came from industries themselves and were sponsored by their respective industrial establishments. As the focus has shifted more and more toward preemployment institution-based

"apprenticeship," the links with industry have declined (NVTI 2007). With the shift toward preemployment training, on-the-job placements had to be set up as the trainees themselves were not coming from industry. Although enrollment in NVTI preemployment training has increased, opportunities for industrial attachment remain few.

Trainee Industrial Attachments and the OJT Taskforce

The on-the-job training (OJT) program is an integral part of the NVTI program. Approximately 44 percent of the entire three years of school-based apprenticeship is spent on OJT (GoG 2006b). However, according to a report of a task force on incentives for OJT (GoG 2006b), the OJT aspects of the formal apprenticeship program are in crisis because of the very limited placement and support to carry through this aspect of the training. Notable among the findings are the following:

- Limited placement opportunities for trainees that cannot meet the increasing demand of the VTIs
- Limited placement avenues for industries to support the OJT program
- Inadequate stipend to sustain the trainees while on the job
- Inadequately trained workshop instructors to support the trainees on the OJT with sound pedagogical skills to build on what has been learned at the centers

Government has recognized the necessity to motivate employers to take on students for on job training (while in school and fresh from school), and in 2006 the Ministry of Finance and Economic Planning Task Force set up a task force on OJT incentives (GoG 2006b). The analysis of the current OJT environment identified five key developments that are crucial for implementing the OJT program:

- Design a structured, comprehensive, and effective OJT program that is well managed, monitored, and supported.
- Strengthen industry and institutional partnership for the development of appropriate OJT schemes and curriculum that is relevant to industry needs.
- Integrate both the formal and informal/micro small medium enterprise sectors into the apprenticeship system.
- Provide appropriate and adequate motivation, incentives, and grants for industry including the informal and micro small medium enterprise sector to participate in the program.
- Provide stipends to students and trainees as well as funding for monitoring and supervision (GoG 2006b).

Incentives for industry include various types of tax benefits and grants for formal sector employers. For micro, small, and medium enterprises, suggested incentives include tax relief (for example, a "tax holiday" for five to eight years), training for the owners, and tool kits.

A three-year pilot was proposed at a cost of more than Gh₵20 million (about $23 million in late 2008). This cost would mainly be for the provision of stipends to students and trainees as well as funds to pay the cost of supervision and monitoring. Twenty thousand NVTI students would be covered, as would 20,000 polytechnic and 16,000 university students. It is notable that no trainees from the technical training institutes, ICCES, Opportunities Industrialization Center (OIC), among others were included in the three-year pilot exercise. Rather, only those institutions with direct representation on the OJT taskforce (the NVTI, polytechnics, and universities) secured a place in the pilot.[23] No information is available on the outcome of this pilot.

Institutional Autonomy and Availability of Information

Institutional autonomy: No data on this.

Extent of data available/collected: In early 2009 the NVTI monitoring and evaluation department came out with a statistical report for 2001–07 (NVTI 2008) that provided much basic data on NVTI activities. However, although useful, the overall reporting focused on outputs—numbers trained, number of tests taken, and number of institutes—but said nothing about the efficiency of the system (for example, dropout and completion rates), about the quality of the system, or about the financing of the system (including estimated unit costs). The NVTI (2008) report did contain discussion of a tracer study of 500 former NVTI trainees that was conducted in 2005/06 with the assistance of a Japanese volunteer. It asked, among other things, about their employment status and found that 46 percent were self-employed, 22 percent wage-employed, and 22 percent unemployed (a further 10 percent did not respond). However, these results should be viewed with caution because the sampling procedure for this tracer study relied on the ability of center managers to locate past trainees rather than a random sample of past trainee lists being used to generate a list of those to be sampled. It is encouraging, nonetheless, that the NVTI has made this effort to generate some outcomes data.

Funding/Financing

Like for other publicly funded training institutions, the GoG covers staff salaries and provides a grant to the NVTI earmarked to cover the costs of administration, service, and investment activities.

Internally generated funds make up about 50 percent of the NVTI's total income. Fifty percent of internally generated funds comes from fees charged by centers (as well as a little production activities at the center level). The other 50 percent comes from trade testing fees and the training of master craftspeople.

Training fees for most courses range from Gh₵150 to Gh₵250 per year (approximately the same in dollars in 2008), though trades like catering can cost up to Gh₵350 per year (approximately the same in dollars in 2008). Meanwhile, the (nine) NVTIs in the three northern regions charged only Gh₵15 per year ($15 in 2008).

Fee Payment and End of Training Certification

Numerous NVTI institutes have problems with trainees paying fees. As a result, it is not uncommon for NVTIs to withholds the results, certificates, and testimonials of indebted students and release these only upon payment of arrears. Some students who through various means are able to collect their certificates abscond without paying their fees. Others abandon their certificates. In some NVTIs there are piles of uncollected certificates.

Other Activities of the NVTI

Apart from the 37 NVTI training centers discussed above, the NVTI headquarters conducts various other activities, noted below.

A major function of the NVTI is standards setting. NVTI centers, as well as other public VTIs (for example, Opportunities Industrialization Center—Ghana, ICCES, and Youth Leadership and Skills Training Centers), all draw their curriculum, standards, and certification from NVTI. This is in the process of changing (since 2012) with the introduction of new standards, certificates, and procedures by Council for TVET (COTVET).

In other words, NVTI does training and provides its own certification, which is a clear conflict of interest. There is also some resentment toward NVTI by the other public training providers, especially those who are also under the MoELR (as NVTI is), because their students do not get any kind of reduction in exam fees even though they are under the same ministry.

The NVTI conducts testing in a large number of trade areas, including building skills, mechanical skills, automotive skills, electrical skills, agricultural skills, dressmaking and tailoring skills, catering and lodging skills, and printing skills.

Over the period 2001–07 on average about 27,021 candidates participated in the full trade test and proficiency examination each year;[24] approximately 20,000 of these were taken by trainees in public and private VTIs (about 20 percent took proficiency tests and 80 percent full trade tests). The remaining 7,000 were (predominantly) proficiency tests taken by workshop-based informal apprentices. The number of informal apprentices currently taking the NVTI proficiency test is small compared with the total number of apprentices.

Over the period 2003–07, total participation in the trade and proficiency tests declined steadily from 29,342 to 26,191. NVTI head office has not yet ascertained the reason for this decline, but one suggestion made by them is that their examination fees may be too high.

Although total participation in the proficiency and trade test remained relatively constant between 2006 and 2007 (numbering 26,246 and 26,191, respectively), a number of trade areas saw significant increases or decreases in the take up of those wanting to be tested in that trade; this may partly reflect which trade areas are in more demand or which trade areas' certification is seen as increasingly useful (table B.5).

In addition to the regular trade and proficiency testing, the National Clerical Training Council of the NVTI drafts curricula and prepares syllabi for training activities in the clerical, secretarial, and related fields. It sets national standards

Table B.5 Number of Trade and Proficiency Tests Taken, 2006 and 2007

	2006	2007	Change from 2006 level
More popular trades to be tested in			
Motor vehicle mechanics	499	1,566	3.1× increase
Masonry	741	2,863	3.9× increase
Building draughtsmanship	144	1,174	8.2× increase
Plumbing	174	471	2.7× increase
General electrical	715	2,333	3.3× increase
Construction electrical	214	706	3.3× increase
Cookery	4,137	4,828	1.2× increase
Computer hardware service	39	338	8.7× increase
Dressmaking	812	2,569	3.2× increase
Less popular trades to be tested in			
Carpentry and joinery	1,337	1,133	0.15× decline
Hairdressing	201	110	0.45× decline

Source: Calcuations based on NVTI 2008.

and conducts secretarial grading examinations in six levels. It conducted an average of 6,000 examinations a year between 2002 and 2007.

Private VTIs are meant to follow some standards set by the NVTI before they are granted mandate to operate. Private VTIs have to apply to be issued with a registration certificate before they start operating. There are currently 335 private VTIs registered by the NVTI (NVTI 2008). There may be as much as 200 unregistered private VTIs. Again, it is expected that this accreditation function that NVTI currently has will be moved to COTVET.

Instructor and Master Craftspeople Training

The Instructor and Master-Craftsman Training Department conducts training courses for instructors from both public and private VTIs who have not acquired any skills in teaching methodology. However, over the period 2001–07, of the total 1,453 persons trained by this department, only 182 (13 percent) were VTI instructors; the bulk of those trained took courses related to driving. This means that between 2001 and 2007, an average of only 26 VTI instructors were trained annually; indeed the NVTI readily admits that training for VTI instructors "has not been a regular training program" (NVTI 2008, 23).

A more significant program organized by the NVTI is the upskilling of master craftspeople (MCs). In 2007 the NVTI organized upskilling for 4,000 MCs all over the country. The NVTI looks at the particular trade area and sees what type of training is required: Some MCs require just entrepreneurship training, others pedagogical training, and others technical training. NVTI advertises that it is going to be putting on a course and then MCs apply and the training takes place. MCs decide what courses to take. When more state-owned enterprises were operating, the NVTI used to oversee the welfare of apprentices. As the number of state-owned enterprises declined in the 1970s, the number of small and medium enterprises increased.

Over the coming few years the priority for the NVTI should be to improve the quality and relevance of all its existing institutions. This was a specific short-term recommendation of the Anamuah-Mensah Report (GoG 2002, 90). This priority is reaffirmed by the current NVTI director who wishes to upgrade, within five years, all the existing 37 NVTI centers to make them centers of excellence, by upgrading the tools, equipment, and staff levels of the institutes.[25] Interestingly, the 2012 budget notes that the NVTIs will be retooled. Opening new NVTI centers should be postponed until all existing NVTIs are rehabilitated. Expansion of the NVTI network was envisaged as a long-term priority in the Anamuah-Mensah Report (GoG 2002, 90). The NVTI director envisages that expansion might start in five years, resources permitting, of course.[26] Other priorities should be to establish closer links with industry, including through a review and reform of outdated syllabi and industrial attachments for trainees (GoG 2002, 82).

The fact that NVTI is not specifically mentioned in the New Education Reform (NER) White Paper has disturbed some in the NVTI Directorate. However, the NVTI board has been trying to reposition the role of the NVTI to engage with the new apprenticeship system as mentioned in the NER; it even proposed changing its name to "National Apprenticeship and Vocational Training Institute" (NAVTI) to better reflect what it sees as its new role: to be both a skill training provider and a coordinator of informal apprenticeship (see NVTI 2007). However, that possibility appears to have receded. As noted in the section, "Social Welfare Centers, Department of Social Welfare," there was some disagreement about which agency should be responsible for the new apprenticeship system under the NER, but COTVET has now (2012) emerged as the clear overall coordinator.

Social Welfare Centers, Department of Social Welfare

Since 1957 one of the activities of the Department of Social Welfare has been to provide vocational skills training to youth.[27]

Coverage and Location
The Social Welfare Centers operate in all 10 regions of Ghana, largely in more urban areas, through a network of 18 vocational training institutes, six of which are rehabilitation centers for people with disabilities.

Access and Enrollment
Enrollment in 2010/11 was approximately 2,350 (about 53 percent female). Clear data are not available on the breakdown of this figure by year. The focus is on disadvantaged youth, who are identified by district officers.

Staffing
The number of teaching staff was 177 in 2010, with 52 percent female. All paid staff are on government payroll, but payment is irregular. Staff are on the government universal salary scale, but they are not highly motivated.

Those doing workshop/practicals are supposed to have an Intermediate Certificate; those teaching theory in the classroom are meant to have an advanced or higher national diploma certificate.

In-service training "is an individual issue" because there is no organized staff training or funds to do so; staff members estimate it has been at least 15 years since there was any organized staff training. Instead, individual staff members have to make their own arrangements for training, such as attending courses.

Training Environment

Equipment in the VTIs is a "shambles," and some students buy their own tools and bring them for the training.

The Social Welfare VTIs follow the NVTI curriculum and so now deliver four-year training programs in line with the new education reform. Trainees now sit for Foundation 1 and 2, which are intended to replace the current NVTI trade tests, as well as Certificate 1 trade tests. In addition to these tests, the Social Welfare VTIs also do internal testing, which leads to a Department of Social Welfare Certificate. Practicals make up about 80 percent of the test time, theory about 20 percent.

Trade areas—which vary institute to institute—include catering, batik tie and dye, dressmaking, hairdressing, welding, plumbing, masonry, carpentry-joinery, shoemaking, rural crafts, electricals, auto mechanics, tailoring, and agriculture. Since about 2010, the Social Welfare VTIs have also been offering examinable core subjects, including English, math, entrepreneurship, and science.

Unlike ICCES, where the majority of infrastructure comes from, for example, community efforts, District Assemblies, and NGOs, for the Social Welfare centers the central government has been involved in, for example, the building of suitable structures. However, the increase in training duration from three to four years, which will result in an increase in student numbers, has not been met with plans to expand infrastructure and facilities.

Labor Market Linkages

There are no staff industrial placements opportunities, no short courses for industry, and no industry representatives on institutional boards.

Industrial attachment for trainees with some formal private companies is rare, but a few attachments have been organized, including with Japan Motors. It is up to the headmistress or headmaster to organize the industrial placements for the students; there are no industrial liaison officers. The cost of transporting the students to attachment is hard to meet.

In general, first-year students do not go on industrial attachment but have 100 percent of training in the training institutions. Year 2 and year 3 students spend a third of their year on industrial attachment.

In regard to posttraining support, District Officers are supposed to follow up with the trainees once they have completed. On graduation, trainees are given tool kits (funded by NGOs, such as the United Nations Children's Fund

[UNICEF]) or at least a few core tools. In 2006 graduates were given about $50 as start-up capital, but this has not happened since 2007.

Institutional Autonomy and Availability of Information

No data are available for institutional autonomy. Real problems exist with keeping clear, up-to-data on basic issues such as enrollment numbers and dates and number of teachers. They claim to have some data on the percentage of trainees according to their background (for example, street children, junior high school [JHS] graduates, school dropouts, people with disabilities, and illiterate people), but this was not readily available. No data are available on quality measures.

Funding/Financing

Social Welfare financing comes under three GoG core programs: Justice and Administration, Child Rights, and Community Care. Under each of these three areas, there is a little money for the training centers. The Social Welfare Centers are not a subvented organization and therefore do not receive government grants to cover institutional running and administration costs.

Training fees, which are kept by the institutions themselves, range from about Gh¢10–20 per year ($10–20 in 2008) in the rehabilitation centers, to about Gh¢50 per year ($50 in 2008) in the regular VTIs.

Production activities apparently represent quite an important source of income at the institutional level, but there are no data on this.

Funding from NGOs has been quite useful. For example, there has been some support from UNICEF and Rotary International, via the Department of Social Welfare headquarters (not individual centers). For example, UNICEF provides some tools and equipment, usually each year about 40–50 tool kits, divided among the 25 centers.

No data are available on either allocation mechanisms or unit costs.

The Integrated Community Centers for Employable Skills

Considerable ignorance and misinformation surround the Integrated Community Centers for Employable Skills (ICCES).[28] This lack of understanding about ICCES is despite the fact that ICCES has the largest number of training centers (57) compared with any single agency or department; NVTI has 36 centers (MoELR), and GES has 36 technical training institutes (TTIs) (MoE).[29]

The 2002 Anamuah-Mensah Report mentions ICCES, although it does not place it within the "vocational institute stream" as might be expected, given that it is a VTI. Rather, the report places ICCES in the "apprenticeship stream" and portrays it as an organization that can impart technology to the informal sector (GoG 2002, 82). Similarly ICCES is presented in the White Paper as an organization that trains apprentices (GoG 2004a, 13–14). Although the Anamuah-Mensah Report notes that ICCES "should be supported by Government to enable them intensify their activities" (GoG 2002, 82), and the 2004 White Paper (GoG 2004a, 13) reiterates the need to support TVET institutions like ICCES, there is a real danger that the misplacement of ICCES will result in resources for vocational institutes being diverted solely to NVTI. Indeed, *all* of the recommendations in the Anamuah-Mensah Report related to the "vocational institute stream" refer solely to NVTI (see GoG 2002, 81–82). In spite of mention in the Anamuah-Mensah Report and White Paper, the reality is that few people in government actually know what is going on with ICCES on the ground. The reason can be boiled down to three key factors:

1. Not much is written about ICCES. Although ICCES has been mentioned in numerous agency or policy-orientated documents, in most cases this is limited to a few lines (for example, Aryeetey et al. 2005; World Bank 2008a) or a short section (for example, Haan and Serrière 2002; UNESCO 2003) or is based on information that dates back to the early 1990s (for example, Boeh-Ocansey 1995). Unlike the Skills Training and Entrepreneurship Program (STEP), which was high on both the political and policy agendas (2003–05), ICCES receives little attention within the GoG. ICCES is not mentioned in either the GPRS I (GoG 2003a), the GPRS II (GoG 2005), or the NYEP (GoG 2006c). The 2008 budget statement, for example, simply stated that ICCES trains youth in "various vocational and handicraft skills mostly in rural communities" (GoG 2007c, 228). The 2012 budget statement made no mention of ICCES (GoG 2011c).
2. Unlike other agencies or departments ICCES has no board to articulate ICCES's needs, raise awareness of ICCES, advise the ICCES Directorate, and lobby for further support.
3. The capacity of the leadership within the ICCES Directorate has been very low.[30]

Coverage and Location
ICCES is an agency under the MoELR with a network of 57, predominantly rural, vocational training centers located in nine of the 10 regions (not in Upper East). ICCES is essentially designed as a provider of preemployment training for the informal economy, and the ICCES Directorate expects that students will become employed—mostly self-employed—upon completion.

Courses and Certification
ICCES trains youth in four-year[31] preemployment courses mainly in traditional trades such as carpentry, masonry, dressmaking, and hairdressing, leading to a NVTI trade certificate and the new Certificate 2. Trade teaching includes both practical and theoretical courses, supplemented by other subjects, principally math, English, agriculture, public education, and entrepreneurial skills.

Access and Enrollment
Total enrollment nationwide was *estimated* at 4,465 in May 2012, with approximately 30 percent female trainees.[32] Complete enrollment data for all centers do not seem to be available from the ICCES head office. The approximate number of students per ICCES center is 76.

According to available time data (2008–11) for four regions (Brong Ahafo, Ashanti, Central, and Eastern) covering 26 ICCES centers, total student enrollment has declined over this period by almost 40 percent. Most of this is because of a catastrophic decline in enrollment in Brong Ahafo Region from 1,100 students in 2008 to 394 in 2011, a decline of about 65 percent. However, all four regions where data are available show enrollment decline.

Although most trainees are JHS graduates, trainees must fulfill no specific entry requirement and ICCES is open to both literates and nonliterates. However, ICCES is definitely not a first choice for most trainees and certainly ranks after SHS, TTIs, and NVTI centers in terms of attractiveness. Most of those that do enter ICCES have very poor aggregate scores at the Basic Education Certificate Examination level, making it difficult to enter into other second-cycle institutions.

However, public perception of ICCES is low; much of this has to do with the perceived and actual low quality of training (see below).

Although disaggregation of national enrollment data is not possible as the ICCES Directorate's data collection ability is very weak (and interest in collecting data apparently very low), it is possible to take a closer look at access and enrollment issues in Ashanti Region. ICCES in Ashanti Region is widely regarded as being the most organized when compared to any other region; this has a great deal to do with the competent regional coordinator. For the last few years it has consistently had about 1,000 trainees in 13 different centers (in nine districts of Ashanti Region); enrollment there alone represents approximately 30 percent of nationwide enrollment in ICCES (table B.6).

Enrollment increased significantly in 2002, in part perhaps because GoG started to pay the salaries of instructors, which in turn would have led to higher attendance of instructors and therefore, perhaps, higher enrollment. Female enrollment as a percentage of total enrollment in ICCES has consistently been about 30 percent since 2001. This is lower than the national average, but much higher than female enrollment in TTIs.

Some individual centers remain very underused; the average number of students per center in February 2012 was 88, but this ranged from just 37 to 196

Table B.6 Enrollment in ICCES Ashanti, 2001–12

Year	Male	Female	Female (%)	Total
2001	267	116	30	**383**
2002	452	222	33	**674**
2003	466	260	36	**726**
2004	690	339	33	**1,029**
2005	596	316	35	**912**
2006 (Jan.)	677	269	28	**946**
2007 (Mar.)	—	—	—	**935**
2008 (Jan.)	647	296	31	**943**
2012 (Feb.)	727	331	31	**1,058**

Source: ICCES Regional Office, Ashanti.
Note: — = not available.

trainees. Part of the problem is lack of student hostels at the centers, which typically serve wide rural catchment areas. Another issue is the perceived low quality and relevance of ICCES training.

ICCES Ashanti has about 151 staff (February 2012) of which 53 percent (80) are full-time permanent instructors on the government payroll. In addition, 9 percent are full-time instructors with their salaries paid direct by their center, and 38 percent of staff are one-year national service volunteers.

No data are available on total teaching staff numbers, but one can extrapolate a national estimate based on the average number of staff per center for Ashanti Region. On average, at each center in the region there are seven permanent full-time GoG-paid instructors, one instructor paid by the center, and four national service volunteers. Based on this, we can estimate that nationwide there may be about 700 teaching staff in ICCES.

It needs to be recalled that many ICCES trainees do not make it to graduation (completing the full course duration). In the Ashanti Region dropout rates are in the 20 percent range on an annual basis; so for a first form intake of 100 students, about half of this number will not make it to graduation. In other words, the completion rate is about 50 percent (in some centers about 70 percent of ICCES trainees from poorer backgrounds drop out). In comparison, the SHS completion rate is 34 percent, and the JHS completion rate is 65 percent (national averages cited in GoG 2007b). Reasons for dropping out of ICCES include the rural nature of ICCES and difficulty in fee payment (despite the low fees), competing demands on trainees' time (many need to work to earn money), and lack of satisfaction with the quality of ICCES training.

Staffing and Training Environment

Up until early 2012, when a new single-spine salary system was introduced for all civil servants across the public sector (which essentially created one salary framework, with salaries pegged to formal qualifications and years of experience on the job), ICCES instructor salaries were not the same as salaries paid by the GES to instructors with identical qualifications. With the single-spine salary introduction, there has been a general increase in staff salaries for those ICCES instructors with formal qualifications.

However, ICCES staff still argues that salaries based only on formal qualifications are not helpful; recognizing prior informal learning and experience and actual competencies are also critical for TVET teaching. For example, some successful center managers with many years of experience are being paid only Gh₵80 a month ($50 in 2012), whereas new GES trained teachers (with no experience) are getting some Gh₵200 a month ($125 in 2012).

Until the introduction of the single salary spine, staff payments were often irregular, sometimes delayed by months. For years, instructors received no pay advice slip (hence staff had no idea of deductions on salary, for example, for income tax, Social Security and National Insurance Trust/National Health Insurance Scheme, or a salary increase). No incentives are available for staff (bonus or additional benefits). Most staff are also not aware of their rights and terms of employment. The rural nature of ICCES also makes it an undesirable work place for instructors, most of whom are from larger towns or cities, since there is a general absence of amenities, services, entertainment, infrastructure, and housing for ICCES instructors. Unsurprisingly there are problems getting and retaining qualified and experienced instructors.

Most ICCES instructors are not trained teachers; in Ashanti, for example, fewer than 5 percent of instructors are trained teachers. At the same time there is no ICCES-organized training of staff (either technical upgrading or teacher training).

Centers do not have sufficient resources to cater for their infrastructural needs, including maintaining existing infrastructure. Typical infrastructural needs include staff accommodation, workshops for the main trade areas, hostels (in some centers most trainees come from outside the community), and student canteens.

Most centers lack basic equipment including tools, books, and materials. Some centers ask trainees to bring a few basic tools with them. However, this policy discriminates against poorer trainees and does not solve the problem of how to obtain communally used equipment (for example, hoes, rakes, watering cans, wheelbarrows for agriculture, block-molding machines for building and construction), nor does it lead to the introduction of more advanced equipment to centers and trainees.

Despite these difficulties, NVTI results for the proficiency exam (a nonwritten test that measures competencies through practical and oral components) are surprisingly good (85–90 percent pass rates in Ashanti); given the difficulties instructors face in delivering quality training, these high pass rates might lead one to question what it actually means to pass these proficiency exams. For the full written trade tests—which are required to progress to further training—the results are not so positive (pass rates are between 41 and 48 percent in Ashanti).

Labor Market Linkages

ICCES training is only weakly in touch with the labor market:

- Staff industrial placements: none
- Trainee industrial placements: none
- Industry liaison officers: none
- Short courses for industry: none
- Industry reps on institutional boards: no explicit policy to this effect

The trade areas taught in ICCES are mostly in traditional areas (carpentry, masonry, dressmaking, hairdressing). There is no needs assessment undertaken to determine whether there might be sufficient employment opportunities in these trade areas in the local area, or whether such trades might already be at a saturation point.

ICCES leavers receive no posttraining support or assisted access to credit facilities. One of the main problems faced by ICCES graduates seeking to enter into self-employment is the difficulty of accessing funds to set up their business.

Institutional Autonomy and Availability of Information

The ICCES head office pays the salaries of most teaching staff in all ICCES centers and determines the number and type of staff (and their hiring, firing, and transfer). The ICCES regional offices require that centers produce quarterly reports on their progress. Apart from those instructors paid by government, centers have a reasonable degree of autonomy and are free to set training, parent-teacher association, and other fees, and free to hire additional staff (teaching and auxiliary) and undertake any income-generating projects they wish. Individual centers can also introduce new courses such as electronics and information technology (IT), so long as they pay the instructor's salary (which is then sometimes subsequently taken over by the head office).

Up-to-date data collection is a serious problem within ICCES. Existing data almost all relate to the supply side of the equation, focusing on numbers of institutes, numbers of trainees, types of trade courses, and numbers of staff. Only in Ashanti Region is up-to-date information regularly available, but here too the focus is on the supply side. There is some limited information available about dropout rates (though not collected by the ICCES head office). No data related to outcomes or financing are collected by the head office.

Funding/Financing

Since 2002 the government through the MoELR and the ICCES Directorate has been paying the salaries of about five instructors per center nationwide. Where centers have more than five instructors, responsibility for their payment still falls upon the center. Before 2002 all salaries had been paid by the centers themselves, which resulted in many centers collapsing, since they were unable to pay the salaries. For those that remained active the funding policy prior to 2002 had a disastrous impact on the quality of training that could be provided.

Apart from this limited support for salary payment, individual centers do not receive any funding from government to meet administration or running costs. Such costs must be met entirely from internally generated funds (including trainee fees and sale of products made by trainees), as well as limited community, District Assembly, private sector, and international support.[33]

ICCES training fees are, on average about Gh₵150 per year ($95 in 2012).

At present, almost all the internally generated funds of a given center go into recurrent costs, leaving virtually nothing for capital expenses. Recurrent costs include payment of instructors (where there are more than five), watchmen, and general operational costs. The situation is made worse because of the difficulty of collecting fees from trainees (despite ICCES fees being less than most, if not all, other vocational training institutes). Because of the rural nature of ICCES, many trainees come from farming families. Many students' families find it hard to pay regularly (partly because of their overall low incomes, partly because of their main income being dependent on harvest times). When a center manager "sacks" the trainees to collect their fees, because of the high percentage of less well-off trainees, once "sacked" many do not return. "Sacking" trainees for fees therefore presents a dilemma to a center. Communities also find it hard to pay for capital costs but can contribute to communal labor. The result is a general inability of centers to finance capital costs, and this has led to a general lack of tools, equipment, books, materials, and infrastructure in ICCES.

It appears that both the MoELR and the ICCES Directorate assume that District Assemblies, through the District Assembly Common Fund, will come in and provide the equipment and infrastructure needs. However, since there is no legal framework or directive to this effect, individual centers are left to negotiate directly with the District Assembly, explaining the need for support; rather than there being a mechanism in place that specifies that a set percentage of the District Assembly Common Fund should be used for TVET or ICCES directly. The result is that many DAs argue that they are too financially stretched and cannot support ICCES.

Since approximately 2009, the ICCES regional offices have not been receiving financial support from the ICCES head office for running costs.[34] They have been told that the individual ICCES centers in their region should contribute some of their internally generated funds to support regional office costs. However, there is no policy in place to this effect (for example, specifying the percentage of internally generated funds that centers are meant to allocate); moreover, even if there was a policy in place, centers cannot afford to finance the running costs of the regional office. As a result, regional coordinators find it very hard to visit and support centers. In Ashanti region, an NGO stepped in (in 2009) to finance running costs, but the amount the NGO is able to provide is still not sufficient to finance fully effective regional support functions. It is not known how other regions finance their running costs or the extent to which they are able to visit centers.

Commitment and Prioritization

Since the mid-1990s the ICCES Directorate has been keener to open up new centers than on consolidating and strengthening existing centers. The objective has been to open ICCES centers in all districts nationwide to offer vocational, agricultural, and entrepreneurial training.[35] In 2008 the number of districts in Ghana was increased to 168. This objective is *far* too ambitious at the present time. ICCES needs to improve to quality of all its existing centers (equipment, tools, books, staffing, staff training, and infrastructure) before opening up any new centers. Although there are currently nearly 60 active centers, approximately half of them are not running well, and many others have collapsed.

The 2004 "White Paper on the Report of the Education Reform Review Committee" committed the government to supporting ICCES. It is therefore hoped that government will take a serious look at ICCES; it should start by setting up a national ICCES board,[36] reforming the ICCES Directorate, and then building quality and capacity in existing centers.

Opportunities Industrialization Center—Ghana

The Opportunities Industrialization Center —Ghana (OICG), operating under the MoELR, has been providing center-based training in Ghana since 1970.[37]

Coverage and Location

There are only three centers nationwide, located in the regional capitals of the Greater Accra, Ashanti, and Western Regions (Accra, Kumasi, and Takoradi, respectively).

Access and Enrollment

The total enrollment in the three centers is 835 trainees (55 percent female) (table B.7). Enrollment significantly decreased over the last 10 years, dropping from more than 1,500 in 2002 to about 800 in 2012. OICG targets unskilled and unemployed disadvantaged youth, mainly JHS and SHS dropouts and graduates between 18 and 30 years old. Although there are no formal entry requirements except being able to read and write, most trainees are 17–25 years old and hold Basic Education Certificate Examination certificates. Since 2001 the annual dropout rate has been only between 5 and 10 percent.

Since the end of 2010, OICG has introduced a new fee payment policy under which students must pay 100 percent of that year's fee in advance; earlier students could pay when they wanted and many students were graduating with fee arrears. This is likely to have impacted on student enrollment since 2010, but does not explain the longer term decline in enrollment over the last 10 years.

Staffing

OICG employs a staff of 107 (33 percent female), but less than 50 percent of these are actually engaged in teaching (about 50); the remainder are nonteaching staff, with the head office employing about 21 staff alone. This is clearly an inefficient use of resources. The ratio of teaching staff to trainees is about 17:1. There is limited availability of in-service training or capacity building interventions for staff. In 2010 the teaching staff went on CBT (about one week's duration). Many of OICG staff are pursuing self-funded courses to increase their qualifications levels. OICG supports them in-kind, for example, by giving staff a few hours of paid leave per week to study, or by providing some of them with soft loans to finance their courses.

Table B.7 Enrollment and Dropout Figures, 2001–12

	Enrollment			Dropouts		
Year	Male	Female	Total	Male	Female	Total
2012	—	About 55%	835	—	—	—
2007	456	554	1,010	33	47	80
2006	497	490	987	48	47	95
2005	598	612	1,210	61	56	117
2004	696	592	1,288	35	26	61
2003	728	716	1,444	69	47	116
2002	702	840	1,542	58	62	120
2001	576	607	1,183	40	38	78

Sources: Private communications with OICG general manager and OICG 2011.
Note: — = not available.

Courses and Certification

The mainstay of OICG is preemployment center-based training; trainees take two-year courses that lead to Certificate 2 certificates.[38] Seventy-five percent of the time is devoted to practical training, while the rest of the contact hours are used for theoretical classes and counseling. Trade areas include, for example, masonry, carpentry, plumbing, electricals, auto mechanics, textiles, graphic art, catering, and office skills. OICG teaches math, english, and entrepreneurship skills as examinable subjects.

Training Environment

OICG's training equipment and tools are out of date and not in line with what industry is currently using (much of it dates to the early 1970s). The infrastructure facilities on the compound are also inadequate.

Labor Market Linkages

Initially there was an industrial advisory committee, a subcommittee of the OICG board. The industrial advisory committee was meant to provide a link to industry, but it has not been functioning since the mid-1990s. Since the membership of the board was purely voluntary, the OICG could not keep industry interested.

Trainees are required to do 16 weeks of industry attachment (after completion of 52 weeks of center-based training). Although this OJT is an integral part of the training it only happens when the trainees can organize it themselves. About two-thirds of all OICG trainees go on industry attachment, but many of these are still not allowed to get fully involved in industry attachments because they lack the required insurance coverage. Companies sometimes complain that trainees can slow down production. Some trainees want a stipend for doing OJT, but companies, rightly, are unwilling to provide this. OICG tries to follow up and seek the opinions of the supervisors of the trainees regarding their strengths and weakness in the world of work; these industry opinions and suggestions are incorporated into the training.

Some industries periodically offer attachments for OICG instructors. In 2007/08, 14 instructors had this opportunity. More generally, staff industrial placements are organized by staff directly. About 10 percent of teaching staff went on multiple-week placements in 2011; their respective center provides them with transport allowance and a small stipend.

Nonetheless, OICG has weak linkages to industry and, in the words of one senior OICG staff member, remains "a little bit distant" from companies.[39]

How can links with industry be improved?

- The industrial advisory committee needs to be revived and government could provide incentives to industry to serve on committees of VTIs (like OICG).
- OJT needs to take place.
- Industry could get more involved in the actual teaching of trainees.

Institutional Autonomy and Availability of Information

Individual OICG institutes appear to have limited autonomy from head office; they can make decisions on specific issues if that issue falls within the institutes agreed plans for that particular year or period. If the issue is outside the policy framework of the year, then it will be referred to the head office for consideration.

There appear to be no incentives to improve performance, only disincentives for performing poorly; poorly performing center mangers receive warnings from the head office and are sacked if performance does not improve.

OICG has limited autonomy from the MoELR with regard to increasing the number of staff (to be paid by government); it has been seeking approval to hire new staff for the last four years without success. OICG has been keen to introduce new trade areas requiring new staff; since the government has been slow at responding, OICG has hired new staff itself using internally generated funds, but it hopes that the government will take over their salaries at some point.

Data on the supply side of the OICG are quite well kept (number of institutes, staffing, enrollment, budget), but apart from gender disaggregation there are no other equity indictors. Few data are available as well on the quality of training being undertaken, although some data are kept on the efficiency (including dropout and completion rates) of the system. Outcomes data for the two-year program are nonexistent (for example, data on the proportion of graduates who found a job after training or those that are using the trade skills).

OICG formerly conducted tracer studies to see how relevant the skills that the trainees had acquired were. There used to be discussions not only with the graduates, but also with the graduates' current employer/superior. Among other things, OICG found that many of its training graduates did not succeed in setting up their own business after completing the training because they could not mobilize sufficient resources (Haan and Serrière 2002). However, these tracer studies proved too costly and have been discontinued.

The MoELR requires OICG to report on its "results," but the feedback form focuses on the number of people trained.

Funding/Financing

Like some other public training providers, OICG is a subvented organization, and therefore the MoELR pays staff salaries and OICG receives some funding for administration, service, and investment activities. However, funding is usually delayed, which seriously affects the execution of activities.

Main sources of funds for the training programs, apart from training fees from the trainees, include some donations from corporate bodies and foreign donors as well as revenues generated by the practical work in the various workshops of the center (Haan and Serrière 2002). Training fees are approximately Gh₵220 per year ($140 in 2012) and are retained by each center. OICG currently offers about 25 full scholarships at any one time.

Since 2001 the Kumasi branch of OICG has also been involved with an apprenticeship training project entitled "Skills Development and Self-employment for Non-literate and Semi-literate Youth." It is funded by the Church Development Service (Evangelischer Entwicklungsdienst), an organization of the Protestant churches in Germany (Baier-D'Orazio 2007). The overhead provided as part of this project has helped to sustain OICG administrative costs.

The Youth Leadership and Skills Training Institutes of the National Youth Authority

The National Youth Authority (NYA),[40] Youth Leadership, and Skills Training Institutes were set up to respond to a felt need: to provide vocational skills and leadership training opportunities for the "teeming unemployed, untrained, needy, and disadvantaged youth" (National Youth Authority 2009), most of whom have completed lower secondary school (JSS/JHS/middle school).[41] The first institute was set up in 1971.

Coverage and Location

All 10 regions have training institutions managed by the NYA (under the Ministry of Youth and Sports): two institutes in Ashanti Region and one each in the other nine regions. All are in rural areas.

Access and Enrollment

There are 11 institutes in the country, with a total enrollment (2011/12) of 1,948 youth (approximately one-third female); the average number of trainees per center is 177. The average dropout rate is about 15 percent per year. Over the period 2001/02 to 2011/12 total enrollment increased significantly from 592 to 1,948 trainees (table B.8), and the number of institutes increased from 6 to 11 over the same period. The increase in enrollment between 2001 and 2008 was due to new institutes opening up rather than expansion of the six institutes; in fact total enrollment in the six institutes from 2001/02 actually decreased over the 2001/02 to 2007/08 period from 592 to 546 trainees. The significant increase from 2008 to 2011/12 is also due to the increase in the duration of training from two to four years long (see below).

The Youth Leadership and Skills Training Institutes are interested in the development and empowerment of youth, especially in rural areas. Target groups are all types of youth, including JHS graduates, SHS dropouts, literate, and semiliterate and nonliterate street youth. Its mission statement notes that it is especially concerned with "needy and disadvantaged youth." According to the director, the

Table B.8 Enrollment Figures, 2001/02 to 2011/12

Year	2001/02	2002/03	2003/04	2004/05	2005/06	2006/07	2007/2008	2010/11	2011/12
Total	592	605	586	688	723	749	786	1,885	1,948
Female (%)	28	27	35	38	33	36	36	34	33

Sources: 2001–08 data computed from National Youth Authority 2009; 2010/11 and 2011/12 data from private communication with NYA (May 2, 2012; May 18, 2012; and May 24, 2012).

approximate breakdown of trainees is as follows: JHS graduates, 50 percent; school dropouts, 25 percent; and young people from tribal conflict areas, orphans, and street children, 25 percent.

The normal entry requirement to the regular vocational skills and leadership training is a JHS result up to aggregate 36. But the institutes take in those with less than this level of formal schooling for some programs. The majority of trainees are boarders, though there are a few day students (9 of the 11 institutes are boarding-only). In the boarding schools, all trainees are provided with three meals a day.

Staffing

In 2011/12 there were 103 teaching staff (about 39 percent female) out of 203 staff in total (table B.9). Staffing levels have remained at the same levels for at least the last five years.

The ratio of teaching staff to trainees is, on average, 1–8, but this varies from as low as 1–3 to 1–28 in different centers.

Prior to 2010, a staff development program was virtually nonexistent because there was no budget; it "exist[ed] only in name" (National Youth Authority 2009, 17). In 2010 the government provided support to 50 teachers to undertake a two-week training course in instructional delivery. But clearly the approach to in-service training is ad hoc.

There are no performance incentives offered to staff.

Courses and Certification

Courses taught (which vary according to the VTI) include general agriculture, masonry, carpentry, cookery, dressmaking, electrical installation, welding, plumbing, secretarial studies, and IT. The focus is on hands-on training, with an emphasis on practical lessons (60 percent) rather than theory (40 percent).

Until 2008/09, the Youth Leadership and Skills Training Institutes delivered two-year NVTI courses, with trainees taking either the NVTI

Table B.9 Number of Teaching and Nonteaching Staff, Various Years

Year	Staff	Female (%)	Total
2007/08	Teaching	39	104
	Nonteaching	—	96
	Total	—	200
2010/11	Teaching	—	105
	Nonteaching	—	109
	Total	—	214
2011/12	Teaching	—	103
	Nonteaching	—	100
	Total	—	203

Sources: Private communication with the director of the NYA on December 2, 2008, and from National Youth Authority 2009.
Note: — = not available.

proficiency or NVTI trade test. In 2009 in accordance with the TVET reforms, the training expanded to four years' duration, and the certification offered was intended to change to Foundation Certificate (end of year 2 test), Certificate 1 (end of year 3 test), and Certificate 2 (end of year 4 test). However, the NVTI examinations are still running in parallel with these new tests.

Furthermore, the previously nonexaminable subjects such as math, English, and entrepreneurship became examinable in the switch from a two- to four-year program.

Training Environment

Infrastructure and training facilities are "mostly lacking or obsolete and in very poor condition" (National Youth Authority 2009, 15). There is a general lack of books, tools, and equipment. In 2012 the NYA was expecting the government to provide some basic equipment for each of its training institutes.

There is no regular budgetary allocation for infrastructural development, improvement, and rehabilitation. However, between 2001 and 2008 most individual institutes were able to undertake some minor improvements and rehabilitation work with funding mainly from internally generated funds, although six institutes received some support from the Enhanced Heavily Indebted Poor Countries Initiative, and others got some support from PTAs and DAs.

The rapid increase in total student enrollment (without an increase in number of institutes) in recent years means that schools are being stressed and there is more and more pressure on the existing infrastructure.

A report from the National Youth Authority (2009, 15) concluded that "the operating conditions of the institutes have been such that it has survived only on the sacrifices and resourcefulness of the training staff and administration."

NVTI examination results show that in 2006/07 the average failure rate among all Youth Leadership and Skills Training Institutes trainees nationwide was 37 percent; female trainees were less likely to fail than male trainees (33 percent of all female and 38 percent of all male trainees failed).

Labor Market Linkages

Since its establishment, the NYA Youth Leadership Training Programs has run five core vocational programs (general agriculture, masonry, carpentry, dressmaking, and cookery with a few of its institutes later adding electrical installation, plumbing, welding, and secretarial studies and IT); these programs have never been reviewed to determine their relevance and impact on trainees in regard to content of training and job prospects. The NYA describes these training programs as "archaic" (2009, 5).

No staff industrial placements have been made. During the first two years of the four-year course, trainees spend 100 percent of time training at the institution. During the third year, trainees are meant to go on attachment, going to train on the job at an industry or in a small business, for one year. However, trainee industrial attachment programs and commitments vary from one institute to another because they are not mandatory; whereas some institutes consider the practice as an integral part of the training program that must be fulfilled to merit completion of training, others consider it peripheral because of problems and challenges in organizing the attachment. The main challenges faced in trainee industrial attachments include the following:

- Difficulty in placing trainees as all the institutes are located in rural areas and not many industries or enterprises are located in the vicinity
- Trainee monitoring and evaluation (although trainee attachment assessment reports are usually completed)
- Trainee accommodation or transport problems
- Trainee vulnerability to occupational hazards

There are no industry liaison officers. The NYA recognizes that this "is a major deficiency which must be addressed" (National Youth Authority 2009, 18). There are also neither short courses for industry nor posttraining support. There is no funding "to do anything about start-up funds and tools."[42] No funding is given for career guidance, but it is done on an ad hoc basis by some individual VTIs.

Institutional Autonomy and Availability of Information

Institutes appear to have some degree of autonomy in terms of seeking resources from PTAs and from DAs, but the extent of autonomy with regard to setting courses, hiring and firing staff, and disciplinary procedures is unknown.

The Youth Leadership and Skills Training Institutes do not appear to have been collecting data on a regular basis. However, following a request for information, the NYA director quickly mobilized resources and instructed staff to make personal visits to all institutes to collect up-to-date data. This was presented in a report of the institutes (National Youth Authority 2009). The data contained in this report included the number of institutes, number of staff (by gender), number of students (by gender), and some data on dropout rates and examination passes, among other things. It is clear that the NYA is serious about collecting data if requests are put to it. No data could be provided about the outcomes of training. In fact, the NYA has developed a tracer study instrument/questionnaire but has never used it because of a lack of funds.

Funding/Financing

Like some of the other public training providers, the Youth Leadership and Skills Training Institutes are a subvented organization and receive a GoG grant to cover salaries of staff, cost of feeding trainees, and general running costs. The GoG grant is regarded as inadequate. Budgeting is top-down, and the NYA has very little say in its budget.

About three-quarters of a typical institute's income comes from a GoG grant, with the remaining quarter coming from internally generated funds (both training fees and some production activities). Training fees were Gh¢100 a year ($100 in 2008 and the same for all categories of trainees). Some district assemblies support a few needy students.

There is no NGO support to the Youth Leadership and Skills Training Institutes as a whole, although individual centers have received limited assistance from their PTAs or DAs, or from the Heavily Indebted Poor Country Initiative and Youth Funds. All institutes solicit and execute small outside jobs and projects.

No data are available on unit costs.

Community Development Vocational/Technical Institutes

In 1957[43] the Department of Community Development, as part of its mandate of improving the socioeconomic well-being of people—including youth—opened its first training center in the Central Region with the main objective to provide the youth with sustainable employable skills and to increase their income.[44] The Department of Community Development is under the Ministry of Local Government and Rural Development.

Coverage and Location
Community development vocational/technical institutes are located in all 10 regions of Ghana in both urban and rural areas.

Access and Enrollment
There are 24 community development vocational/technical institutes (20 are all female, four are mixed). Total enrollment was 3,072 (68 percent female) in 2011/12; enrollment over the period 2001/02 to 2011/12 has been more or less stagnant, with a slight decline in the most recent year (table B.10).

The target group includes lower secondary (middle school, junior secondary school [JSS], JHS) leavers and school dropouts. The normal entry requirement is the Basic Education Certificate Examination. School dropouts require a testimonial to their character.

The management does not keep detailed records on dropouts but estimates that the survival rate to grade 3 is 75 percent, which implies an annual dropout rate of about 10 percent.[45]

Staffing
The total number of staff is 308, of which 60 percent are teaching staff. Of the 186 teaching staff, 84 percent are female (table B.11).

The increase in the number of staff—despite stagnation in student numbers—was due to the need to recruit additional staff to teach the new examinable subjects such as math, english, and entrepreneurial skills development (see below).

Table B.10 Enrollment, 2001/02 to 2011/12

No. of students	2001/02	2002/03	2003/04	2004/05	2005/06	2006/07	2007/08	2010/11	2011/12
Girls	2,876	2,800	2,769	2,579	2,303	1,939	2,553	1,970	2,084
Boys	544	595	655	790	766	695	967	—	988
Total	3,420	3,395	3,454	3,369	3,069	2,634	3,520	—	3,072

Source: Author interviews (see source information for this appendix).
Note: — = not available.

Table B.11 Total Number of Teaching and Nonteaching Staff, 2008 and 2012

	2008	2012		
	Total	Male	Female	Total
Teaching staff	153	29	157	186
Nonteaching staff	90	—	—	122
Total staff	243	—	—	308

Source: Author interviews (see source information for this appendix).
Note: — = not available.

Some of the teachers in the institutions still only hold NVTI certificates, which are not really adequate for effective teaching. Plans are in the pipeline for these teachers to improve themselves and, for those who cannot, to be employed on contract and eventually phased out from the system. It is also planned that in future the minimum qualification for the instructors and teachers should be a degree or higher national diploma.

Adequate capacity building for teaching staff is lacking even as most of the teachers need to upgrade their skills. There used to be subject teacher trainings organized on a regular basis, but currently it is all ad hoc.

Courses Offered

Training is offered in 13 different examinable areas (for example, catering, dressmaking, hairdressing, block laying, or concrete work) following the NVTI curriculum. Since January 2009, other subjects including English, math, and entrepreneurial skills have been taught as (nonexaminable) subjects; since 2011 these subjects (and information and communication technology [ICT]) have become examinable. Under the 2007 educational reforms the training program was extended from three to four years. The focus is on both practical and theory classes, with approximately 50 percent of time allocated to each. At the end of year 2 students take the proficiency 2 test; at the end of year 3, the certificate 1 test, and at the end of year 4, the certificate 2 test.

Training Environment

Most institutions have long had inadequate infrastructure; most need libraries, assembly halls, demonstration blocks, toilets, and the like. With the shift to four-year duration of courses, the pressure on infrastructure has increased. There is also inadequate accommodation for staff and students in the institutions; this limits the number of students who wish to attend the vocational institutes both as day students and boarders. Some institutions face acute water shortages, which poses many problems for the students and staff in the institutions affected.

A four-year initiative (2009–13), the Gender Responsive Skills and Community Development Project (GRSCDP), funded by the African Development Bank, is supporting the Community Development Vocational/Technical Institutes. Each of the 24 institutes is to receive training equipment and tools and five computers and have their infrastructure rehabilitated and expanded (based on need). In addition, the GRSCDP was to support curricula revision to focus on CBT, as well as teacher training on CBT approaches. It should also provide scholarships to 500 girls from poor households.

Labor Market Linkages

Labor market links with the Community Development Vocational/Technical Institutes are very weak. The Directorate does not engage with industries for advice.

No staff industrial placements have been made. Trainee industrial attachment has only taken place in the area of catering, dressmaking, and, of late, hairdressing. Headmistresses provide students with attachment forms, and they have to find their own attachment. Challenges faced in organizing the attachments are as follows:

- Inadequate monitoring of students due to distances to place of attachment
- Most of the service providers prefer polytechnic students
- Some of the service providers are not comfortable with the monitoring of the students by the institutions
- Complaints of verbal and sexual harassment of the students
- Employment after attachment often does not materialize
- Some of the students are made to perform odd jobs most of the time, instead of working in the specialty in which they have been training

There are no industry liaison officers and no short courses for industry. Guidelines for the composition of institutional board members do not include the suggestion to include industry representatives.

No posttraining support is given. The management claims that there is no money to do this, so there is no startup or equipment support for graduates. The head office hopes to link up to the Local Enterprise and Skills Development Program (LESDEP) (see section "Local Enterprise and Skills Development Program"), so that the graduates of the Community Development Vocational/Technical Institutes can access equipment.

Institutional Autonomy and Availability of Information

In terms of institutional autonomy, here is some degree of decentralization. For example, individual institutions can take the following administration decisions:

- Those related to minor discipline of students and staff in the institutions
- Minor infrastructural repairs at the various institutions
- Purchase of some minor logistics needed by the individual institutes
- Raising funds for the institutes through income generating activities like the operating of canteens, running of small shops, sale of ice water, pig raising, vegetable farming, poultry farming, sewing of uniforms, and goat rearing
- Employment and payment of part-time teachers.

Decisions that need to be approved by the Community Development Directorate in the regions include fixing of school fees in the institutions even though a minimum amount is fixed by the head office. Decisions taken by the Community Development Directorate at the head office include those related to staff recruitment, promotion and placement of staff, curriculum development and fixing of the school calendar, organization of courses for the teaching staff, financial allocation, provision of infrastructure and major repair works on the infrastructure.

Most of the data supplied by the Community Development Vocational/Technical Institutes relate to supply-side issues (numbers trained, number of institutes, staffing, etc.). No data are available on efficiency (dropouts, completers, repeaters), quality, outputs (including examination passes/failures), or finance (for example, there is no reporting of the centers' financing data to the head office, and no data on unit costs). There are no tracer studies conducted and very little monitoring and evaluation undertaken. There is only anecdotal evidence of what graduates get up to.

Funding/Financing

Staff salaries are paid direct by the government. However, the Community Development Vocational/Technical Institutes are not subvented and therefore do not receive a GoG grant to cover general running costs.

Training fee levels are not standard in all institutions; they ranged from the lowest fee of Gh₵4 per year ($4 in 2008) in one of the poorest districts (Bongo) to the highest fee of Gh₵200 per year ($200 in 2008) (Madina). Fee levels are determined by the parent-teacher association and the Board of Governors. The training fees are collected and used by the institutions without any interference from the head office or the regional office.

The institutions get some extra assistance in the form of equipment, infrastructure development, sponsorship of poor students, training of teaching staff, and other means from, for example, NGOs (World Vision, Actionaid, Vocational Training for Females, Valco Trust Fund, etc.), private individuals, and DAs. The institutions also engage in income-generating activities such as vegetable farming, sewing of uniforms, operating canteens, hair salons, sale of drinking water, goat rearing, and contracts to construct doors, windows, and other items.

Short-Term Priorities
- Obtaining buses for all institutions
- Fencing of all of the unwalled institutions to prevent land encroachment
- Provision of administration blocks for the institutions
- Toilet provision for both sexes
- Provision of demonstration blocks for the institutions that do not have them
- Providing water facilities for institutions having water problems
- Providing electricity for institutions lacking a steady source
- Dealing with staff inadequacies and in-service training

Ghana Regional Appropriate Technology Industrial Service

The government of Ghana established the Ghana Regional Appropriate Technology Industrial Service (GRATIS) as a project in 1987 with support from the European Union and the Canadian International Development Agency to promote small-scale industrialization in Ghana.[46] In 1999 its status changed from a project to a foundation. The GRATIS Foundation is a technology transfer and training organization. The mission of GRATIS is to develop, promote, and disseminate marketable technologies and skills for the growth of industry, particularly micro, small-, and medium-scale enterprises in Ghana and the West Africa subregion. Its vision is to become a reputable technology development and skills transfer organization in Africa.

Coverage and Location
GRATIS operates in all regions of Ghana and has a network of nine institutes and three rural technology services centers nationwide.

Access and Enrollment
GRATIS undertakes a variety of training programs, lasting from several days to several years (box B.3). Training is aimed at equipping male and female adults and youth with technical, vocational, and entrepreneurial skills for self-employment. Extension training programs are also held to support the development of rural industries for employment and income generation.

Box B.3 Training Services Offered by GRATIS

Training of master craftsmen and technical apprentices in areas including metal machining, welding and fabrication, casting, blacksmithing, woodworking, and pattern making. The duration is one to three years, and target groups include JHS, SHS, and vocational/technical institute leavers (for the technical apprenticeship training) and informal sector craftsmen (for the MC training).

box continues next page

Box B.3 Training Services Offered by GRATIS *(continued)*

Engineering skills upgrading program in areas such as AutoCAD, improved welding techniques, metal fabrication, occupational health and safety, engineering drawing, productivity, and quality management. The duration is three to 10 days, and target groups include (1) engineers, technicians, designers, and MCs; (2) students and graduates of engineering institutions; and (3) engineering firms and factories.

The visiting apprenticeship program is aimed at providing artisans, MCs, and their apprentices with retraining and the acquisition of new skills in areas including metal machining, welding and fabrication, pattern making, and foundry work.

Practical/industrial attachment aims to provide practical hands-on training to back up the theoretical knowledge of students from higher technical/engineering institutions. The duration is 2–12 weeks, and target groups include students from universities, polytechnics, and technical and vocational institutes.

Textile training is aimed at providing men and women with employment and income-generating skills in the areas of batik, tie and dye cloth making, screen printing, and narrow and broadloom weaving. Training duration is from 4 to 12 months, and target groups include school leavers, "housewives," pensioners, and persons older than 18 years seeking employable and income-generating skills.

The skills and rural enterprise training program aims to provide skills and new/improved technologies to micro and small enterprises in rural and urban areas. Skill areas include tailoring and other skills for the garment industry, soap making, pomade and powder making, bee keeping, mushroom cultivation, snail farming, grasscutter[47] rearing, and brass wax casting. The duration is 5–10 days, and target groups include groups, associations, and communities.

GRATIS provides technical support for community-based projects in areas such as cassava processing, vegetable oil extraction, cereal and grain processing, jam, marmalade, hot pepper sauce, bread and pastries production, and confectionery production. Training duration is 5–10 days.

Source: GRATIS 2006.

The only enrollment data available by year are for the preemployment three-year "Technical Apprentice Training Program"; in this program enrollment has been declining steadily for at least the past seven years, and in 2007/08 there were 245 trainees (table B.12).

Table B.12 Enrollment in the Three-Year Technical Apprentice Training Program, 2001/02 to 2007/08

Academic year	National enrollment
2001/02	280
2002/03	275
2003/04	273
2004/05	264
2005/06	261
2006/07	253
2007/08	245

Source: GRATIS 2008.

Participation in the other training programs that GRATIS offer varies, but since the mid-1980s GRATIS has been responsible for providing training and posttraining support to a sizeable number of individuals (box B.4).

Box B.4 Training Output and Other Services Offered by GRATIS since Its Establishment (to 2006)

- 21,164 people (38 percent female) have received technical assistance and entrepreneurial training (1988–2006).
- 1,865 young men and women have been trained under the three-year Technical Apprentice Training Program (1988–2008) (2007–08 data added from GRATIS, 2008).
- 2,126 people (85 percent female) have been trained under the batik, tie dye, and screen print training (up to 2006).
- 200 blacksmiths provided with training to upgrade their skills (1990–92).
- Over 1,600 entrepreneurs were assisted to improve and expand businesses (up to 2006).
- 498 people have been assisted with working capital to start and expand businesses (up to 2006).
- 102 people have been assisted with equipment on hire purchases to improve operations (up to 2006).

Source: GRATIS 2006.

Staffing

GRATIS has 9 training officers and instructors with back-stopping support from a team of more than 18 engineers and 32 technicians in such fields as mechanical, agricultural, manufacturing and design engineering, metallurgy, material science, and food technology.

Training Environment

The institute is not an NVTI (students receive GRATIS's own certificates), and students also take NVTI exams if they wish. Main training areas for GRATIS include the following:

- Manufacturing with a focus on agriculture and agroprocessing, environment, and sanitation equipment
- Technology-based training including
    - Manufacturing of items related to agriculture, agroprocessing and food security, for example, dryers, ovens, stoves, farming implements, tools, and animal traction equipment
    - Manufacturing of items related to environment and sanitation: for example, open and closed solid waste containers, garbage push trucks, hospital equipment, steel wells, and concrete molds
    - Training in equipment installation, repair, and maintenance services.

The training approach used is based on theoretical training through lectures, hands-on-training in actual jobs, industrial attachment in industry, entrepreneurial skills training, and examinations. Although the training environment is regarded as being of higher quality than many other public TVET institutions, a high number of trainees are still failing exams, which may be an indication that the training environment is failing them; of all the craft certificate examinations that took place in the summer of 2007, 40 percent ended in trainees failing (table B.13).

Labor Market Linkages

There are no staff industrial placements. In terms of trainee industrial placements, as part of the "Technical Apprentice Training Program," trainees do three months industrial attachment. Training managers serve as the industrial attachment liaison officers.

GRATIS offers a large variety of short courses (see above). GRATIS board members are selected from the sector ministry (Ministry of Trade and Industry), the country's education system, Association of Ghana Industries, the private sector, and small and medium enterprises.

For posttraining support, GRATIS makes trainees aware of the National Board for Small-Scale Industries business advisory centers and opportunities for accessing startup capital.

Institutional Autonomy and Availability of Information

GRATIS operates in a decentralized manner, with the regions/centers being led by managers. Regional managers have authority to allocate funds (up to Gh₵50,000 in 2008, equal to $50,000 that year); anything above this needs to go through the GRATIS head office. The head office is also responsible for the recruiting of senior staff.

Centers have authority to purchase materials for the execution of contracts and can also undertake income-generating activities. The centers need approval from the head office before they can recruit even junior staff or if they wish to sell off GRATIS property.

The focus of available data is on the supply side: numbers trained in programs, number of staff, etc. No data are available on efficiency, quality, or outcomes.

Funding/Financing

GRATIS, which is under the Ministry of Trade and Industry, receives a grant from the GoG. The budget allocation is determined by the GoG.

Table B.13 Craft Certificates Examination Results, May/June 2007

	Passed		Failed		Total	
	n	%	n	%	N	%
Male	100	58.8	70	41.2	170	100
Female	3	60.0	2	40.0	5	100
Total	103	58.9	72	41.1	175	100

Source: GRATIS 2008.

The Canadian International Development Agency had a project supporting GRATIS (2000–09) to the amount of US$5 million, the main activities being vocational training and providing business support and services.

Each of the training programs GRATIS offers charge fees, but the only information on fees available at the time of writing is for the three-year "Technical Apprentice Training Program"; fees were $100 per term (in 2006), although this varies from center to center. Trainees on this program are sometimes able to obtain paid work at the centers during their second and third years.

National Apprenticeship Program

A National Apprenticeship Program (NAP) in Ghana has been a decade in the making.[48]

The 2002 President's Committee Report (GoG 2002) noted that "since apprenticeship is mainly [a] private initiative, Government policy with regard to apprentice training should be to effect the registration of apprenticeship providers, and to standardize the content, duration of training programs and certification" (GoG 2002, 152). In other words, the advice was to formalize and then regulate *certain aspects* of the largely private apprenticeship system, not for full direct state sponsorship/subsidy of this large private training system. As COTVET's National Apprenticeship Strategy 2010–14 notes: "The Professor J. Anamuah-Mensah Committee on Education Reform has recommended … a State-sponsored (i.e. publicly financed) apprenticeship" (COTVET 2010, 18). It was the 2004 White Paper that brought in the state sponsorship aspect when it was pledged that the "Government [would] assume full responsibility for the first year of all approved apprenticeship programs" (GoG 2004a, 13)—although quite what this meant was not spelled out (Palmer 2009a). In 2007 and 2008, the government, through the NVTI, designed a national apprenticeship program that unfortunately did not build on the lessons of earlier interventions or good practice elsewhere (see Palmer 2009a for a discussion). Implementation was then delayed further because of the change in government—and political party—in early 2009.

By the time the government had got itself organized to launch the NAP, in 2011, it was on a much smaller scale than what was originally intended; the original NAP proposal was to cover about 65,000 youth, but only 8 percent of this number (5,000) ended up being included.

As it stands, the NAP is a publically funded program that, in its first phase,[49] was to provide funding[50] to 5,000 JHS graduates who could not gain admission to SHS. The NAP was piloted in 78 selected metropolitan, municipal, and district assemblies, each of which chooses the apprentices within its jurisdiction. It was launched in the three northern regions in November 2011, and as of August 2012 it had reached 5,000 apprentices in all districts except Greater Accra (this region is expected to account of the remaining 1,000 NAP apprentices for phase 1). The second phase (8,000 apprentices) was planned to commence in September 2012. NAP is being implemented by COTVET through the National Apprenticeship Committee (NAC) (COTVET 2012a, 2012b).

Components of NAP

Program duration and target group: Duration of the program is one year. JHS graduates identified at the various districts after the *Computerized Schools Selection* and *Placement* System (CSSPS) has been completed. The DAs do the selection of the apprentices. In theory, selection is based on set criteria including, completion of JHS, parental/guardian statement of interest, the individual's own interest in learning a trade, the trade area they select and the places available for that trade, and their age (preference is given to older JHS graduates, meaning that the government wishes to create opportunities for JHS leavers within the year of their graduation is being subverted). Moreover, in some districts it is suspected that political party motivations have influenced the selection of apprentices. In practice, it is not only the immediate JHS graduates who are taking part in NAP; there appears to be so loose a definition that any relatively recent JHS graduate can apply (for example, even five years after completing JHS, many such people still find their way on to the NAP). In the three northern regions, even school dropouts have become NAP apprentices during NAP phase 1.

Cost: There is no commitment fee or other payment by the JHS graduates for the training, and the Ghanaian media report that NAP is "free apprenticeship for JHS leavers" (GNA 2011). However, the parents or guardians have to sign a commitment form to provide the NAP apprentice with basic support (food and transport money). The program pays MCs Gh₵150 ($95 in 2012) per student for the one-year apprenticeship. Currently no stipends are paid to the majority of NAP apprentices, although this was included in the budget for the NAP phase 2. The unit cost for phase 1 NAP apprentices was approximately Gh₵600 in 2012 ($380 in that year), while this increased to Gh₵750 ($475 in 2012) for the planned phase 2 of NAP; the increase in cost is justified by COTVET as largely being the result of increases in equipment costs.

Trade areas: Cosmetology (for example, hair dressing and manicures/pedicures), tailoring and dressmaking, auto mechanics, electronics, ICT, welding and fabrication, carpentry and joinery, and block laying and concreting.

Startup kit: The government pays for a tool kit that the apprentice will use during the one-year NAP apprenticeship; during the year this is kept by the MC and is given to the NAP apprentice upon completion of the year.

Trainers: MCs are selected to serve as the key trainers on the NAP. The selection criteria of MC trainers includes the following:

- Their enterprise is registered with the local district assembly for tax purposes
- Experience (more than five years in training apprentices)
- Availability of basic equipment in their workplace
- Good reputation among citizens in the locality
- Membership of relevant trade associations
- Availability of space to train apprentices

MCs receive basic training in CBT teaching approaches[51] and are given training manuals to serve as reference materials.

Monitoring and Evaluation: No baseline survey was conducted for the NAP phase 1 apprentices, and instruments do not yet exist (May 2012). It is claimed that after the completion of the one-year NAP, there will be an evaluation to assess whether the NAP training has been sufficient to allow NAP apprentices to start up on their own. In 2013/14 USAID is financing an impact assessment of the NAP using a randomized-control trial approach for new cohorts of trainees.[52]

A Comment on NAP

Palmer (2009a) provided an early comment on the design of the NAP, and most of these comments stood as of May 2012; these comments covered issues related to the one-year duration of NAP, the training given to MCs, the limited coverage of the NAP, the lack of an integrated approach, as well as concerns related to inadequate monitoring and evaluation. It is worth repeating several here, as well as noting a few other issues related to the most recent version of the NAP.

After one year—then what? Since most informal apprenticeships take about three years, the issue of what will happen to NAP apprentices after the one-year program is of concern; experience from Ghana has shown that one year is too short to adequately train an apprentice (Palmer 2009a). What is quite surprising is that this was exactly the same conclusion of an evaluation report of an International Programme on the Elimination of Child Labour one-year apprenticeship project: "Effectiveness of the project has not been fully achieved because of the one-year duration which is too short for mastery of skills acquisition. Effective competency requires 2–4 years of apprenticeship" (Pealore 2007, 26–27). What is most interesting is that the author of this evaluation, Pealore, is now the COTVET Board Chairman and sits on the National Apprenticeship Committee.

A 1 percent program: The NAP is not a program that is designed for the approximately 440,000 youth currently in informal apprenticeship (GLSS 2005/06 data in Nsowah-Nuamah et al. 2010), but is a program for a small fraction of annual JHS leavers (the first one-year batch covered 5,000 youth, which represents only 1 percent of all 440,000 youth in informal apprenticeship). It is not designed, therefore, to improve the functioning of the regular private informal apprenticeship system. Instead, it is introducing a parallel, publically funded version of informal apprenticeship. Although on a small scale, such actions risk substituting public for private finance at local levels.

The one-year, 1 percent NAP is somewhat removed from the grander vision of COTVET's National Apprenticeship Training Policy, which states it plans to do the following:[53]

- Reform and strengthen the formal and informal apprenticeship system by infusing a CBT and assessment system
- Develop training systems and mechanisms to facilitate the articulation of the informal level and standards of skills acquisition with those of the formal TVET system

- Encourage the formation and recognition of trade associations as a means of delivering training-related assistance to members
- Integrate informal apprenticeship training into the National Qualifications Framework
- Provide guidelines for governmental and private/NGO activities in the informal sector training and apprenticeship

Local Enterprise and Skills Development Program

The Local Enterprise and Skills Development Program (LESDEP) is a public-private initiative, launched in 2011, that provides technical and vocational skills training to local communities, with the aim of "empowering the youth through the acquisition of technical and entrepreneurial skills … [to] … creat[e] gainful employment for the youth" (GoG 2011c, 183, 240).[54]

Registered under the auspices of the Ministry of Local Government and Rural Development, LESDEP received Gh₵12 million in funding from government in 2011 ($8 million in that year), and in 2012 this jumped to Gh₵84 million ($53 million) (GoG 2011c); this combined amount is more than the entire Skills Development Fund budget ($60 million) (World Bank 2011a).

Prospective participants register for free, undertake short-term training, and are then given a basic tool-kit or equipment on a soft-loan basis (payable back after a couple of years).

Training courses under LESDEP include IT, mobile phone and laptop computer repairs, local garments and fashion, beauty care, event organization and decor management, bead making, local food and catering services, fish farming, grasscutter rearing, agroprocessing, welding and fabrication, agriculture, photography, and construction.

Training is implemented in collaboration with MoELR and other agencies including the Ghana Youth Employment and Entrepreneurial Agency,[55] the National Youth Council, ICCES, OIC, and the National Board for Small-Scale Industries. The LESDEP program has opened offices in all 170 metropolitan, municipal, and district assemblies in Ghana. In other words, LESDEP is not working directly *through* the existing TVET-providing departments and agencies at the regional and district levels, but has set up parallel organizational structures and then links to these existing providers. As of May 2012, COTVET had very little, if anything, to do with LESDEP and started meeting with them only from that month.

As a government-funded short-term training program that operates with parallel structures outside the main TVET providers and without coordinating with COTVET, LESDEP represents an inefficient way to utilize resources. Furthermore, the program may actually cause localized market distortions. For example, since LESDEP is offering to provide basic training equipment (on a soft-loan basis) to those who complete a few weeks or months of training, it is quite possible that trainees will drop out of regular (long-duration) formal TVET provision and informal apprenticeships specifically to access the LESDEP training equipment. This is more or less what was reported to have happened under the earlier STEP program (where instead of an equipment/loan, participants expected to be offered microcredit—most of which never actually materialized) (Palmer 2007b).

The Skills Training and Entrepreneurship Program

Another type of public skills delivery mechanism was the short-duration modality, organized on a periodic basis.[56] The 2003–05 Skills Training and Entrepreneurship Program (STEP) offered 3–12 months of training to youth with the intention that the STEP graduates would immediately enter self-employment. STEP was a highly politicized program that largely had disappointing outcomes (Palmer 2007a).

Following the 2001 unemployment census in Ghana, which revealed that most of the unemployed wanted to acquire skills to enable them to be self-employed or employable, the Skills Training and Employment Placement Program was initiated (it was later renamed the Skills Training and Entrepreneurship Program (see why below) with the same acronym. STEP, a government-supported training program, was intended to reduce poverty by providing short-duration, modular, employable skills and other assistance (including access to microfinance) to those who had registered as "unemployed," thus enabling them to join the workforce. Funding was made available by allocations from the HIPC fund.

While socioeconomic data are unavailable for former STEP participants, from a poverty perspective it is interesting to note that of the one million people who registered as "unemployed" in the 2001 unemployment census (and who provided the majority of STEP participants), 82 percent had completed lower secondary school and a further 8 percent had a post–basic education. Most STEP trainees, it appears, already had at least a basic education. Hence it is quite accurate to assert that the most vulnerable and excluded did not participate in STEP.

STEP comprised three principal components:

1. *Skills training delivered through vocational training providers*: About 27,500 "unemployed" were trained through formal public and private training providers. STEP training courses ran for 3–12 months in 58 training areas, from textiles and soap production to welding, carpentry, and painting.
2. *Skills enhancement for master craftspeople and skills training delivered through apprenticeship placements*: MCs go through a few days' training with GRATIS to make them more effective trainers. Skills training is then delivered by attaching up to 10 trainees to a MC to undertake a workshop-based apprenticeship for up to 12 months.
3. *Microfinance component*: This component, launched in December 2004, had the intention of providing startup and working capital to enable those trained under the STEP program to set up their own enterprises. Funding was meant to be made available from HIPC funds to microfinance institutions for lending to qualified trained STEP graduates. Two microfinance institutions

participated: Women's World Banking Ghana (WWBG) and a rural bank network under the Association of Rural Banks APEX (ARB APEX).

A number of problems hindered the outcomes of the STEP program:

1. *Lack of demand for these types of skills*: The STEP program was highly centralized: Skills needs assessments were conducted at NVTI headquarters in Accra. But there was no real attempt at establishing demand for skills and product types at the local level, and one ILO-commissioned review noted that DAs sometimes complained about STEP delivering "useless" courses (Preddey 2005, 22).
2. *Weak training environment*: Many MCs who were given apprentices to train could not provide a safe training environment, for example, providing protective clothing, and were ill-resourced in tools and equipment. MCs complained about receiving insufficient funding to adequately train apprentices. The duration of training was not considered long enough, especially in trades such as welding and carpentry, leading to the creation of "half-baked" apprentices. Training was also criticized for having a traditional approach to production, one that was not competitive and not productive.
3. *Inadequate posttraining support:* There was inadequate posttraining support and huge delays in STEP graduates accessing microfinance; by October 2006 only 10 percent had received loans. The failure of the microfinance component had much to do with the unrealistic expectations of the government with regard to private sector microfinance institutions. The microfinance institutions with which the government tried to work, WWBG and ARB APEX, viewed the capacity of STEP graduates to understand the conditions of lending as inadequate. They considered that providing microfinance to STEP graduates was a social program and not commercially viable. STEP borrowers were seen by the microfinance institutions as a higher risk than other borrowers, being new "customers" with low educational attainment. No follow-up or impact assessment of STEP was made; instead politicians were—and still are (in 2012)—keen to portray the program as meeting its objectives and creating employment. But, for the majority of STEP graduates, this is unlikely to be the case. Although it has been claimed that young people trained under STEP have started their own businesses or secured employment, it is probably telling that STEP was renamed the Skills Training and Entrepreneurship Program (in 2005), as it had signally failed to connect with job opportunities the very large number of young people who registered.
4. *Employment outcomes unknown*: Except for anecdotal evidence, no one really knows what has happened to the substantial number of STEP graduates since the program's inception. There is concern that many (if not most) STEP graduates are not faring well in the labor market. Because of the failure of loan delivery as part of STEP, many of those who participated in this training program became disillusioned. More worryingly, as the director of one of the

main agencies under the MoELR noted, "whatever they [the trainees] learned in STEP has now become useless" since training was often of mediocre quality, not up-to-date, and not responsive to local demand.[57]

5. *A numbers game between total reach of STEP and total demand*: The total number trained under STEP was about 27,000, a small percentage of the annual approximately 150,000 lower secondary graduates who finish school and cannot enter further formal training.

The Rural Enterprise Project (IFAD, 1995 and Ongoing)

Experience from Phase II (2003–12)

The Rural Enterprise Project second phase (REP II) ran from June 2003 to June 2012 and was implemented in 53 districts in all regions nationwide.[58] The overall goal of the REP II was to alleviate poverty and improve living conditions in the rural areas and in particular to increase the incomes of women and vulnerable groups through increased self- and wage employment. The project was funded mainly by the government of Ghana, the IFAD, and the African Development Bank.

The REP II design involved four interrelated components:

1. Business Development Services through establishment and operation of business advisory centers in 53 participating districts. Business advisory centers provided business management training to MSEs in those districts.
2. Technology Promotion and Support to Apprentices Training through establishment of rural technology facilities in 21 selected districts. The rural technology facilities promoted, tested, and disseminated technologies, supported apprenticeship training for traditional and technical apprentices, and fabricated and serviced equipment adapted to rural MSEs.
3. Rural Financial Services were made through continuation of the REP I Rural Enterprises Development Fund.
4. Support was given to MSE Organizations and Partnership Building (Institutional Support).

Technology Promotion and Support to Apprenticeship Training (REP II, component 2)

The Technology Promotion and Support to Apprentices Training component was implemented through the rural technology facilities in a partnership arrangement with the District Assembly and GRATIS. The rural technology facilities served as a focal point for the promotion and upgrading of MSE technologies in the districts.

Rural technology facilities train three categories of clients under the Technology Promotion and Support to Apprentices Training: MCs, traditional apprentices, and technical apprentices (young people without any previous employable skills who were enrolled by the rural technology facilities for a period of three years to acquire a vocational skill).

The rural technology facilities organized training for apprentices and MCs in both general[59] and trade-specific issues (for example, for carpentry, blacksmithing, welding and fabrication, and spraying upholstery). General training courses typically lasted up to five days, and trade-specific training up to 10 days.

Basic training needs assessments were conducted to ensure training relevance, particularly for the trade-specific training courses; these involved trade associations, as well as direct discussion with MSE owners.

The rural technology facilities organized separate training sessions for MCs and traditional apprentices. The facilities enrolled a maximum of 20 MCs and 25 traditional apprentices for a typical trade-specific training session.

An apprentice in the rural technology facility training program paid 10 percent, and a MC paid 20 percent of the total training cost.

Posttraining Support and Follow-up

The rural technology facilities and business advisory centers provided posttraining support to their clients: They gave them posttraining follow-up counseling and start-up kits, facilitated access to credit, and facilitated certification (for example, by the NVTI).

Start-up kits: Although limited in scale, the provision of start-up kits for graduate apprentices made considerable impact in the district and served to motivate the entrepreneurial poor to avail themselves of skill enhancement. The districts received about 60 start-up kits each year for selected apprentices based on predetermined criteria including the type of kit available, sex, level of needs (disadvantaged person), and geographic location.

- *Impact (2003–10)* (IFAD 2011)
- 7,481 apprentices trained (47 percent female), against a target of 6,000 (IFAD 2011).
- The delivery of start-up kits for graduate apprentices commenced in 2007 with an average of about 60 start-up kits per district per year provided to selected apprentices. By the end of December 2010, a total of 3,182 apprentices (42 percent women) had received start-up kits (IFAD 2011; Okorley 2011).
- A total of 5,860 apprentices (57 percent female) were assisted to take the NVTI certification examination (Okorley 2011).
- 2,889 master craftspeople trained (11 percent female), against a target of 5,000, particularly in the development of the metal and agro-processing industry.

Challenges included the following: (1) Time of training: The rural technology facilities reported a drop-out rate of 10–20 percent mainly because apprentices and masters were unable to commit to 5–10 days away from their workshops. The rural technology facilities responded by splitting up the training and scheduling it from 9 am to 2 pm to allow participants to work the rest of the day in their enterprise or conduct other activities necessary for their daily survival (Okorley 2011).

(2) Targeting the poor: REP II successfully reached the "entrepreneurial poor" (IFAD 2011) but was unable to reach out directly to the poorest. IFAD expected that "enterprise growth [as a result of REP II] would benefit the very poor by increasing opportunities for employment" (IFAD 2011, 8). Okorley (2011, 6) comments that "there [was] very little effort in terms of strategies and indicators to identify and include the poor."

Private Vocational Training Institutes

Access to Training

There is a huge range and diversity of private for-profit and nonprofit skills training institutions in Ghana.[60] The exact number of private VTIs involved in skills training in Ghana is not known; only those schools that are officially registered are recorded. But the total number of registered and nonregistered private VTIs is estimated at around 445.

Data compiled from a survey of 293 sampled private VTIs by NACVET (2005) show a concentration of schools in the southern part of the country. In general, private for-profit VTIs are located in urban and metropolitan areas, religious VTIs are in both urban and rural areas, and nonprofit VTIs run by NGOs are usually found in rural areas (UNESCO 2003). About 92 percent of private VTIs offer training in the low-capital-intensive trade courses (mostly the vocational trades) because of the high capital investment and recurrent cost associated with the technical trades, whereas only 30 percent offer training in the technical trades.

A small field survey conducted for this report on 10 private VTIs in the Greater Accra area in late 2008/early 2009 revealed that almost all VTIs (9 out of 10) were operating under capacity; most had experienced a continuous decline in student enrollment since 2006. Interest in TVET provided by these private VTIs appears to be high—as evidenced by the large number of enquiries from parents that these VTIs report. However, effective demand is significantly less than this potential demand.

The reasons for the low enrollment of the private VTIs include the following:

- Parents and the students (some who support not only themselves but also their family) find it very difficult to afford the school fees.
- The low social status of TVET discourages some parents and students to consider it as a means of acquiring a trade for the world of work.
- Lack of quality training and flexibility in paying school fees makes it difficult for most parents to keep their child in school.

Although many private VTIs are experiencing a decline in enrollment, there are exceptions to this. For example, at the Don Bosco Technical Institute (Tema)—a nonprofit private VTI that provides skills to the destitute and the under-privileged in society—the enrollment figure is always high and currently the school is operating above its capacity, a situation attributed to the quality of training and flexibility in paying school fees (see box B.5).

Box B.5 Don Bosco Technical Institute, Ashaiman (Tema)

Background:[61] The Don Bosco Technical Institute at Ashaiman was a privately run Catholic missionary and educative institution, run by the Salesians of Don Bosco. It was established in 1999 to provide a better future for boys and girls, especially for those who found themselves in difficult economic and social situations (orphans, dropouts, street children, and others from poor families). The objective was to train young people for the world of work with the aim of making them self-reliant. There were four main trades (secretarial studies, electronics, electrical installation, and auto mechanics), with each being three to four years' duration.

The school had the capacity to take up to 300 trainees. In 2006 the trainee population was 165 (45 secretarial studies, 40 electronics, 45 electrical installation, and 35 auto mechanics), and it increased to 230 (50 secretarial studies, 40 electronics, 63 electrical installation, and 50 auto mechanics) in 2007 and further increased to 323 (60 secretarial studies, 50 electronics, 70 electrical installation, and 65 auto mechanics) in 2008.

Access: The minimum entry requirement was a Basic Education Certificate Examination certificate and the ability to read English. Applicants also wrote an entrance examination, and those who lacked the ability to write English were prepared for the proficiency test. The fundamental requirement for entry was the expression of interest in the trade (this requirement aimed to eliminate undermotivated trainees).

For the 2008 new entrants, the yearly school fees were Gh₵300 (approximately the same in dollars in 2008) for each of the four areas of training. These school fees were set annually by the head and staff of the school and presented to the Board of Directors for approval. The main factor considered in determining the fees was the recurrent cost of the school. When trainees did not pay their fees they were sent home to bring their parents or guardians to negotiate flexible payment terms with the school. At times the school helped by providing paying jobs on campus for the trainees. Some very needy trainees were often helped by their teachers to pay their fees. The school also offered some bursaries to needy but talented trainees; 25 trainees (about 15 percent) had full scholarships in 2006, 50 trainees (about 22 percent) had varied levels of partial scholarships in 2007, and 75 trainees (about 23 percent) benefited from such support in 2008. In addition, all the trainees were provided with one meal a day. Trainees did not usually drop out because the school had mechanisms in place to support them. It has been observed that most parents/trainees prefer to pay fees for examinations and materials for practical exercises rather than paying tuition fees.

Generally, trainees were allowed to write their examinations while still owing the school, but they had to pay all arrears before collecting certificates, result slips, or testimonials. The majority (60 percent or more) of the trainees were poor, defined as those who pay school fees in small installments, those that do not get enough to eat at home, and those who work outside to earn money. A further 25 percent were very poor, defined as those whose parents could not easily pay school fees, provide transportation, and materials needed for practical lessons; those who could not afford one decent meal; those who worked to earn money and were often late or absent; and those with nonworking parents or parents with very low income (those in petty trading, subsistence farming, or fishing).

box continues next page

Box B.5 Don Bosco Technical Institute, Ashaiman (Tema) *(continued)*

Quality of training: Don Bosco had excellent training facilities (classrooms, well-equipped workshops, offices and auditorium, hostel, compound for extra-curriculum activities, canteen) and a conducive environment for studies. The workshop equipment, tools, and machines were modern and in working condition.

All four core trades were studied together with six compulsory subjects (math, english, integrated science, moral ethics, entrepreneurship, and ICT), and the type of examinations written were the NVTI, National Coordinating Committee for Technical and Vocational Education and Training (NACVET), and GES Intermediate. The number of teaching staff was 24 (21 males and 3 females), all permanent teachers. Their level of qualification ranged from higher national diploma (minimum) to degree (maximum), and their gross monthly salaries fell between Gh₵100 and Gh₵400 inclusive (approximately the same in dollars in 2008). In the academic year 2007/08, the ratio of students to teachers was 14:1.

The school instituted a very effective teaching monitoring system that included inspecting lesson plans, trainee evaluating teachers, and the principal consulting with the class prefects on the performance and effectiveness of their teachers. The quality of training and flexibility in paying school fees impacted positively on the trend of new entrants' enrollment: the number rose from 165 in 2006 to 230 in 2007 to 323 in 2008.

Relevance of training to the labor market: The continuous engagement with industries through the industrial attachment and the provision of services to the public enabled the school to deliver the trades to meet the needs of the labor market. Engaging the trainees in the live jobs built their confidence and enhanced their practical skills.

The trainees in auto mechanics and electrical installation easily found employment or set up their own shop. Because of that, new entrants often chose those two trades. Electronics was least patronized because it was limited to repairs of home electronic gadgets. The requirements for industry are of a higher level of knowledge and skills than what is acquired at the institute, limiting job opportunities in industry for graduates. Some past trainees are working in the armed forces, police service, and shipping industries.

Some of the teachers were sent for skills upgrading training in Italy and Germany (on soft/hardware, solar panels, vehicle repair and servicing, and vehicle gas installation). Occasionally retired teachers of some schools overseas came on visits to impart their knowledge and skills to the Ghanaian teachers and trainees.

Posttraining support: The institute provided microfinance support for serious graduates who wanted to set up their own business. They were encouraged to form groups and present a business proposal (trainees were assisted to write these proposals when necessary) for soft loans from the Don Bosco Youth Empowerment Scheme (Don Bosco YES), a revolving fund. The scheme was managed by a board made up of a lawyer, the school principal, and three entrepreneurs, who evaluated the business proposals and approved the loan.

Funding: The funding of the school came from the school fees paid by the trainees and the Catholic Church. The school did not receive any support from government. Other external social support institutions, such as the Catholic Action for Street Children, provided the electronics workshop with discarded computers for practical work, and the AFW Province provided some form of social support and funding for very needy trainees. Only 35 percent of the

box continues next page

Box B.5 Don Bosco Technical Institute, Ashaiman (Tema) *(continued)*

school budget was financed from the school fees and alternative income (hiring out school facilities such as the social hall and the sports field, and providing automobile repair services to the public), while the remaining 65 percent came from the Catholic Church and NGOs. Though the payment of fees was not regular, it did not impact the effectiveness of training because the institution had an internal mechanism in place for borrowing when in financial need. External sources of financing, made up of donations, were the same amount for the several years but were slashed by half in 2012. This meant that the institution had to find a way of making up the drop in income either through internally generated income or by increasing the training fees, which will make the training not accessible to the poor and vulnerable.

Sources: Research Consortium on Educational Outcomes and Poverty interviews, July 2006 and World Bank interviews, December 2008.

The standard entry requirement for private VTIs is a Basic Education Certificate Examination certificate. However, some VTIs offer school dropouts and those who could not read or write in English the option to enroll for the (nonwritten) proficiency examination. The training fees of the private VTIs are set by management (including the owner), and they vary widely with the trade program and from one school to another. To remain competitive, most private VTIs do not charge the full cost of training. A trade-off often results between the number of pupils enrolled and the level of training fees. Some of the schools cut on teacher costs by using part-time staff as means of making savings for other recurrent costs, including the cost incurred in cutting down on the training fees. Scholarship awards are available in very few schools for brilliant but poor students, while others (such as the Family Strengthening Program of the SOS Hermann Gmeiner VTI in Tema) have programs that help underprivileged and vulnerable students, most of whom support themselves by combining work with the training.[62]

UNESCO (2003) collected data on training fees in 30 private VTIs and found fee levels to be higher for private VTIs compared with public VTIs.

Quality of Training

A great diversity is seen in the quality of training offered. The effectiveness of imparting skills and knowledge to students depends significantly on the level to which the school is equipped with training materials and qualified instructors. Facilities and equipment used in many private VTIs are woefully inadequate and in most cases obsolete. A study conducted by EMIS in 2007/08 found that 84.8 percent of the instructors in private VTIs surveyed had technical qualifications, with only 45.9 percent having training in teaching (table B.14).

This suggests that about 54 percent of the instructors (those who were not trained) may not have acquired adequate pedagogical skills. Just over half (50.4 percent) of the instructors in the private VTIs indicated that they hardly ever receive in-service training. Many VTI students who are trained by these

Table B.14 Number of Instructors in TVET Providers

Type of TVET providers	Number of instructors	Instructors with technical qualification (%)	Trained instructors (%)
Private TVET providers	1,180	84.8	45.9
Public TVET providers	2,375	87.1	62.6
Total	**3,555**	**86.4**	**57.0**

Sources: Compiled from EMIS Survey 2007/2008, GoG 2008c.
Note: TVET = technical and vocational education and training.

instructors, especially those with little or no industry exposure, may find themselves deficient in knowledge and practical skills.

For most of the other schools, it has been difficult operating with qualified and experienced instructors. Under certain circumstances, quality instructors are passed over for part-time inexperienced instructors, a situation existing with most private schools. Some private VTIs have instituted effective teaching monitoring and evaluation systems, which entails inspecting teachers' lesson plans, making unannounced visits to the classrooms to inspect the student's notes and observing how the training is being delivered, trainees evaluating teachers and the principal confirming with the class prefects the performance and effectiveness of their teachers; assessing teachers' competence, as well as challenges and problems that relate to the training; and using external examination results of students as a measure of evaluating teachers' performance.

The contact hours for the 10 private VTIs surveyed by Ahorbo (2009a) vary greatly from 17 to 40 hours per week. Some of the compulsory subjects taught alongside the trade course—to widen the academic scope of the students—include math, English, general science, french, information technology, social studies, entrepreneurship, and moral ethics (the subjects vary among VTIs). The main types of examinations held by the schools (at that time) were GES and NVTI examinations.

The other factors that could be contributing to the poor quality of training are the existence of unregistered schools that may be offering low-quality training.

Relevance of the Private VTI Skills Training to the Labor Market

In general it might be expected that private for-profit VTIs would provide better quality—and more relevant—training compared to public VTIs (or nonprofit private VTIs receiving grants from other sources); as businesses, these for-profit VTIs would close if the public perceived the quality to be low or the relevance of the training offered to be minimal. Indeed, the decline in enrollment in many private VTIs may be the result of this.

Although it is difficult to generalize—because of the diversity of private for-profit and nonprofit VTIs—it is clear that some private VTIs do make efforts to engage with the world of work through trainee industrial attachment and through the provision of services directly to the public. This enables some private VTIs to deliver the trade courses to meet the needs of the labor market. It also helps the schools to identify some of the skill mismatches and deal effectively with the practical issues faced by the graduates in the labor market. Some private VTIs offer postindustrial attachment seminars—organized at the end of any industrial attachment—which have helped reshape course delivery to make them more relevant to the labor market.[63] Engaging the students in live jobs during practical lessons has built their confidence and enhanced their practical skills.

To sustain an adequate inflow of workforce with appropriate technical and vocational skills, TVET providers must create better links with industry and recognize that industry has a better perception of its own needs; it is best positioned to identify and flag trends in the marketplace that may render the current training focus at TVET providers irrelevant (Kodzi 2008).

The absence of labor market information has even made it difficult to tailor training to respond adequately to the specific skills in demand, a situation that has significantly contributed in the low level of theoretical knowledge and practical skills found with the graduates on the labor market. The private VTIs need to follow their graduates to know how well they are surviving with the knowledge and skills they have acquired from training.

To be well positioned to meet the demands of an increasingly technological labor market, it is necessary to have a good mix of practical skills and theoretical understanding. Until TVET activities move in tandem with the changing technology and workplace requirements, TVET graduates will always remain inadequate in knowledge and practical skills. Amid all this, the poor basic education of incoming students also limits subsequent skills attainment.

Posttraining Support

Some private VTIs encourage their graduates to present a business proposal to access a soft loan, whereas others steer their graduates to seek employment opportunities with organizations and industries that have long-standing relationships with the school. Private VTIs also assist their graduate students with introduction letters, testimonials, and certificates to help them to apply for salaried employment.

Financing of the Private VTIs

To a large extent financing is secured from fees paid by students and from donations. The unreliability of the fees—which is the main source of financing—affects the operation of many private VTIs. Since private TVET delivery is comparatively expensive because of the demanded practical experiences within the trade, it has become crucial to find a reliable sustainable source of financing.

An analysis of the income and expenditure statements of the private VTIs by Ahorbo (2009a) indicated that the main source of income of schools that do not receive financial support from outside are the school fees collected from students. Such schools spend between 18 and 79 percent of their income on staff salaries. However, donor-supported private TVET providers spend more than the school fees collected on salaries. Generally the salaries of the private VTIs form more than 50 percent of the school expenditure. In certain situations the salary forms 80 to 90 percent of the total expenditure. The spending on training and learning materials has been as low as 1–3 percent of the total income in most of the schools.

On average, private VTIs manage to survive the challenges of low enrollment and high operating cost by passing on the cost of operation to their clients. This is reflected in the portion of income spent on training and learning materials, salaries, and other related costs in other to make savings.

There could be three approaches to providing reliable financing to TVET providers, such as the following:

- Income-generating activities that relate to the general activities in which the institute has its core strength, a situation that could serve two good purposes: providing reliable income to the school and providing an opportunity for the students to acquire practical exposure.
- Passing on part of the financial responsibilities to the government: finding a way to rely on the state to provide some relief in the form of subvention.
- Setting up a fund to contribute to TVET financing and related skills development. Such a fund could be a special avenue to sustainable financing, to which the government and all corporate bodies in the country would contribute.

Government Commitments to TVET

Government (via COTVET) should set and assess standards of the private VTIs, and the schools that achieve these standards should be accredited and provided with grants and/or salary subsidies. Government efforts to expand formal TVET opportunities in the country should include assistance to formal private training providers to enable them to increase enrollment and reach their capacity.

Informal Apprenticeship Training

The general features of informal apprenticeship training in Ghana are well known (Ahadzie 2003; Palmer 2007a; Donkor 2012) and similar to those described in other countries in West Africa (for example, see Haan 2006; Johanson and Adams 2004).

Access and Equity

As noted earlier, more than 440,000 Ghanaian youth 15–24 years of age (53 percent female) were participating in informal apprenticeship (GLSS 2005/06 data in Nsowah-Nuamah et al. 2010).[64] Informal apprenticeship training remains the largest provider of vocational skills in Ghana; it is responsible for 80 percent of all basic skills training, compared with 7 percent from public training institutions and 13 percent from for-profit and nonprofit providers.[65] To put it another way, the numbers involved in informal apprenticeship in Ghana are about four times higher than all the youth in all public and private formal TVET providers combined.

Apprenticeship has become more important over time as a means to acquire skills for employment, especially for young women. Currently, about one of every three youth in the 20–30 age group has experience as an apprentice, compared to one in four youth 15 years ago. The percentage of young women doing an apprenticeship has doubled in the last 15 years (World Bank 2008a).

Gaining entry to informal apprenticeships is easier than to formal VTIs, and hence apprenticeships often serve important target groups (illiterates, rural populations, and urban poor). Costs are generally lower than for formal training, and parents can usually pay over time. They represent an important source of technical and vocational skills in manufacturing/service trades for those who cannot access formal training institutes (Palmer 2007a).

However, although it is widely acknowledged that informal "apprenticeship training can be the least expensive way to get skills training" (Johanson and Adams 2004, 131), the training fees associated with apprenticeship, combined with the tools and other items apprentices have to bring before training can commence, can serve to exclude the poor (and certainly the very poor). Apprenticeship may be more accessible to disadvantaged youth than formal TVET, but they can still face significant barriers to entry and completion of apprenticeship training. According to the GLSS, in 2005/06 the percentage of those in the highest standard of living quintile who have had an apprenticeship, 47 percent, is more than four times the percentage of those in the lowest standard of living quintile (World Bank 2008a). However, it is also true that—according to the same data—the poorest youth (those in the lowest quintile) are almost 20 times more likely to be doing an informal apprenticeship than formal TVET. JHS graduates who fail to transition to SHS—for numerous reasons—see TVET, and especially informal apprenticeships, as their only option.

Unlike formal TVET, there are no formal educational entry requirements for informal apprenticeships; yet the majority of youth (75 percent) entering informal apprenticeships in Ghana now do so after completing lower secondary schooling (Palmer 2007a; Monk et al. 2008; World Bank 2008a), although they most likely performed poorly in the leaving examination. However, the majority of those in the poorest part of the population—who are not even able to attain lower secondary schooling—are not participating in apprenticeship training, as the GLSS data demonstrates. Although, on average, 75 percent of youth doing apprenticeships have completed basic education, there appear to be clear differences in the education levels of apprentices following different apprentice trades (see Ahadzie 2003; Palmer 2007a).

Among those youth who are able to access informal apprenticeship training, education level, gender, and poverty level all appear to contribute to a social fragmentation of the informal apprenticeship training system. Educational fragmentation of informal apprenticeship occurs when some trade areas attract more educated, and hence less-poor, youth.[66] Evidence from Ghana suggests that there appears to be a degree of clustering of more educated youths in hairdressing, tailoring, auto mechanics and welding, whereas the more traditional trades of carpentry, dressmaking, and weaving still attract significant numbers of those with less than 9 years of schooling (table B.15).[67] Gender fragmentation of informal apprenticeship is also an important issue, especially from a poverty reduction perspective (Johanson and Adams 2004; Palmer 2007a; Haan 2008). Overall, most male informal apprentices train in traditionally male trades (for example, carpentry, auto mechanics, welding), whereas young women have fewer opportunities in apprenticeship; those opportunities that do exist for women are usually in traditional trade areas for which the market demand is often limited.

Table B.15 Apprentices in Ghana with Less Than a Complete Basic Education

Trade area	Less than basic education (%)
Hairdressing[a]	25
Tailoring[b]	27
Auto mechanics[b]	35
Electrical installation[b]	35
Welding[b]	36
Carpentry[b]	50
Carpentry[a]	40
Dressmaking[b]	49
Dressmaking[b]	49
Weaving[a]	59

Sources: World Bank.
a. Palmer 2007a.
b. Ahadzie 2003.
Note: Nine years of schooling.

The educational and gender fragmentation of informal apprenticeship suggests that the poor, and especially poor women, are less able (either through cost, education level or gender) to be able to access the more popular, and more lucrative, trade areas under the present status quo.

Poverty levels can also determine the choice of apprenticeship because some apprenticeships (such as auto mechanics, electrical installation, and welding) cost more than others, both in terms of the fee paid to the master craftsperson and the cost of the basic tools and equipment needed to start working in that trade area.

Relevance and Quality

The informal apprenticeship system is more relevant to the real world of work and more effective at linking training with work than pre-employment center-based training. The on-the-job training:

- Is work-based and practical, and there is a close link between training and production
- Allows for a gradual building up of informal enterprise networks (for example, with suppliers, customers, other business owners and apprentice masters), the development of general business-related skills, including customer-relation skills, and apprentices are able to "learn the mechanics of being self-employed" (van Dijk 1997, 107)
- Allows apprentices to develop their institutional networks (for example, with informal sector associations and credit and business support agencies)
- Is more effective than formal preemployment training as trainees are usually more mature and motivated
- Offers apprentices the possibility of finding employment with their master on graduation.

However, the informal apprenticeship system finds it hard to connect to technological advances; new product designs and production technologies are difficult to introduce as the technology level and understanding of the master is reproduced in the apprentice. Training is delivered in enterprises of varying quality[68] and provides trainees with little, if any, theoretical understanding of the on-the-job processes that they learn. The training–production balance is usually biased toward production, which means that more often than not what apprentices learn depends on what is produced (Palmer 2007a).

Funding

Costs are borne by apprentices and their family with no input from government[69] or communities. Unlike preemployment training there is no need for a training center or separate tools/equipment for training. In Ghana there has been no tradition of government support, control, or supervision. Instead there is a history of sustainability. There are often many different types of fees related to informal apprenticeship training.

- In many cases training fees are made up of two types of fees, commitment and graduation fees, paid at the start and end of training respectively.[70]
- In addition, some MCs ask for in-kind contributions, commonly a crate of minerals (soft drinks) or malt (malt beer), a bottle of alcoholic spirits, cigarettes, or a goat (Breyer 2007).[71]
- Furthermore, in addition to the training fees, apprentices usually have bring certain items before they can commence training. For example, carpentry apprentices usually have to bring some basic tools (hammer, chisel, measuring tape), while dressmaking apprentices need to bring their own sewing machine, scissors, and tape (Breyer 2007; Palmer 2007a).[72]
- MCs often provide apprentices with a small amount of money on a daily basis to cover feeding costs (known as "chop money") (Breyer 2007; Palmer 2007a).[73]

Breyer (2007) conducted some detailed work on the costing of informal apprenticeship training in urban areas (Accra). The average commitment fee, usually charged at the start of training, was approximately $85 (2007) (ranging from $22 to $336). The graduation fee, at the end of training, averaged $93 (ranging from $11 to $440). Adding up the different fees (commitment fee, in-kind contribution, and graduation fee), the average total amount of fees charged for an apprenticeship was $160, ranging from $22 to $616. Furthermore, in 2006 the average cost of a toolbox that prospective apprentices were usually asked to bring along before commencing training was $45 (ranging from $6 to $224) and varying considerably between different trades.

Apprenticeship fees are generally lower in rural areas compared to urban areas (and likely to be lower in urban areas outside of Accra). One study of rural apprenticeships (Palmer 2007a) asked about the total fees paid by apprentices and did not disaggregate the "commitment fee" and the "graduation fee." This study, based on data from rural Ashanti Region in 2005, estimated the average total fee to be $42 with a range from $13 to $173.

Interventions to Improve Informal Apprenticeship Training in Ghana

There have been several well documented projects that have attempted to improve the informal apprenticeship system in the recent past; but these have had little overall impact on the system. These include the following:

- The Vocational Skills and Informal Sector Support Project (VSP), 1995–2001 (Palmer 2007b; World Bank 1995, 2001)
- The Rural Enterprise Project Phase One (REP I), 1995–2002 (GoG/IFAD 2000)
- The Skills Training and Entrepreneurship Program (STEP), 2003–05 (see section "The Skills Training and Entrepreneurship Program (STEP)")
- The Rural Enterprise Project Phase Two (REP II), 2003–12 (see section "The Rural Enterprise Project (IFAD, 1995 and Ongoing")).

Other than the National Apprenticeship Program (see section "National Apprenticeship Program"), the most recent attempts to support skills training in the informal sector include: the informal sector window of the Skills Development Fund (SDF) and the GIZ-financed Ghana Skills Development Initiative Project.

The SDF (see report, chapter 5) contains four funding windows, one of which focuses on skills development for informal MSEs. Funding will focus on informal MSEs, and the upper ceiling is expected to be $60,000 per grant. It is not expected that individual MSEs would come forward with training proposals, but rather that groups of MSEs, informal sector associations, NGOs, or other training providers would. The $60,000 ceiling per grant is expected to cover the costs of 30–40 trainees with the expectation that the duration of training is one year or less. Beneficiaries are expected to provide 10 percent in-kind matching support (not funds), including internships and work opportunities to be provided to the trainees during the training period (World Bank 2011a).

The Ghana Skills Development Initiative (GSDI)[74] (January 2012–June 2014)[75] is funded by the German government through GIZ and Kreditanstalt für Wiederaufbau (Reconstruction Credit Institute; KFW). GSDI aims to strengthen Ghana's informal apprenticeship system and will involve capacity building for informal sector stakeholders (COTVET, informal sector trade associations), as well as direct training of MCs and apprentices.

The project will be piloted in three regions: Greater Accra, Northern Region, and Volta Region. The six pilot sectors are construction, electronics, auto mechanics, welding, tailoring, and cosmetology/hairdressing.

Components are the following:

- Capacity development for COTVET.
- Strengthen the role of informal sector trade association in TVET, including

their involvement in the development of CBT standards, quality assurance of training, expanding their services for informal enterprises, and developing and offering training courses in consultation with COTVET.
- Train MCs in CBT (who then deliver training to their apprentices). The current (May 2012) intention is to train 30 MCs in each of the six pilot sectors, in each of the three pilot regions: 540 MCs altogether. Each of these CBT-trained master craftspeople would then train five apprentices, making about 2,700 apprentice beneficiaries. It was expected that the training of the apprentices by the masters would not start until mid-2013.[76] Unlike in the National Apprenticeship Program, the MCs would not be paid to train apprentices, but the apprentices themselves would pay fees as they usually do (ibid.).
- Support public and private training providers in developing and implementing training courses for master craftspeople and apprentices. The project will involve a training voucher system for the apprentices; the apprentices would select where to use the voucher, choosing from a list of approved formal TVET providers (a mechanism similar to the 1995–2001 World Bank vocational skills and informal sector support project). The training institutes shall be put in a position to offer complementary needs-based training courses to master craftspeople and apprentices. The program will work with both public (TTIs, NVTIs) and private training providers. The duration and mix of practical versus theoretical training, as well as the type of certification to be offered was still to be determined as of May 2012.

As of May 2012, it was still unclear as to how the GSDI would interact with the NAP, and discussions between the GSDI team and COTVET were underway around two scenarios: (1) that the GSDI works with the same apprentices who have completed the one-year NAP (the option COTVET is in favor of) and (2) that the GSDI works with a new "batch" of young people (non-NAP).[77]

Private Formal Enterprise-Based Training

Skills Upgrading in Industry

The survival and profitability of industries in Ghana and elsewhere hinges firmly on the skills of the workforce and how effectively these skills are harnessed and coordinated to achieve the set targets of the industry.[78] Changes in technologies, systems, or processes call for new skills—hence the need for upgrading employees' skills at all levels in industry.

A small survey was conducted in 2009 by Ahorbo (2009b) on seven industries, four industry associations, and support agencies in the Greater Accra area. Below, these new data are merged with existing knowledge about private formal enterprise-based training.

Formal training is found in the wage sector of the economy, which is small in Ghana, accounting for about 16 percent of employment, based on the 2006/07 Ghana Living Standards Survey (World Bank 2008a).

A 2007 enterprise survey in Ghana (www.enterprisesurvey.org), conducted by the World Bank, found that firms of all sizes offer formal training, but that medium and, especially, large firms are more likely to offer such training compared to small firms.

Generally all the industries surveyed by Ahorbo (2009b) acknowledged that there is skills mismatch in the labor market, which results in industry having to spend heavily on skills upgrading, especially on fresh TVET graduates employed by them. The situation appears to be getting worse with each passing year. Industry considers that TVET providers are not turning out graduates with the appropriate skills required for industry; and almost all TVET graduates lack sufficient practical experience.

A 2006 Ghana Employers Association (GEA) Skills Gap Survey—which surveyed some 90 employers—found that 40 percent of employers are addressing the situation of hard-to-fill vacancies through on-the-job training, and 13 percent turn to expatriates for the hard-to-fill vacancies (figure B.1). Together, this is an indication that a lot of the industries are investing in training to bridge the skills gap.

Johanson and Adams (2004) noted that most formal companies in Sub-Saharan Africa put shop-floor employees through some kind of training; this could include both formal training that takes the trainee off the job site (and is delivered mainly in classrooms), and organized OJT. However, the duration, rigor, and formality depended largely on the nature of the tasks to be learned and the size of the enterprise.

In Ghana, Ahorbo (2009b) found that most fresh TVET graduates selected for a job in industry have to be started as (formal) apprentices and retrained. They are taken through a one- or two-year in-house apprenticeship training program to strengthen their foundation in science and math together with building their knowledge and fundamental skills in basic technical trades (for example,

Figure B.1 Key Actions to Address Hard-to-Fill Vacancies

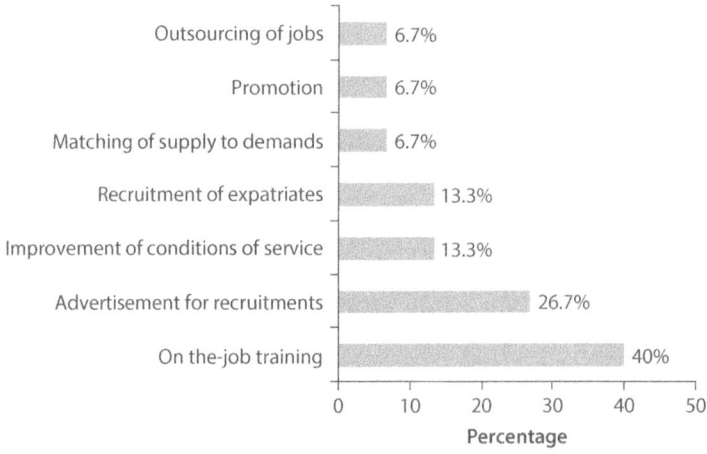

Source: GEA 2006.

plumbing, electrical wiring, welding, and machining). Some industries in Ghana have even established a training workshop where new graduates undergo intensive training before being put on the job. Currently industries have a lot of interest in technicians who have appreciable knowledge and skills in one or more other trades in addition to the specialized trade for which they have been trained.

Ahorbo (2009b) found that in an effort to help TVET teachers to be up to date with current technologies and manufacturing processes of industries, attachment programs are organized by some industries for teachers during school holidays.

Ahorbo (2009b) also found that training for employees in industry appears to take place as and when the need arises: for example, when there is the introduction of new equipment or a new manufacturing process. However, in some industries, health, safety, and environmental compliance training is conducted regularly. Industries tend to prefer to use trainers with a great deal of experience for their training programs. Some companies encourage their employees to initiate their own private capacity-building programs for which the cost is fully borne by the company if it is relevant to the work of the employee. For example, Anglogold Ashanti estimates that it spent about $427 to train each formal apprentice in 2006, rising to $519 per apprentice in 2007. Fan Milk Limited calculated that the unit cost of training a staff is in the neighborhood of $400. The CocaCola Bottling Company estimates the cost of training a new employee from a TVET school to attain the desired skill for the job to be about $200.

The Ghana Industrial Skills Development Center

Outline

The[79] Ghana Industrial Skills Development Center in Tema with a strong emphasis on demand-driven, industry-responsive training was regarded as very much in touch with one strand of thinking in the TVET reform process: the focus on short, modular competency-based training rather than a long-term supply-driven approach. The center was not under one of the traditional ministerial sponsors, like MoE or MoELR. It was a public-private partnership, and its links with qualification and certification bodies were international, not national. The model that was developed at GISDC was considered among the most progressive, promising ones in the area of skills development in Ghana. It was based on strong industry links, on a sound strategic- and business-development mentality that included clearly defined expected outcomes by which effectiveness could be measured, as well as on keen awareness of the resource potential (including participation of industry and of beneficiaries of training in financing the program). However, in 2011 the GISDC suffered a fatal collapse and closed, as we will explain.

Origins

The initiative to set up GISDC came from the Technical Director of Vlisco, a Dutch textile firm in Tema. He felt such an organization could fulfill a need, after contacting a number of industries about the problem of the lack of practical skills, of good quality, and the mismatch between the skills available (for example, among graduates from the public TVET institutions) and those required by industry. There was a feasibility study carried out in May 2004 that confirmed that many formal sector firms were facing the same problem. The situation forced many firms to set up their own in-house training programs.

Others saw the establishment of the GISDC as a response to the failure of the government to deliver TVET reform; one senior development partner official commented that the GISDC initiative was indicative of "a sign of frustration on the side of the private sector that it has taken 10 years [for the TVET policy] to go nowhere."[80]

The initial intention was to set up a full-time technical school (one-year course). But industries pushed instead for short one-to-two-week courses for retraining or upskilling of those already in industry.

Significant delays were seen in the setup of the GISDC; the first training session, which was due to start in September 2006, did not start until mid-2008. The delay was due to time required to get land registration for the organization's site (required by the Dutch funders) and the slowness of the initial industry contributions.

Courses, Curriculum, and Certification

The GISDC may well have been one of the first (albeit short-lived) examples of the new demand-driven approach to training envisaged in Ghana's TVET reform. Following a training needs analysis by the Scottish Qualifications Authority in December 2005, four main training areas were decided upon: Mechanical Engineering, Electrical Engineering, Process Engineering, and Core Skills (modules in Health and Safety, IT, etc.). The curriculum was to be modified on an ongoing basis following feedback from trainees and from industry (the latter through periodic discussions with industry and the industry board members, who together comprise the majority of the GISDC board). There was to be ongoing market assessment. It was also expected that as industry identified new specific training needs they could discuss them with the GISDC, which would then identify and design courses. Courses were one-week modules, and each of the main areas (for example, electrical engineering) was divided up into about 20 modules. Capacity was about 80 trainees at a time in the GISDC, but courses were limited to 16 trainees per module. Certification came from the Scottish Qualifications Authority, which caused some concern in the MoE as it was not clear how the GISDC courses and certificates would have fit into the TVET qualifications framework. From the GISDC perspective, however, the emphasis was not on individuals graduating from the center, but rather individuals getting certification for blocks/modules taken.

Contributing to the Achievement of the Millennium Development Goals?

It was clear that the GISDC was oriented to the formal sector of the economy, and not to the large number of petty producers in the informal economy.[81] But the Dutch government offered to provide a bonus to the GISDC if it could find a way of bringing a more poverty-focused dimension to the center. The GISDC planned to do this by letting a certain number of "unemployed" individuals register for courses for free. The "Yes Ghana" organization was meant to source needy students to train for free with the intention that "Yes Ghana" would help these needy students to set up on their own after completing a course.

Funding

The GISDC was registered as a nonprofit NGO and was a public-private partnership. It was initially meant to be a 50:50 partnership, 50 percent of funding from the Dutch government and 50 percent from Ghanaian industry. But in reality by February 2008 the funding ratio was more like 80:20 (80 percent public and 20 percent private funds, with most of the "public" money being foreign public money). The total set-up cost of GISDC as of mid-February 2008 was almost 1 million euros: 753,000 from the Dutch government and about 200,000 from approximately 20 industrial partners. In addition, the United Kingdom provided technical advice and a link to the Scottish Qualifications Authority; the government of Ghana provided land within Tema Technical Institute. Even if GISDC did not reach the 50:50 goal in funding from public and private resources, the very effort and the partial success was encouraging.

Funding from the Dutch government and from Ghanaian industry was a one-off contribution, and one of the most attractive features of GISDC was how it was planned to work based to a large extent on user fees. Courses were designed around one week modules and cost Gh₵250 per person per week. The GISDC needed to "sell" about 1,000 modules each year (an income of about Gh₵250,000) to meet recurrent costs (the center needs about Gh₵15,000 a month for salaries and other running costs) and still have money set aside for upgrading machinery and up-skilling trainers.

Collapse

Despite its very promising focus and beginnings, by mid-2011 the GISDC had collapsed after only a couple of years of operation and has since been taken over by GRATIS. It failed to attract enough industry partners with their Gh₵10,000 contribution, and courses were too expensive and therefore demand was low. In addition, construction and equipment costs were higher than expected, leaving fewer funds than expected to be used as working capital. Meanwhile, staff salaries were high, and ultimately the GISDC ran out of funds to operate.[82]

Notes

1. In total there were some 730,000 adults (15–64 years old) engaged in apprenticeship in Ghana in 2005/06 (Nsowah-Nuamah et al. 2010).
2. Private communication, May 2012.
3. Authors' calculation based on enrollment data in all TTIs over the period 2009/10 to 2011/12.

4. Authors' calculation based on enrollment data in all TTIs over the period 2009/10 to 2011/12.
5. Private communication, November 20, 2008.
6. Private communication, May 1, 2012.
7. RECOUP interviews at Tema Tech and ATTC, July 2006 and other interviews at ATTC in February. 2008.
8. TVED director, private communication, November 2008.
9. Private communication, February 22, 2008.
10. Private communication, May 1, 2012.
11. ATTC principal, February 21, 2008.
12. In some TTIs responsibility for finding an industrial attachment is with the trainees alone.
13. Block release refers to industry employees being released from work for a period (block) of time for training purposes.
14. RECOUP interviews, July 2006 and other interviews at ATTC in February 2008.
15. ATTC principal, February 21, 2008.
16. Private communication, July 27, 2006.
17. Private communication, July 27, 2006.
18. Private communication with senior government official May 3, 2012.
19. Former and current ATTC principal, November 19, 2008, and April 15, 2008. Internally generated funds are short courses for industry, 5 percent; custom projects, 10 percent; income from hiring out premises, 5 percent.
20. The per capita cost is the total expenditure on that level of education divided by public enrollment at that level. The unit cost is the recurrent expenditure divided by public enrollment at that level. Data for 2011 are not shown here because these have been distorted due to reasons outline in GoG (2012, 49–54).
21. Unless otherwise stated, the material in this subsection is based on interviews with the NVTI director on December 1, 2008, and April 23, 2008, as well as NVTI (2008).
22. Estimate based on a one-third increase in the total number of students.
23. For a list of the OJT taskforce, see GoG (2006b, 3).
24. The proficiency test is a nonwritten test, whereas the full trade test contains both written and practical components and also covers theoretical issues.
25. Private communication, February 20, 2008.
26. Private communication, February 20, 2008.
27. Information here is from a report from the Department of Social Welfare prepared in response to a questionnaire sent by one of the authors (see Department of Social Welfare 2008), as well as from interviews with the Chief Technical Officer on November 26, 2008, and May 3, 2012.
28. Information here, unless otherwise specified, is from one of the author's personal experience of ICCES 2001–12, during which time he has worked for ICCES (more than one year) and followed ICCES developments very closely.
29. By enrollment size, however, TTIs remain the largest public providers with some 29,000 trainees in 2011/12, compared to about 7,000 for NVTI and about 3,500 for ICCES.

30. Although there are one or two individuals in the ICCES Head Office who have a genuine commitment to developing ICCES, the overall capacity of Directorate staff is low.
31. Under the New Education Reforms (since 2007), training duration increased from three to four years. There is some talk that this may revert back to three years.
32. Data supplied by senior MoESW official (May 2012). Estimate based on full enrollment data for four regions, extrapolated nationwide based on the number of known centers.
33. International support includes small grants made by foreign embassies or international NGOs to individual centers, support in the form of foreign volunteers (for example, through JOCV, VSO) and support to individual centers from former volunteers.
34. Private communication from senior official in ICCES Directorate, May 2, 2012.
35. In fact, the objective of opening up ICCES centers in every district of Ghana was first set in 1996 and was thought achievable in one year.
36. Senior officials in the MoELR are aware that ICCES needs a board, but no action has been taken. Some of these officials are waiting for the ICCES Directorate itself to set up this board. This would be a mistake. The ICCES Directorate is itself part of the problem and should not be tasked with setting up a board to oversee it; if they are, the ICCES Directorate are likely to suggest people for the board who are happy to maintain the status quo, and no reform of the ICCES management is likely to take place.
37. Unless otherwise stated, information on OIC Ghana comes from private communication with the OIC Ghana general manager on February 20, 2008, November 21, 2008, January 16, 2009, and April 30, 2012, as well as OICG (2011).
38. Until recently, the examination at the end of year two was the NVTI II trade test.
39. Private communication, February 20, 2008.
40. Unless otherwise stated, the following information is from private communication with the director of the NYA on December 2, 2008, and from responses to a questionnaire; see National Youth Authority (2009).
41. In 2011 the National Youth Council (NYC) changed its name to National Youth Authority (NYA); the latter is used in this report. To avoid confusion, the report from NYA in 2009 is referred to here using this name, even though it was NYC at that time.
42. Director, private communication, December 2, 2008.
43. Information in this appendix is from a report produced for the authors (Department of Community Development 2008), from an interview with the director of the Department of Community Development and the director of the Community Development Vocational/Technical Institutes, on November 27, 2008, with a follow-up interview on May 3, 2012.
44. Information is from a report produced for the authors (Department of Community Development, 2008), from an interview with the Director of the Department of Community Development and the Director of the Community Development Vocational/Technical Institutes, on November 27, 2008, with a follow-up interview on May 3, 2012.
45. Since the four-year course has only recently been introduced, very few students are currently in grade 4 at these institutes. The estimate that by the management can make is to the end of year 3.
46. The following draws on GRATIS's response to the authors' questionnaire (GRATIS 2008), on GRATIS (2006), and on research work undertaken in July 2006 as part of

the DFID-funded Research Consortium on Educational Outcomes and Poverty. Readers may also wish to visit www.gratis-ghana.com.
47. Or greater cane rat (*Thryonomys swinderianus*), a type of rodent that is popular to eat in Ghana.
48. Unless otherwise stated, information here is from the informal sector coordinator at COTVET, May 7, 2012. The comments on NAP are the authors'.
49. The first phase is expected to last a year.
50. Gh₵3.0 million (from the GETFund) for the first group of 5,000 JHS graduates.
51. In 2011, 400 MC nationwide were trained in CBT (GoG 2011c) to train the first group of 5,000 apprentices.
52. See http://www.usaid.gov/div/portfolio/ghana-national-apprenticeship.
53. http://www.cotvet.org/national-apprenticeship-policy.php#nap.
54. Unless otherwise stated, information is from http://lesdepgh.org.
55. Formerly known as the National Youth Employment Program (NYEP).
56. This section on STEP draws on Palmer (2007a). See also Debrah (2007), who holds a view of STEP similar to that of the present authors.
57. Private communication, October 19, 2007.
58. This case study draws on and summarizes the key findings from IFAD (2011) and Okorley (2011). For details on the first phase of the rural enterprises project (1995–2002), see Haan (2006) and GoG/IFAD (2000). The REP aims to upscale and mainstream the district-based MSE support system piloted by REP-II and I to at least 161 municipalities and districts in all the 10 regions of the country from 2012 to 2020.
59. For example, business planning, costing, pricing, accounting, record keeping, occupational safety, product quality, and finishing.
60. This section draws heavily on a background paper (Ahorbo 2009a).
61. In 2012, the Don Bosco institute was taken over by the Ministry of Education (MoE), so the information here below is a historical case study of how the institute previously operated.
62. This program assists the student by absorbing the cost of training for a maximum period of three years. It also providing livelihood skills to a member of the student's family so that they are better able to earn income to support their child.
63. For example the Don Bosco VTI, Tema.
64. In total there were some 730,000 adults (15–64 years old) engaged in apprenticeship in Ghana in 2005/06 (ibid.).
65. This estimate is based on there being 440,000 informal apprentices, about 40,000 in public TVET institutes and about 73,000 in private TVET institutes (see main report, chapter 3). About 10 years ago, Atchoarena and Delluc (2001) had a similar estimate: that informal apprenticeship was responsible for 80–90 percent of skills training, public training institutions 5–10 percent, and private providers 10–15 percent.
66. This assumes that youth with less than a complete basic education are more likely to be poor than those that have, or exceed, this level of schooling.
67. The cost of some of these trades, like auto mechanics, electrical installation, and welding are also usually higher than those such as dressmaking and carpentry—which might be a further reason for this fragmentation by education level.

68. Since training occurs on-the-job, the training environment is intimately linked to the state of the work environment in the micro and small enterprises (MSEs), and evidence suggests that this is generally of low standard in Ghana (especially from an occupational safety and health perspective) (Morton 2004).
69. The National Apprenticeship Program (see section "National Apprenticeship Program") is an attempt by government to finance apprenticeship.
70. In Breyer's (2007) urban survey, 65 percent of master craftspeople charged a graduation fee, and 97 percent charged a commitment fee.
71. Breyer (2007) found that 75 percent of enterprises in her urban survey charged this type of in-kind fee.
72. In Breyer's urban survey, 81 percent of apprentices were asked to bring along their own set of tools.
73. In Breyer's urban survey, 75 percent of master craftspeople (MCs) paid their apprentices chop money. Palmer (2007a) found that overall 52 percent of rural MCs paid their apprentices chop money; disaggregating by gender, however, revealed that 75 percent of male apprentices were paid chop money (in the trade areas of carpentry, masonry and mechanics), but only 20–25 percent of female apprentices (in dressmaking and hairdressing) were paid chop money.
74. Unless otherwise stated, this section on GSDI draws on GIZ (2011).
75. The project has initially been funded for 2½ years, but there is some assurance that the project would be funded for an additional 2½ years.
76. Private communication, GSDI consultant, May 4, 2012.
77. Private communication, GSDI consultant, May 4, 2012.
78. This appendix on private formal enterprise-based training draws heavily on a background paper produced for this report by Ahorbo (2009b).
79. Unless otherwise stated, information in this section comes from RECOUP interviews with the GISDC management in July 2006 and interviews with GISDC management by the author in February 2008. Note: In 2011 the Ghana Industrial Skills Development Center collapsed; see below. This is, therefore a historical case study.
80. Private communication, July 22, 2006.
81. This slogan used to appear on the top of every page of the (now closed) GISDC website, but without the question mark. This slogan was later changed on the website to describe the GISDC as "a leading sustainable centre of excellence for demand-driven industrial skills."
82. Private communication from a member of the now defunct GISDC Board, May 3, 2012.

References

AfDF (African Development Fund). 2012. "Development of Skills for Industry." Project Appraisal Report, April, African Development Bank, Abidjan.

AGI (Association of Ghana Industries). 2013. "The AGI Business Barometer." First quarter, Summary Report, AGI, Accra.

Ahadzie, W. 2003. "Non-formal Training: A Study of the Traditional Apprenticeship System in Ghana." Doctoral thesis, University of Ghana, Legon.

Ahorbo, G. 2009a. "Rapid Assessment of Supply, Demand and Financing in the Private TVET System in Ghana." Unpublished draft report, February, World Bank Accra.

———. 2009b. "Industry and MSE Skill Needs in Ghana." Unpublished draft report, March, World Bank, Accra.

Akyeampong, O., and A. B. Asiedu, eds. 2008. "Tourism in Ghana: A Modern Synthesis." Assemblies of God Literature Centre, Accra.

Almeida, R., J. Behrman, and D. Robalino. 2012. *The Right Skills for the Job? Rethinking Training Policies for Workers*. Washington, DC: World Bank.

Amankrah, Y. 2007. "Labor Market Study to Determine Apprenticeship Trades with Market Potential, Commissioned by the Ministry of Manpower, Youth and Employment and the ILO International Program on the Elimination of Child Labor, Ghana Time-Bound Program (TBP) Support Project." Draft, September, Accra.

Appaw-Agbola, E. T., S. Afenyo-Dehlor, and A. K. Agbola. 2011. "Human Resource Issues in the Development of Tourism in Ghana: A Survey of Small/Medium Hotels in the Volta Region." *World Review of Business Research* 1 (1): 115–31.

Aryeetey, E., A. Laryea, T. Antwi-Asare, W. Baah-Boateng, E. Turkson, E. Codjoe, and C. Ahortor. 2005. "Globalization, Employment and Poverty Reduction: A Case Study of Ghana." ISSER, University of Ghana, Legon.

Atchoarena, D., and A. Delluc. 2001. "Revisiting Technical and Vocational Education in Sub-Saharan Africa: An Update on Trends, Innovations, and Challenges." IIEP/Prg. DA/1,320. IIEP, Paris.

Baier-D'Orazio, M. 2007. "Mid-term Evaluation and Assessment of the OIC/EED Project: Skills Development and Self-employment for Non-literate and Semi-literate Youth in Kumasi Metropolis." Mimeo, Opportunities Industrialization Centre Ghana, Kumasi Program.

Boeh-Ocansey, O. 1995. "Education and Training for the Informal Sector: Ghana Country Study." In *Education and Training for the Informal Sector*, edited by F. Leach, vol. 2, *Country Studies*, Education Research Paper 11. London: DFID. http://r4d.dfid.gov.uk/PDF/Outputs/Misc_Education/paper11.pdf.

Bortei-Doku Aryeetey, E., D. Doh, and P. Andoh. 2011. "From Prejudice to Prestige: Vocational Education and Training in Ghana." City & Guilds Centre for Skills Development/COTVET, Accra.

Botchie, G., and W. Ahadzie. 2004. "Poverty Reduction Efforts in Ghana: The Skill Development Option." Mimeo, CSPS/ISSER, University of Ghana, Legon.

Breyer, J. 2007. "Financial Arrangements in Informal Apprenticeships: Determinants and Effects. Findings from Urban Ghana." Working Paper No. 49, Social Finance Program, International Labour Organization, Geneva.

Campbell, M. 2002. *Learn to Succeed: The Case for a Skills Revolution*. Bristol: Policy Press.

CIA World Fact Book. 2009. https://www.cia.gov/library/publications/the-world-factbook/geos/gh.html.

COTVET (Council for Technical and Vocational Education and Training). 2009. "Skills Development Fund Operations Manual." Draft zero, February 1, COTVET, Accra.

———. 2010. "National Apprenticeship Strategy 2010–2014." COTVET, Accra.

———. 2012a. "2011 Annual Report." COTVET, Accra.

———. 2012b. "A Five Year Corporate Plan for the Council for Technical Vocational Education and Training (COTVET), 2012–2016." Draft, COTVET, Accra.

CPTC (COTVET Preparation Technical Committee). 2006. "Report on Operationalizing COTVET Act." Technical Vocational Education and Training Support (TVETS), COTVET, Accra.

CREATE (Consortium for Research on Educational Access, Transitions and Equity). 2011. "Making Rights Realities: Researching Educational Access, Transitions and Equity." University of Sussex, Brighton.

Danida (Danish International Development Agency). 2009. "Support to Private Sector Development—Phase II (2010–2014)." Ref. no. 104.Ghana.809-200. Danida, Danish Ministry of Foreign Affairs, Copenhagen.

Davidson, R. 1993. *Tourism*. 2nd ed. London: Pitman.

Debrah, Y. 2007. "Promoting the Informal Sector as a Source of Gainful Employment in Developing Countries: Insights from Ghana." *International Journal of Human Resource Management* 18 (6): 1063–84.

Department of Community Development. 2008. "Report on the Community Development Vocational/Technical Institutes." Unpublished report, Accra.

Department of Social Welfare. 2008. "Vocational Training Report." Unpublished report, Accra.

DFID (Department for International Development). 2008. "Jobs, Labor Markets and Shared Growth: The Role of Skills." DFID Practice Paper, September, DFID, London.

Dieke, Peter U. C. 2003. "Tourism in Africa's Economic Development: Policy Implications." *Management Decision* 41 (3): 287–95.

van Dijk, M. 1997. "Economic Activities of the Poor in Accra." In *Farewell to Farms*, edited by D. Bryceson and V. Jamal. Aldershot: Ashgate.

Donkor, F. 2012. "Reasons for Non-Completion among Apprentices: The Case of Automotive Trades of the Informal Sector in Ghana." *Journal of Vocational Education & Training* 64 (1): 25–40.

European Commission. 2005. "ICT and Electronic Business in the Tourism Industry: ICT Adoption and e-Business Activity in 2005." European Commission Sector Report No. 09.

http://ec.europa.eu/enterprise/archives/e-business-watch/studies/sectors/tourism/documents/Tourism_2005.pdf.

Fasih, T. 2008. *Linking Education Policy to Labor Market Outcomes*. Washington, DC: World Bank.

Figgis, J., and A. Standen. 2005. "Training Skilled Workers: Lessons from the Oil and Gas Industry." National Centre for Vocational Education Research: Adelaide, Australia. http://www.ncver.edu.au/research/proj/nr3016.pdf.

Foster, P. 1965a. *Education and Social Change in Ghana*. London: Routledge and Kegan Paul.

———. 1965b. "The Vocational School Fallacy in Development Planning." In *Education and Economic Development*, edited by C. Anderson and M. Bowman, 142–46. Chicago: Aldine.

G20DWG (G20 Development Working Group). 2011. "Working Draft of Paper on Developing Indicators of Skills for Employment and Productivity: An Initial Draft Framework and Approach for Low-Income Countries." Mimeo, OECD and World Bank, Washington, DC.

GEA (Ghana Employers Association). 2006. "Skills Gap Survey." GEA, Accra.

GISDC (Ghana Industrial Skills Development Centre). 2005. "Scoping and Training Needs Analysis for Establishing a Technical Training Centre in Ghana." Unpublished report, Accra.

GIZ (Deutsche Gesellschaft für Internationale Zusammenarbeit). 2011. "Ghana Skills Development Initiative (GSDI), Project Description." GSDI Office, Accra.

GNA (Ghana News Agency). 2011. "Free Apprenticeship for JSS Leavers." http://www.ghanaweb.com/GhanaHomePage/NewsArchive/artikel.php?ID=214593.

Gondwe, M., and J. Walenkamp. 2011. *Alignment of Higher Professional Education with the Needs of the Local Labor Market: The Case of Ghana*. The Hague: C. Anderson and M. Bowman.

Government of Australia. 2005. "Prospecting for Skills: The Current and Future Skill Needs in the Minerals Sector. Report by the National Centre for Vocational Education Research and the National Institute of Labor Studies (Flinders University), for the Chamber of Minerals and Energy (Western Australia) and the Minerals Council of Australia." http://www.minerals.org.au/__data/assets/pdf_file/0013/9040/Propin_or_killull.pdf.

GoG (Government of Ghana). 1970. "The National Vocational Training Institute Act, 1970." Act 351. Government Printer, Accra.

———. 1978. "Legislative Instrument No. 1154. National Vocational Training Board (Apprentice Training) Regulations, 1978." Government Printer, Accra.

———. 2002. "Meeting the Challenges of Education in the Twenty First Century." Report of the President's Committee on the Review of Education Reforms in Ghana, October, Accra.

———. 2003a. "Ghana Poverty Reduction Strategy (GPRS) Paper. An Agenda for Growth and Prosperity 2003–2005." IMF Country Report No. 03/56, Government Printer, Accra.

———. 2003b. *Education Strategic Plan 2003–2015. Volume I: Policies, Targets and Strategies*. Accra: Ministry of Education.

———. 2003c. *Education Strategic Plan 2003–2015. Volume II: Work Program*. Accra: Ministry of Education.

———. 2004a. "White Paper on the Report of the Education Reform Review Committee." GoG, Accra.

———. 2004b. "Draft TVET Policy Framework for Ghana." August, MoEYS, Accra.

———. 2004c. "Draft TVET Policy Framework for Ghana." January, MoEYS, Accra.

———. 2004d. "Preliminary Education Sector Performance Report." October, MoESS, Accra.

———. 2005. "Growth and Poverty Reduction Strategy (GPRS II). The Coordinated Programme for the Economic and Social Development of Ghana (2006–2009)." Final draft, September, National Development Planning Commission, Accra.

———. 2006a. "Preliminary Education Sector Performance Report." June, MoESS, Accra.

———. 2006b. "Report of Task Force on Incentives for 'On the Job Training.'" Ministry of Finance and Economic Planning, Accra.

———. 2006c. "Youth Employment Implementation Guidelines (Ghana Youth Job Corps Program)." March, MoMYE, Accra.

———. 2006d. "Modernising Traditional Apprenticeship." PowerPoint Presentation, MoMYE, Accra.

———. 2006e. "Council for Technical and Vocational Education and Training Act." GoG, Accra.

———. 2006f. "Report on Basic Statistics and Planning Parameters for Technical and Vocational Education in Ghana 2005/2006." EMIS Project, MoESS, Accra.

———. 2007a. "Report on Basic Statistics and Planning Parameters for Technical and Vocational Education in Ghana 2006/2007." EMIS Project, March, MoESS, Accra.

———. 2007b. "Preliminary Education Sector Performance Report." June, Ministry of Education, Science and Sports, Accra.

———. 2007c. "2008 Budget. A Brighter Future." Ministry of Finance and Economic Planning, Accra.

———. 2007d. "Technical and Vocational Education and Training (TVET) Sub-committee Final Report." February, National Education Reform Implementation Committee, Accra.

———. 2008a. "Preliminary Education Sector Performance Report." July, Ministry of Education, Science and Sports, Accra.

———. 2008b. "PowerPoint presentation by the Technical and Vocational Education and Training (TVET) Thematic Group." June 19, Education Sector Annual Review, Accra.

———. 2008c. "Report on Basic Statistics and Planning Parameters for Technical and Vocational Education in Ghana 2007/2008." EMIS Project, March, MoESS, Accra.

———. 2009a. "Report on Basic Statistics and Planning Parameters for Technical and Vocational Education in Ghana 2008/2009." EMIS Project, March, MoE, Accra.

———. 2009b. *Education Strategic Plan 2010–2020. Volume 1: Policy, Strategies, Delivery, Finance.* Accra: Ministry of Education.

———. 2009c. *Education Strategic Plan 2010–2020. Volume 2: Strategies and Work Program.* Accra: Ministry of Education.

———. 2011a. "Preliminary Education Sector Performance Report, May 2011." Ministry of Education, Accra.

———. 2011b. "Report on Basic Statistics and Planning Parameters for Technical and Vocational Education in Ghana 2010/2011." EMIS Project, April, MoE, Accra.

———. 2011c. "Budget Statement and Economic Policy of the Government of Ghana for the 2012 Financial Year. Presented to Parliament on Wednesday, November 16." Ministry of Finance and Economic Planning, Accra. http://danquahinstitute.org/docs/2012%20budget%20print%20latest.pdf.

———. 2012a. "Education Sector Performance Report 2012." Draft, May, Ministry of Education, Accra.

———. 2012b. "Legislative Instrument No. 2195." Council for Technical and Vocational Education and Training Regulations, Government of Ghana, Accra.

———. 2013a. "Budget Statement and Economic Policy of the Government of Ghana for the 2013 Financial Year Parliament, on Tuesday, 5th March, 2013. Theme: Sustaining Confidence in the Future of the Ghanaian Economy." Government of Ghana, Accra.

———. 2013b. "Education Sector Performance Report 2013." June, Ministry of Education, Accra.

GoG/IFAD (International Fund for Agricultural Development). 2000. "Rural Enterprises Project, Republic of Ghana. Interim Evaluation, vol. 1." Report No. 1097, IFAD, Rome.

GoJ (Government of Japan). 2004. "Evaluation Study on Japan's ODA to the Education Sector in Ghana, Summary Report." March, Earth and Human Corporation, JICA, Tokyo.

GRATIS (Ghana Regional Appropriate Technology Industrial Service). 2006. "GRATIS Foundation. Corporate Profile." GRATIS Foundation, Tema.

———. 2008. "Response to a Questionnaire on Gratis Activities." Unpublished note, November.

GSS (Ghana Statistical Service). 2008. "Ghana Living Standards Survey, Report of the Fifth Round (GLSS5)." GSS, Accra.

———. 2010. "2010 Population and Housing Census." http://www.statsghana.gov.gh/docfiles/2010phc/2010_POPULATION_AND_HOUSING_CENSUS_FINAL_RESULTS.pdf.

Haan, H. 2006. *Training for Work in the Informal Micro-Enterprise Sector: Fresh Evidence from Sub-Saharan Africa*. Dordrecht: Springer.

———. 2008. *Training for Work and the Informal Economy*. Geneva: Skills and Employability Department, ILO.

Haan, H., and N. Serrière. 2002. *Training for Work in the Informal Sector: Fresh Evidence from Western and Central Africa*. Turin: ITC/ILO.

IAWG (Inter-Agency Working Group on TVET Indicators). 2012. *Proposed Indicators for Assessing Technical and Vocational Education and Training*. Geneva, Paris, Turin: ETF, ILO, UNESCO.

IFAD. 2011. "Project Evaluation. Republic of Ghana, Rural Enterprises Project. Phase II, Interim Evaluation." October, IFAD, Rome. http://www.ifad.org/evaluation/public_html/eksyst/doc/prj/region/pa/ghana/rep.pdf.

ILO (International Labour Organization). 2009. "High-Level Tripartite Meeting on the Current Global Financial and Economic Crisis." March 23, ILO, Geneva.

———. 2010. *A Skilled Workforce for Strong, Sustainable and Balanced Growth: A G20 Training Strategy*. ILO, Geneva. http://www.ilo.org/wcmsp5/groups/public/---dgreports/---integration/documents/publication/wcms_151966.pdf.

———. 2012. *Global Employment Trends 2012: Preventing a Deeper Jobs Crisis*. ILO, Geneva. http://www.ilo.org/wcmsp5/groups/public/---dgreports/---dcomm/---publ/documents/publication/wcms_171571.pdf.

IMF (International Monetary Fund). 2011. *World Economic Outlook, September 2011. Slowing Growth, Rising Risks*. Washington, DC: IMF.

———. 2012a. "Statement at the Conclusion of an IMF Mission to Ghana." Press release no. 12/64, March 2. http://www.imf.org/external/np/sec/pr/2012/pr1264.htm.

———. 2012b. *World Economic Outlook, October 2012. Coping with High Debt and Sluggish Growth*. Washington, DC: IMF.

Johanson, R., and A. Adams. 2004. *Skills Development in Sub-Saharan Africa*. Washington, DC: World Bank.

King, K., and R. Palmer. 2006. "Education, Training and Their Enabling Environments." Centre of African Studies, University of Edinburgh, Edinburgh. http://info.worldbank.org/etools/docs/library/244489/day9TVET.pdf.

———. 2007. "Briefing Paper on Technical and Vocational Skills Development." http://www.unevoc.net/fileadmin/user_upload/docs/technical-vocationalDFID.pdf.

———. 2010. "Planning for Technical and Vocational Skills Development." Fundamentals of Educational Planning No. 94, UNESCO and IIEP, Paris. http://unesdoc.unesco.org/images/0018/001895/189530e.pdf.

King, K., S. McGrath, and P. Rose. 2007. "Beyond the Basics." *International Journal for Educational Development* 27 (4): 349–57.

King, K., R. Palmer, and R. Hayman. 2005. "Bridging Research and Policy on Education, Training and Their Enabling Environments." *Journal of International Development* 17 (6): 803–17.

Kodzi, E. 2008. "Harmonization of the Education Strategic Plan. Report of the Local TVET Consultant for Industry Engagement." Mimeo, World Bank, Accra.

Lall, S. 2000. "Skills, Competitiveness and Policy in Developing Countries." QEH Working Paper Series QEHWPS46, Oxford.

Levine, V. 2008. "The Revised Education Sector Plan and 2009 Budget: Policy and Planning Issues." Final report submitted to the Ghana Ministry of Education, Science and Sports Planning, Budgeting, Monitoring and Evaluation Division. Mimeo, June 7, Accra.

Mensah, I. 2011. "(Re)Structuring Ghana's Tourism Industry for Socio-Economic Development." http://www.ghanaweb.com/GhanaHomePage/features/artikel.php?ID=226275.

Monk, C., J. Sandefur, and F. Teal. 2008. "Does Doing an Apprenticeship Pay Off? Evidence from Ghana." RECOUP Working Paper 12. Paper for DFID-funded research project, University of Oxford, Oxford.

Morton, P. 2004. "Job Quality in Micro and Small Enterprises in Ghana: Field Research Results." SEED Working Paper No. 68, ILO, Geneva.

NACVET (National Coordinating Committee for Technical and Vocational Education and Training). 2005. "Technical and Vocational Institutions in Ghana." NACVET, Ministry of Education and Sports, Accra.

National Youth Authority. 2009. "Skills Development in Ghana: An Assessment of Supply, Demand and Financing in the TVET Sector. Responses to Questionnaire—National Youth Council Skills Training Institutes." Unpublished report, February, National Youth Authority, Ghana.

References

NDPC (National Development Planning Commission). 2008. "Medium-Long Term National Development Plan (2008–2015)." February, Government of Ghana, NDPC, Accra.

———. 2010a. *Medium-Term National Development Policy Framework: Ghana Shared Growth and Development Agenda (GSGDA), 2010–2013. Volume I: Policy Framework.* Accra: Government of Ghana, NDPC.

———. 2010b. *Ghana Shared Growth and Development Agenda (GSGDA), 2010–2013: Costing Framework. Volume II: Costing and Financing of Policies and Strategies.* Accra: Government of Ghana, NDPC.

Nsowah-Nuamah, N., F. Teal, and M. Awoonor-Williams. 2010. "Jobs, Skills and Incomes in Ghana." WPS/2010-01, Centre for the Study of African Economies, Oxford University. http://www.csae.ox.ac.uk/workingpapers/pdfs/2010-01text.pdf.

NVTI (National Vocational Training Institute). 2002. "NVTI in Perspective." WPS/2010-01 National Vocational Training Institute, Accra.

———. 2007. "The Role of the National Vocational Training Institute in the Technical and Vocational Education and Training Environment." Position paper by the NVTI board, NVTI, Accra.

———. 2008. "Statistical Report 2001–2007." NVTI, Accra.

———. 2010. "Vocational Institutes Registered under NVTI." NVTI, Accra.

OBG (Oxford Business Group). 2011. "Ghana Country Report 2011." OBG, London.

———. 2012. "Ghana Country Report 2012." OBG, London.

OECD (Organisation for Economic Cooperation and Development). 2012. *OECD Skills Strategy. Better Skills, Better Jobs, Better Lives: A Strategic Approach to Skills Policies.* Paris: OECD.

OICG (Opportunities Industrialization Center Ghana). 2011. "Annual Performance Report 2011." OICG, Accra.

Okorley, E. 2011. "IFAD Supported Training and Apprenticeship within the Rural Enterprises Project Phase II in Ghana. A Field Study of Training Approaches and Outcomes. Initiative for Mainstreaming Innovation." IFAD, Rome.

Palmer, R. 2005. "Beyond the Basics: Post-basic Education and Training and Poverty Reduction in Ghana." Post-Basic Education and Training Working Paper Series No. 4, Centre of African Studies, University of Edinburgh, Edinburgh.

———. 2007a. "Skills Development, the Enabling Environment and Informal Micro-Enterprise in Ghana." Doctoral thesis, Centre of African Studies, University of Edinburgh.

———. 2007b. "Skills for Work? From Skills Development to Decent Livelihoods in Ghana's Rural Informal Economy." *International Journal of Educational Development* 27 (4): 397–420.

———. 2009a. "Formalizing the Informal: Ghana's New Apprenticeship System." *Journal of Vocational Education and Training* 61 (1): 67–83.

———. 2009b. "Skills Development, Employment and Sustained Growth in Ghana: Sustainability Challenges." *International Journal of Educational Development* 29 (2): 133–39.

Palmer, R., R. Akabzaa, and L. Casely-Hayford. 2009. "Skill Pathways Out of Poverty. Technical and Vocational Skills Development: Breaking the Cycle of Poverty for Poor Youth and Young Adults in Ghana?" Unpublished note on preliminary findings, January, RECOUP, Accra.

Palmer, R., R. Wedgwood, R. Hayman, K. King, and N. Thin. 2007. "Educating Out of Poverty?" DFID, London. http://www.dfid.gov.uk/r4d/PDF/Outputs/PolicyStrategy/ResearchingtheIssuesNo70.pdf.

Paterson, A. 2006. "The Growth of Information and Communication Technology Research and Development Networks in South Africa: Leading or Following the Economic Sector?" In *Creating Knowledge Networks: Working Partnerships in Higher Education, Industry and Innovation*, edited by G. Kruss. Pretoria: HSRC Press.

Pealore, D. 2007. "Report of the Final Evaluation of the Regional Project for Skills Training Strategies to Combat WFCL in Urban Informal Sector in Sub-Saharan Anglophone Africa. "Synthesis Report, Ghana, Kenya and Tanzania." ILO/IPEC, Geneva.

PLANCO Consulting. 2011. "TVET Voucher Program, Ghana. Program Design and Feasibility Study for Demand-Oriented TVET Financing." Prepared on behalf of KfW Entwicklungsbank, Hamburg.

Preddey, G. 2005. "Skills Training and Employment Placement (STEP): The Program Document and Performance Appraisal, and Proposals for Enhancement. Ghana Decent Work Pilot Program–ILO." Skills and Employability Department, ILO, Geneva.

RSA (Republic of South Africa). 2007. "National Master Scarce Skills List for South Africa." Ministry of Labor, Johannesburg. http://www.skillsportal.co.za/download_files/professional/NSDS-Scarce_Skills_List_2007.doc.

Tan, J., R. McGough, and A. Valerio. 2010. *Workforce Development in Developing Countries: A Framework for Benchmarking.* Washington, DC: Human Development Network, World Bank.

Teal, F. 2007. "Formal and Informal Employment in Ghana: Job Creation and Skills." Background paper prepared for the study on "Linking Education Policy to Labor Market Outcomes,'" World Bank, Washington, DC.

UNDP (United Nations Development Program). 2011. "Human Development Report 2011. Sustainability and Equity: A Better Future for All." UNDP, New York.

UNESCO. 2003. *Synthesis of Main Findings From Two Case Studies Carried Out in Ghana and Zambia on Private TVET* (Phase II). Paris: IIEP

———. 2011. "The Hidden Crisis: Armed Conflict and Education." Education for All Global Monitoring Report 2011, UNESCO, Paris.

———. 2012a. "The Shanghai Consensus: Recommendations of the Third International Congress on Technical and Vocational Education and Training." May 14–16, Shanghai.

———. 2012b. "Transforming Technical and Vocational Education and Training: Building Skills for Work and Life. Main Working Document." May 13–16, Shanghai.

———. 2012c. "Youth and Skills. Putting Education to Work." Education for All Global Monitoring Report 2012, UNESCO, Paris.

———. 2013. "Global Trends and Issues in TVET: A World Report." UNESCO, Paris (forthcoming).

Wegner, L., and A. Komenan. 2008. "Technical and Vocational Skills Development in Africa." Presentation at the ADEA in Africa Biennale on Education in Africa, Maputo, May.

World Bank. 1995. "Vocational Skills and Informal Sector Support Project." Staff Appraisal Document, Report No. 13691-GH, World Bank, Washington, DC.

———. 2001. "Implementation Completion Report on a Loan/Credit/Grant to Ghana for Vocational Skills and Informal Sector Support Project." Report No. 23406, World Bank, Washington, DC.

———. 2004. "Education Sector Project, Project Appraisal Document." Report No. 26090 GH, World Bank, Washington, DC.

———. 2010a. *Skills Development Strategies to Improve Employability and Productivity: Taking Stock and Looking Ahead.* Washington, DC: World Bank.

———. 2010b. "Improving the Targeting of Social Programs." Report No. 55578-GH, World Bank, Washington, DC.

———. 2010c. "Stepping Up Skills for Jobs and Higher Productivity." Report No. 55566, World Bank, Washington, DC.

———. 2010d. "Rapid Assessment of Information and Communication Technologies (ICT) Sector Skills Demand and Supply in Ghana." Unpublished Consultancy Report, March, World Bank, Accra.

———. 2010e. "Rapid Assessment of Construction Industry Sector Skills Demand and Supply in Ghana." Unpublished Consultancy Report, May, World Bank, Accra.

———. 2010f. "Rapid Assessment of Oil and Gas Industry Skills Demand and Supply in Ghana." Unpublished Consultancy Report, World Bank, Accra.

———. 2010g. "Rapid Assessment of Livestock Sector Skills Demand and Supply in Ghana." Unpublished Consultancy Report, May, World Bank, Accra.

———. 2010h. "Rapid Assessment of Hospitality and Tourism Sector Skills Demand and Supply in Ghana." Unpublished Consultancy Report. World Bank, Accra.

———. 2011a. "Ghana Skills and Technology Development Project, Project Appraisal Document." Report No. 59529-GH, March, World Bank, Washington, DC.

———. 2011b. "Education in Ghana Improving Equity, Efficiency and Accountability of Education Service Delivery." Report No. 59755-GH, February, World Bank, Washington, DC.

———. 2008a. "Ghana Job Creation and Skills Development Draft Report." Version of January 29. Volume I: Main Document. Report No. 40328-GH, World Bank, Washington, DC.

———. 2008b. "Ghana Job Creation and Skills Development Draft Report." Version of January 29. Volume II: Background Papers. Report No. 40328-GH, World Bank, Washington, DC.

———. 2009. "Study on National Oil Companies and Value Creation." Unpublished Consultancy Report, World Bank, Accra.

———. 2012a. "Basic Education beyond the MDGs in Ghana: New Challenges in Equity, Quality and Management." Draft, October, World Bank, Washington, DC.

———. 2012b. *Improving Skills Development in the Informal Sector: Strategies for Sub-Saharan Africa.* Washington, DC: World Bank.

World Economic Forum. 2011. "The Global Competitiveness Report 2011–2012." WEF, Geneva.

———. 2012. "The Global Competitiveness Report 2012–2013." WEF, Geneva.

Young, M. 2005. "National Qualifications Frameworks: Their Feasibility for Effective Implementation in Developing Countries." Skills Working Paper No. 22, InFocus Program on Skills, Knowledge and Employability. ILO, Geneva.

Environmental Benefits Statement

The World Bank is committed to reducing its environmental footprint. In support of this commitment, the Publishing and Knowledge Division leverages electronic publishing options and print-on-demand technology, which is located in regional hubs worldwide. Together, these initiatives enable print runs to be lowered and shipping distances decreased, resulting in reduced paper consumption, chemical use, greenhouse gas emissions, and waste.

The Publishing and Knowledge Division follows the recommended standards for paper use set by the Green Press Initiative. Whenever possible, books are printed on 50 percent to 100 percent postconsumer recycled paper, and at least 50 percent of the fiber in our book paper is either unbleached or bleached using Totally Chlorine Free (TCF), Processed Chlorine Free (PCF), or Enhanced Elemental Chlorine Free (EECF) processes.

More information about the Bank's environmental philosophy can be found at http://crinfo.worldbank.org/wbcrinfo/node/4.

www.ingramcontent.com/pod-product-compliance
Lightning Source LLC
Chambersburg PA
CBHW082120230426
43671CB00015B/2749